anne
...h my compliment.
...a very special lady.
Arnold L.
13584

10/13/00

FROM BENDZIN TO AUSCHWITZ

A Journey To Hell

Arnold Shay after the liberation 1945 in concentration camp uniform.

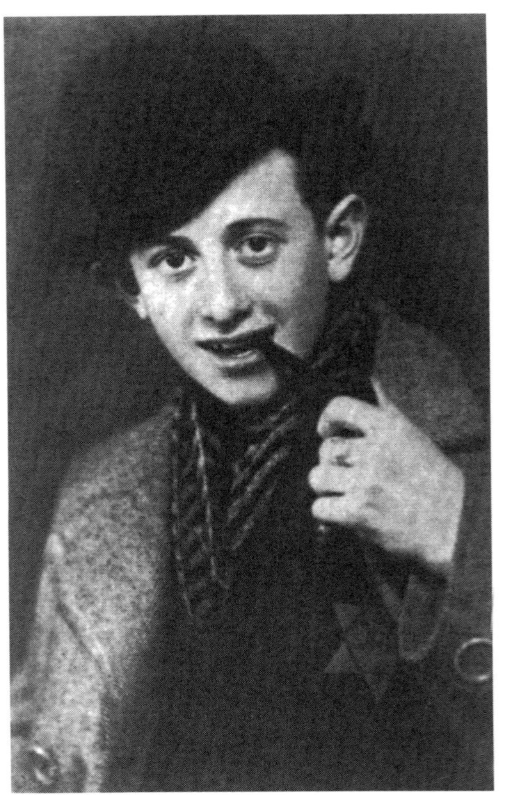

Arnold Shay wearing the Jewish Star in the Bendzin Open Ghetto 1940.

FROM BENDZIN TO AUSCHWITZ

A Journey To Hell

by Arnold Shay, Survivor of the Holocaust

Founded 1910
THE CHRISTOPHER PUBLISHING HOUSE
HANOVER, MASSACHUSETTS 02339

Library of Congress Catalog Number 95-74984

ISBN: 0-8158-0518-7

PRINTED IN THE UNITED STATES OF AMERICA

Dedication

I dedicate this book to all the Jews who perished at the hands of the Nazis.

To all the Jews from Bendzin who perished.

And all the survivors who had to endure all the hardships while fighting to survive.

My deepest gratitude goes to all those who wrote about Bendzin-Sosnowiec and Zaglembie to remember.

You, the writers, were my inspiration,

Thank you.

Contents

List of Illustrations

Preface

On 1 September 1939, the order was given by the Führer to the Wehrmacht commanders to begin the invasion of Poland. This was Hitler's plan to destroy the nation, and its "inferior people," so that the land could be used for settlement by the blond, blue-eyed Teutons of Nazi Germany.

Arnold Shay was one of the thirty million "inferior people" to be destroyed. In fact, his demise was to be scheduled quickly due to two basic plans: (a) he was Polish and (b) a Jew. Hitler's schedule called for the eventual elimination of the Poles, but the Jews were to be exterminated at once. The Einsatzkommando followed his orders to the letter. They killed Jews at random, burned their homes, buildings and confiscated anything of value that had Jewish ownership. The real tragedy of this experience was the aid the Germans got from the Poles, who thought they would be spared by cooperating.

Probably the greatest crime committed by the Germans was the total elimination of the Jewish heritage in Eastern Europe, never to return. The author goes to great effort to present what community life was like in Poland before World War II. He then narrows it down to his own life in the Jewish sector of Bendzin. He exposes the fact that pre-war Poland was just as anti-Semitic as Hitler Germany, but that the Poles never went to the harsh extremes of the Nazis. Shay indicates that the Poles could have taught Hitler a lesson or two in how to deal with the Jew.

The author was one of the very few who lived through the Holocaust, and is qualified to historically record what happened to the Jew from 1939 to 1945. Before writing his story, Shay went back to Bendzin to recap memories of this dark era only to find that Communists finished the job left undone by the Nazis. Because of this post-war condition in Poland, Shay's written record is most important to future generations as proof that the Holocaust for the Jews did, indeed, happen no matter how hard the effort by many today to sweep it under the rug. Don't believe those who say that it never happened, and that it is propaganda for Israel. Through Shay, the truth will out!

DONALD GREY BROWNLOW
Major, USA-ret.,
195144018

Foreword

When I started writing this book my intentions were to write two books. One on Bendzin where I was born and raised for seventeen years until the Nazis came, and the second one about Auschwitz where most of my people and relatives from Bendzin perished in the gas chambers.

No matter how hard I tried to separate those two cities, I could not separate them.

I wanted to write of the Jews of Bendzin as far back in time as it was humanly possible. I read and researched every book on Bendzin, every pamphlet, every article I could get hold of. I searched my own mind in sleepless nights of every detail I could remember, and recorded it.

In a few details I may have failed, but in most of my research I think I was successful.

My wife Eva saw to it that I have the best computer and printer to make it easy for me to do my work.

A big and hearty thank you goes to my wife's son Dr. Frank Laski who is in Los Angeles at UCLA Molecular Biology Institute, whom I bothered at home and in his office when I got stuck at the computer and did not know how to proceed. Thank you Frank, you were a life saver.

I gave credit to every writer that ever mentioned anything on Bendzin. I quoted writers and their books, pamphlets and articles and anything that had something to quote on Bendzin.

With all these efforts on my part and with all the help of previous writers on Bendzin and Auschwitz, I could not separate those two cities. Most of the Jews of Bendzin-Sosnowiec-Zaglembie were killed in Auschwitz.

From you, the reader, all I ask is; try to understand, as impossible as it is, what happened to the Jews of Bendzin and for that matter to the six million Jews we lost in that war. Innocent lives. How we had to live and die under the most inhumane conditions, under the Nazi rule.

You, the reader, will have to judge the Germans by the atrocities committed against the Jews. By the joy the Germans got from torturing the powerless Jews.

Bendzin Jewry flourished in poverty and under Polish anti-Semitism, and we brought pride and civility to the cities we lived in.

Now Bendzin as we knew it is no more, and will be no more. There is only one single Jew living in Bendzin now. Last time I was in Bendzin was 1990 and only one Jew was there, Mr. Szwarc. Sick, deaf, old and still hated by the Poles.

Why any Jew stayed after the war in Bendzin, and for that matter anywhere in Poland, is beyond my comprehension.

You, the reader, Jew or Christian, please say "Kadish" for the Bendzin Jewry, and do not forget the six million.

All of Poland is one big Jewish cemetery. The grounds are soaked with Jewish blood.

I will say "Kadish" for as long as I live. ("Kadish" is prayer for the dead, and yet in that prayer there is no mention of death at all.) Please remember them.

Chapter One

The good and bad years in Bendzin where I was born and lived for the first seventeen years of my life.

Bendzin of Old

The history of the city of Bendzin is a long one and so is the history of the Jews who lived there. The beauty and joy of our youth in Bendzin, the hunger, the happy years and years of disappointments.

That conglomeration of our lives in Bendzin that so many of our Jewish people want to forget, for many good reasons, mind you, I for one cannot and will not forget. Something in my life, in my youth, in my hunger and disappointments, makes want to remember.

About my life in Bendzin, my youth, my trials and tribulations, I will try to recall later in my story.

I would like to begin the story of my book with the history of my home town Bendzin. The history of that town is so very rich, that when I started to write this book and when I started to collect different historical information on Bendzin I just could not stop.

The history of the Jews in Bendzin is as rich and as colorful as probably the largest cities in Poland, and so is the misery, the poverty, and most noticeable anti-Semitism.

The church in Poland was very anti-Semitic and still is. Most of the news of the world's going on, the Poles received on Sunday in the church and it never was complimentary to the Jews. The contrary so is true. The priest at his Sunday sermon would preach venom against the Jews, and when the congregants left the church, they were ready to kill every Jew. Many, many died after those Sunday sermons. When the priest was supposed to preach brotherly love, he preached hatred against the Jews. We have learned to live with it, because we were powerless to do something against those Sermons.

I read many books on the city of Bendzin and the more I read, the more I wanted to know about Bendzin. I only hope that you the reader will get to understand my enthusiasm for that book as you will be lead through the history of that city.

In the first half of the twelfth century, Bendzin was, in the historical terminology, described as "Ziemia Krakowska," belonging to the Krakow District, bordering with Malopolska and the rivers Wisla and Przemsza. This, however, was not the oldest border of Malopolska.

In 1179, Bytom, Siewierz and Oswiecim was taken away from the Krakow District and handed over as a "gift" by Kazimierz Sprawiedliwy to Mieszko Raciborski. It is a bit confusing since (considering) in 1179 Bendzin as well as Chrzanow and Siewierz belonged to Mieszko Pietonogi who died in 1211. (In those days the land owners were very few with great amounts of land. Those were the Barons, that the land as well as people on it belonged to them.)

Then it has to be recognized, that the latest 1231, when Henryk Brodzki took over the reigns of Malopolska, the Gardens of Bendzin returned to Malopolska. However, since there is no documentation left after so many wars and destruction, it is assumed that Bendzin was not included as the gift to Kazimierz Sprawiedliwy.

From the eleventh century to mid thirteenth century the Gardens, that later became Gora Zamkowa (Hills Fortress or Hills Castle) at the time of Kazimierz the Great in the fourteenth century in Bendzin, as well as other gardens in Bendzin, were specifically for the guarding of the borders of the Malopolska Region from the Silesien side.

Upper Silesia, where the Zaglembie Dombrowskie is located, of which the City of Bendzin is a part, is a variation of geological findings for many centuries like coal, iron, limestone and many others. Coal is in the greatest abundance.

The climate of Bendzin and the whole Silesien Region is treacherous. It has a lot to do with the distance from the ocean. The climate is what is called Continental. The winters are colder and the summers are much hotter than in the other parts of Poland, with temperatures 7 to 8 degrees Celsius in winter and 18 to 19 degrees Celsius in summer, with about 2 degrees in the month of January.

Bendzin is located between two rivers, the Czarna Przemsza and the Biala Przemsza. The two rivers of Przemsza meet, taking in smaller rivers, from its left the Sztela and the Jawirznik and from its right the Centuria and the Borek. (Last time when I was in Bendzin, in 1990, those two Przemsza rivers were just small canals. All this was done by the Germans in World War II.)

Geographically and topographical, the circumstances are altogether different today. In the days of then, the Gardens were strictly for defend-

The Lackier Seal of the City of Bendzin at the end of the XIIth Century.

Stancil Seal of the City of Bendzin at the end of the XIIIth Century.

Wax Seal of the District Bendzin from the year 1800.

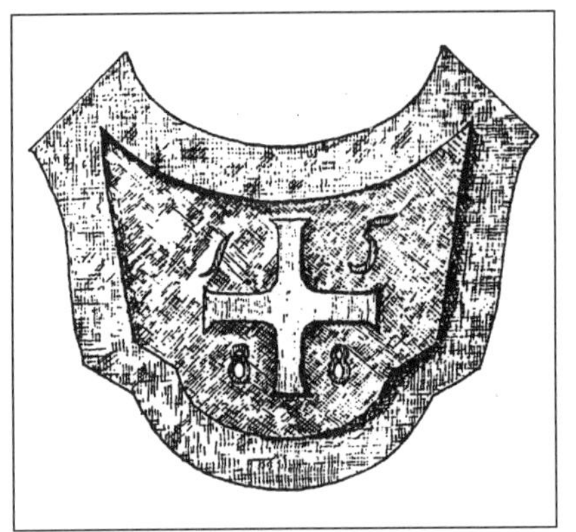

A stone built into the wall, to commemorate "The Bendzin Pact" of 1588.

Herb miasta Bedzina.

Bendzin. Coat of Arms.

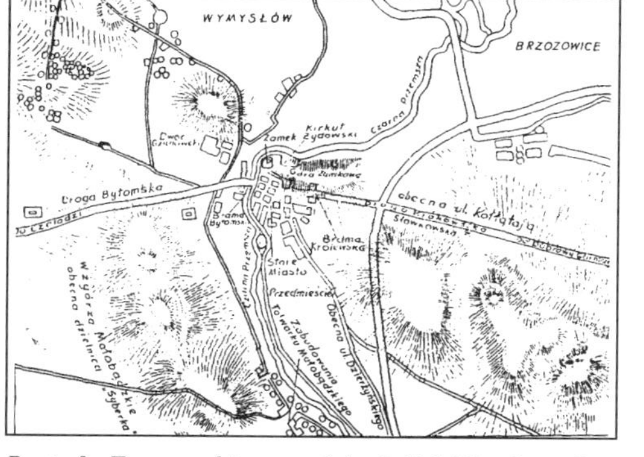

Part of a Topographic map of the Polish Kingdom of 1839. By Richter 1843. With a very detailed map of the City of Bendzin.

The River Basin of the Brynica and the Biaka Przemsza.

Part of a map of Malopolska from the year 1572, according to M. Hellwig. In the collection of the Sileslen Library in Katowic.

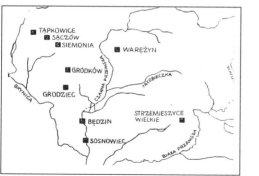

Part of a Topographic map of the Polish Kingdom of 1839. By Richter 1843. With Bendzin prominently showing.

Bendzin Castle according to Flech XIXth Century. Buildings along the bottom of the walls of the castle. Photo 1890.

Bendzin Castle with some walls in need of repair 1907. The huts at the bottom are where mostly Jews lived. I, too, lived in one of those wooden houses. A bit nicer and better. Probably of a later date.

ing the borders, where today there are beautiful gardens and the Castle on the Gora Zamkowa is a place for dancing, relaxation and tourism.

The Capital of Zaglembie Dombrowskie was Bendzin and the main city for industry and commerce was Dombrowa.

In 1975, the Administration of the region was again in Bendzin and to the Bendzin District belonged Czeladz, Dombrowa Gornicza, Grodziec, plus eleven villages and sixty-two hamlets.

In 1915, Zaglembie Dombrowskie was occupied by the German armies and was divided between Germany and Austria. The largest part of Zaglembie Dombrowskie, with Bendzin and Sosnowiec, was left to Germany and the rest with Dombrowa Gornicza and Niwka was in the hands of the Austrians.

After 1918 Bendzin belonged to the Kielce District. Bendzin played a major part in Zaglembie Dombrowskie as the capital of that region, being close to the train lines of the Warsaw-Vienna lines. As of this writing, Sosnowiec took over as a young and vigorous fast rising town. It is seen, however, by many in Poland, that regarding that territory, the administrational functions should and will be conducted in Bendzin as the capital of the Zaglembie Dombrowskie.

Bendzin was always a very important city for commerce, because of the easy crossing between the Atlantic and the Pacific, as well as many other commercial routs. The routs of Silesia cut through Poland, Germany and Tshechoslovakia. Those are the main reasons why foreign armies could and did so easily occupy those parts of Poland. (Hitler's main objective was the so called "Corridor" that he wanted and needed to the Baltic ocean.) That is, too, why the Gardens and the Castle on the Gora Zamkowa in Bendzin, played such an important role in defending that region.

With all that, Bendzin does not have a personal full monographic description of old. The only monograph to be found, comes from the 1930s done by Kantor-Mirski, entitled "From the past of Zaglembie Dombrowskie," containing a very rich monographic documentation of materials and texts of documents and privileges of kings of which the largest part no longer exists. As of now, nobody really undertook to describe completely a synthetic work which would encompass the whole history of Bendzin. Some information can be found in the following works; *Universal* by Gutenberg, *The Illustrated* by Tarski, Evert and Michalski, and a bit more of Bendzin in the "Slownik Geograficzny Krolestwa Polskiego," *(The Geographical Dictionary of the Polish Kingdoms).*

Some, too, can be found in the works of Balinski and T. Lipinski "Starozytna Polska" *(Old Poland).* We can also include "Przewodnik O Zaglebiu Dombrowskim" *(Guide to Zaglembie Dombrowskie)* published just before the outbreak of the Second World War in Sosnowiec. Only 50 copies were printed of that work. There too is another one "Samorzad Miejski" *(Self Governing City)* by Jankoz Czarnowa, published in 1826.

Bendzin as well as all of the Zaglembie Dombrowskie, counts among the richest parts of their past. Proof to it are the archeological finds in the last few years. In the thirteenth century most of the documentation from Bendzin was plundered by the occupying powers, with the largest part of it now housed in the Central State Archives in Leningrad.

Wars, fires, foreign occupations, and especially the last two wars, have caused a lot of loss in the archival depositories, even the city books of Bendzin from old Poland are missing.

Among the important documents found in the main archives of the past in Warsaw is a document of privileges afforded to the Jews during the reign of Jan III, as well as documents concerning privileges for Jews

by	Zygmunt August	in 1535
	Zygmunt III	in 1589
	Zygmunt III	in 1589 April 17
	August III	in 1701 May 22
	Stanislaw August	in 1766 December 11
	Stanislaw August	in 1767 June 18

The above mentioned documents state privileges for Jews in "Commerce in market places, Tree cutting in the forests and so on." Among other books found is a most informative book from the end of the sixteenth century and the beginning of the seventeenth century which encompasses the years of 1572 to 1644, and contains protocols about buying and selling, exchanging, inheritance, gifts of property on the terrain of Bendzin as well as courts and verdicts. In the above mentioned books, original documents were found in one of the Russian books, and mention is made of the privileges given to the Jews of Bendzin by Kings Stefan Batory and August III. It is worthwhile to mention that those books are in many languages.

The writing of the name of the city of Bendzin in the book *Boqutha de Bandzin* by Casten Petriov in "Ksiegi Grodzkie Piotrkowske" of 1399 states how the name of the city was spelled, BENDZIN, BEDZIN, BANDZYN. Liber in 1520 spelled it; BEDZINEK, BEDZIN. In 1522 Pawlinski writes Warsaw 1866 the name was spelled; BADZYN, pod

BEDZYNEM. In diplomatic codex's of Malopolska of the year 1364 the name is mentioned as BANDZYN, BANDZIEN, BANDZIN and BADZYN. In the dictionary "History and Geography of the District Krakow" it mentions the name of the city of Bendzin in the middle ages as BANDEN, (in 1301 BANDIN) BANDZIEN, BANDZEY, BONDIN, BADZEN, BANDZIN, BANDZYN, BENDZIN, BANDZEN and BADZIN.

Bendzin was always known for the beautiful gardens on Gora Zamkowa and the Castle of Kazimierz the Great of the fourteenth century. In 1918 an organization was formed to rebuild the Castle and the Gardens. The most active time this organization had was from 1925 to 1939 when the war broke out. From 1939, during the German occupation, nothing was allowed to be done, and after the war in 1945, very few of the old members were alive and it had to be started all over again. A museum was built. Among the first undertakings of the newly formed committee was the privilege of having a stamp put out of the "Zamek," the Castle, in 1946 with a five zloty postage value.

In 1958 Bendzin celebrated its 600th birthday as a city, even though the city dates back many more years. (At least 400 more years to about 966.)

Poland accepted Christianity in A.D. 966. Not only did this consolidate the country politically but it also started a new epoch in building of the first stone houses and churches. A new era of labor and commerce started all around the Gardens in Bendzin. Artisans built their shops around the gardens of the Gora Zamkowa.

For many centuries, up until 1939 at the occupation of Poland by the Germans, Jews lived around the Gardens. I, even though I lived there for the first 17 years of my life, never knew why the main Jewish quarters were around the Gardens and the Castle. It seems that all the wealthy land owners and all the Kings that lived either around the Gardens or in the Castle employed the Jewish artisans for centuries.

After the war when the newly formed committee to rebuild the Castle wanted to do some work on the Castle, it was found that the walls were very much in need of repair and primarily because of the fire that the Germans caused when they burned down the Jewish quarters and the synagogue. There is mentioning in a statement that "the walls around the Gardens cracked from the intensity of the heat." "In 1916 there was a fire inside the Castle and the Fortress and the walls cracked but not as severe as after the burning of the Jewish quarters."

The walls were 2.40 meters wide and were used to transport water to the Castle and the Gardens. There was once a well and the water was coming from the Gzarna Przemsza River, hitting the mountainous rocks. When the Germans occupied Bendzin, the Czarna Przemsza River was regulated as well as the Biala Przemsza River, making room for a highway towards Germany.

At the end of the nineteenth century, the terrain near the Castle has been occupied by the Jews all through the twentieth century until the Germans burned it down. The Jews built and lived around the walls of the Gardens. They built their own homes and businesses there.

In 1942 there was some cleaning of the rubble of the burned out Jewish homes in the Jewish quarters. I mention Jewish homes because the non-Jewish home and the church there as well as the home on Plebanska #2 where the priest lived were not destroyed.

In 1988 I was back in Bendzin, for the first time since 1945. The rubble in the former Jewish quarters was still as I left it in 1939. The city changed but only for the worst. The houses were not painted since before the war. Most of the Jewish homes not in the Jewish quarters were destroyed by the Poles after 1945. I guess they did not want the Jews back. Of which according to accounts only 150 Jews of Bendzin survived.

The left hand side of the Kollontaja street, coming from the Stary Rynek, is completely gone. Bozniczna, Zamkowa, part of Czeladzka, Browarna and all the small streets in between are gone. They were all Jewish homes.

The Poles are happy now that the Zamek (Castle) and the church are visible from everywhere in the city and beyond. After the war during the cleaning of the rubbles on Plebanska street to be able to fix up the walls of the Gardens on the Gora Zamkowa, the workers found human remains in the burned out Jewish homes. They, the Jews, could not even get a decent burial. There are no Jews in Bendzin to give these people burial and the Poles for sure do not care.

The blind street Grobla that brings to Grzichow is still there and the road to Krakow, Grodziec Beuthen, Lagisza and Czestochowa, in the olden days cutting through in the middle of the Grobla could bring you to the Czarna Przemsza River and to the Castle as through the old street Nadrzeczna, later Podzamcze, is still the same even now at my last visit in 1990. We have to add to it that the closed territory of old was heavy populated; the Gardens on Gora Zamkowa, Dorotka in Grodziec, the cemetery in Sosnowiec-Pogonia and Lagisza and later, about the beginning of the middle-ages, in Strzemieszyce as well as the populated area in Siewierz-Kuznica of the Hoky Jon. All this brought in people.

The entrance now via the old city is assumed to be after the erecting of the Castle in the fourteenth century.

In 1301, Bendzin was a village, run by a Soltys (administrator), named Stanislaw. Not until 1335 was it recognized as a city when it bordered at the waters of the Brinica and the Czarna Przemsza Rivers. Between the eleventh century and the thirteenth century a very unsettling, thundering, commercial, political and social revolution was taking place in Bendzin. The revolution had a character of progression, new settlements were being erected fast. This marks the times between the middle-ages and the time of the King Kazimierz Sprawiedliwy 1173 to 1174, who in 1178 gave Mieszko Pietonogi; Bytom, Chrzanow-Siewierz. This gift was politically motivated to strengthen the borders.

The Gardens in Bendzin occupied 0,78 hectares of land, and the back gardens had about 1.2 hectares. These Gardens had a strictly military function.

As I mentioned before, the oldest records of Bendzin come from the years of 1301 and then 1325 to 1327, 1328 to 1334, and 1336 to 1358. Thc years of 1241, 1246 and 1259 are mentioned as the middle-ages. Those, too, were troublesome years of constant harassment by the Tartars. In the middle of the twelfth century a project is born, the laws will be according to the rights of Magdeburg.

September 5, 1358, Bendzin receives the document as a localized entity. At the time of King Alexander in 1502 where it is written that "Kazimierz the King of Poland gives Hink Ethiop the realization to give the city, rights according to the laws of Magdeburg," and at that time the city was named BANDZIEN, Bedzin. And Hinko (Jon) Ethiopus was named Wojt, administrator, chief officer of the village, monitor and receives land for his own use, a store, bread, meat and a shoemaker, and the citizens of the city received grounds for their own use with gardens within the city and will have the rights to fish in the Przemsza river, and for the next six years all citizens now living in Bendzin as well as ones now moving to Bendzin, are exempt from paying any duty or tax.

"These rights are different than the German rights. However, if any citizen wants to sue, it will cost him 60 grosze to be paid to the political leaders, and may as well hand it over to the German Courts located on the Zamek Krakowski (the Krakow Castle), for decisions.

"After the six years are over the citizens of Bendzin will have to pay all regular taxes and the names of the people responsible for collecting the taxes are mentioned in the document." That document, however, does not mention the place where the market should be or where the markets now in existence are located, what the fee will be for having a place in the market, or even where the borders of the city are.

The study of the city as reconstructed, show the following streets: From the gardens of the church down to Kollontaja street and further, Zamkowa street, Zaulek and Podwale to the Czeladzka street and back to Podzamcze leading to the walls of the Castle at the bottom.

The second building made from stone was the church. First built as a house of prayer for habitants of the Castle. There is mention in that document about the church of the year 1327 to 1355, but it is not known if the church was then of stone or just a wooden structure, but the place was the same, the Plebanska street.

However, in 1977 when reconstruction work was done on Stary Rynek (the Old Market Place), the now highway to Katowice, basements and walls were found from the fifteenth century to the eighteenth century and according to plans found of 1823 Bendzin had three houses of stone and 256 wooden buildings. It is proof enough that there were many more stone houses in Bendzin than it was previously known.

Supposedly in the fifteenth century there was already a city hall in Gothic style in Bendzin in the market. That same layout is even now in existence. It is known that there were different important commercial roads, the layout of the city streets of the middle-ages is very well documented.

The most important layout is constructed from the following streets: Koscielna, Plebanska, Zamkowa, Swietego Jana, Czeladzka, Berka Joselewicza, Rybna and Podwale. (Berek Joselewicz, a Jew, was very much recognized in Polish history as a leader in the army and a fearless fighter and so was his son Josek Berkowicz.) It is interesting that all of those streets mentioned in that document were so called Jewish streets. Jews must have been living in those streets for centuries. I for sure remember those streets as Jewish streets.

It is presumed that the first city hall in Bendzin, before the fifteenth century, was at the corner of Stary Rynek and Czeladzke streets, and it is also assumed that in the same time there was near the city hall a Gothic style structure for the "Assembly" of the city of Bendzin, as well as the surrounding communities.

In mid 1364 the highest and most respected guest of that time was the

German Tsar who visited the walls and the gardens in Bendzin, which as mentioned was used as a fortress. With the German Tsar came the King of the Czechs, Karol the IVth. There is no doubt that the then King Kazimierz the Great, who also was a great architect, wanted those two guests to know that Bendzin is a power to be reckoned with.

As I mentioned before, when the Germans in 1942 demolished the remainder of the Jewish quarters still left standing after they burned it down in 1939, the walls of the church were completely showing especially from the Koscielna and Plebanska streets. Those two streets were the most used roads to the church. And it was no secret that the Poles did not want any Jews in those streets. For that matter they did not want any Jews anywhere in Poland.

I remember when the Germans were asked why they burned down that part of the city they said that the Poles had plans to demolish that sector around the church to get rid of the Jews near the church, but they did not have money to compensate those Jews for their properties.

The defense of the city was the wall around the fortress on the Gora Zamkowa. However, there were other walls that do not exist any more except a small reminder, one of the walls is running on Zawale street along the Jewish cemetery. The other side of the city of Bendzin has natural borders with the Czarna Przemsza River.

Work on the Zamek, the Castle, was done 1588, 1616, 1660 and 1834, after a few fires and the onslaught of the Swedes in 1655 after they burned down the city of Bendzin.

The register of the city of Bendzin shows that in the times of Kazimierz the Great there were living 240 heads on a terrain of 48 km./2, this is five heads to each 1 km/2. This was not much, since the neighboring Beuthen had in the same time 1,440 heads on the same amount of grounds; that is, 26.7 heads for each 1 km/2. It is hard to verify some numbers since most of the documents from that period are missing. However, it is known that in 1540 Bendzin had at least 100 houses and had over 800 people. It is even harder to verify the structure of commerce. However, records do show that taxes were paid in 1564 towards the king's booty.

Backers paid sixteen groszy, this came to five groszy each, ten shoemakers four groszy each, the bath-house had to pay 96 groszy in silver, the pottery makers (wood and other) had to pay 96 groszy in silver for using the markets five times, the beer sellers paid 48 groszy in silver for a barrel of beer, and the keeper of the bridge paid 60 zloty in silver (in those days

Bendzin. The temporary bridge on the Czarna Przemsza River after the destruction of the old bridge in 1939 to halt the onslaught of the Germans. Photo by Podebski, 1944.

The bridge on the Czarna Przemsza River around the end of the XIXth century.

Bendzin. Art by Artur Winer.

Podzamcze Street.

this was a small fortune), which was probably the highest amount any one had to pay, or more than all the others had to pay together.

In 1443 the Bishop of Krakow, Zbigniew Olszenicki, bought from the Siewierz Kingdom the suburbs of Bendzin with the neighboring settlements included as well as the villages of Malobadz and Grzichow. It seems that even then the church had the most money.

Missing too, are the documents of the structure of the population, like the different religious groups. For instance, there were Jews in Bendzin long before the census, long before the established Jewish group was counted in Bendzin in the beginning of the fifteenth century. The Jews had settled outside the walls of the Gardens on Gora Zamkowa, as well as outside the city. The Jews that came later settled at what in my time was known as Zawale street, and even later at Rybna and Targowa streets, in the same region near Targowa street, in the second half of the fifteenth century, taking advantage of the privileges accorded the Jews of Bendzin by the King Kazimierz Jagiellonczyk.

In 1453 a synagogue was erected. In the same time a Jewish cemetery was established, not only for the Jews of Bendzin but Mislowitze and Bytom, as well as Tychy, and part of the city of Sosnowiec-Siedlce, that lasted until the middle of the eighteenth century.

The cemetery was in the back of the city walls on Zawale street and all the way along that street. The Jewish community paid the care taker for the cemetery fifteen groszy a year. (Records from 1568)

All the people of Bendzin were working for the erection of the Zamek, the Castle, as well as other kinds of buildings. While the city was growing, more people were working in food supplies, butchers, sugar making, shoemakers, in leather, furriers, weavers, tailors, smith, woodworkers, masons, pot makers as well as the making of tiles. There were also farmers and people who raised chickens and animals for food.

As early as the sixteenth century there were already protests lodged with the authorities against paying too much taxes by the artisans that had to pay every year more and more.

As much as 90% of the city was surrounded by walls and sand fortifications. Bendzin had a military character, proof to it is that there was never another church built, unlike other Polish cities. Bendzin was proud in that respect.

In retrospect, we have to mention that the city was divided into three different quarters. The fortress, the church and the city proper. In the fifteenth century the suburbs encompassed the homes along the east side of the city across from the church, outside the city walls starting from across the church on the tract leading to Krakow and the road to Zagorze. Every one of the three parts "walls" had their functions, military, political and to defend the borders of the Polish State. Ideologically Bendzin was the center of Catholic and Jewish culture.

In the middle of the sixteenth century, Bendzin became a larger town than Kielce which was considered a large city in those days.

The Jews during the reign of King Stefan Batory, and all other people living now in large numbers in the fore-city of Bendzin "Zagorskie" received the privilege to live inside the city and take part commercially on the city markets.

The Big Synagogue seen from the street.

The synagogue in the Jewish sector of Bendzin mid XVIIth century. Photo by I. Tloczek in the 1930s.

Part of old Bendzin with the synagogue and castle, the symbol of the city.

The Bendzin Cemetery in Czeladz.

The old cemetery in Bendzin. "Untern Berg" (At the bottom of the hill)...

Chapter Two

None of the groups — the Aristocracy, the Church, the Leviathans — was willing to accept a change ...All these vulnerable interest groups were willing to exploit anti-Semitism to its fullest...

"The Jews of Eastern Europe"

Historically to remember of Bendzin, is the invasion of Maximilian of Austria, who in October of 1587 came to Krakow with his army and collaborators, ready to take over the throne of Poland. In 1588 when the Poles won the war with Maximilian, he was for a short time Jan Zamojski's prisoner in the Castle in Bendzin. After some days Maximilian was sent as a prisoner to Krasnostaw. That same year there was a gathering in Bendzin of representatives of the Polish government and delegates for the Tsar Rudolf II to discuss the release of Maximilian.

The so called "Pact Bendzinski," the Bendzin Pact, was signed by Urzini von Rozenberg for the Tsar's delegation and by Jan Zamojski for the Polish delegation. The signing took place in the city hall (Magistrate) in Czeladz the 9th of March 1588. After the signing of this document, Maximilian was brought back to Bendzin on the 6th of September 1588, then in company of Wawrzyniec Goslicki, Mikolaj Zebrzydowski and a company of Polish Hussars sent to the border point in Brynica near Czeladz. On the Austrian side he was accepted by Andrzej Wroclawski, accompanied by some gentleman from Germany. Since the Polish soldiers could not cross the borders, Maximilian had to take an oath on the bridge, that he is renouncing the rights to the Polish Crown. The 9th of March 1589 the "Bytomsko-Bendzinski Pakt" was signed by Habsburg and the Polish King Zygmunt III Waza.

In the beginning of the sixteenth century, the king signed many privileges for the citizens of Bendzin, and as many privileges for the Jews.

In 1527 Zygmunt I is giving special privileges to the Jewish merchants, which was according the Jews the same privileges as the Christians.

During the reign of Stefan Batory, the Jews are given the rights to live within the city limits and carry on the business of selling their merchandise on the markets. This was then a very special and important privilege for the Jews.

In 1559 Jan Kazimierz is dissolving the "Kaduk" rights as a good deed for the Jews.

In 1592 King Zygmunt III had ordered the protection of the Jews of Bendzin and to guard their rights.

In 1644 Wladislaw IV extended the rights of the Bendzin Jews to be the same as all other citizens.

In 1669 Michal Korybut gives the Jews the privilege to do business without any restrictions.

In 1685 Jan II Sobieski is signing a new document that all until now accorded privileges to the Jews are valid.

In 1702 a number of Jews that had fled the persecutions in Slask settled in Bendzin at the Slawkowa street, now Kollontaja, and in mid seventeenth century more houses are being built by the Jews living in Bendzin.

In 1739 August III decreed to all bordering towns, that all Jews who were dislocated from Slask, to settle in Bendzin. In that year a large number of Jews come to Bendzin and settle mostly outside the city gates. Mid seventeenth century, the Jews count one quarter of the population of Bendzin.

In 1766 Stanislaw August Poniatowski sealed all the former privileges accorded to the Jews as binding. The number of Jews living in Bendzin in the sixteenth century is not recorded.

In 1787 there are 978 people in Bendzin of which 250 are Jews. In Bendzin by then there are already 40 houses belonging to the Jews.

In 1789 Bendzin counts 700 population of which 332 are men, 368 women, and the city has 207 houses, three bars, a brewery, 60 wooden houses, 24 shacks with gardens, 32 shacks without gardens, 35 houses for artisans, 42 Jewish homes and a Jewish school. City homes are: the Castle, two churches, the chaplain's house, an institution, house for the vicar, and city hall as well as a house for the mayor of the city.

The structure of the population is as follows: 40 farmers, 25 peasants, 11 shoemakers, four tailors, three smiths, two furriers, barrel makers, cabinet makers, burial men, 38 ordinary workers, two bars, four businessmen, 14 traders, two hat makers and a soap maker. It is not specified how many Jews were in certain trades.

The Jewish population counts 207 including a Rabbi, a school teacher, four tailors, a smuggler, a lease holder, a doctor, a butcher and a hat maker.

In 1791 there are 166 homes, one district farm, three district houses, four noblemen houses and a hospital for 652 patients.

Towards the end of the eighteenth century, the city had 279 houses. In

Bendzin and surroundings there are 1,200 people. The city is suffering from stagnation, the income is lower, the bridge on the Przemsza River is bringing in to the city 60 zloty per year for the district, the Starosta is bringing in 1,000 zloty from the farmers and 5,470 zloty from the Gardens.

The privileges for the middle class and the Jews signed or broadened by Zygmunt August in 1535, and Zygmunt III Waza in 1589, are upheld by the King Stanislaw August in documents of 1766 and 1767, still preserved.

In mid eighteenth century, the Jews are building a new synagogue and the street is named Bozniczna street (Synagogue street), and a new synagogue and street on the mountain side of the Gora Zamkowa is born to the Jews of Bendzin.

From 1736 to 1789 the last Starosta or district Forman, Stanislaw Mieroszewski, has killed almost all income to the city through his incompetence. He forbade fishing on the Czarna Przemsza River, took for himself the forests, mills and most of the grass land bordering Gzichow. The city completely collapsed.

Between the years of 1793 and 1807, Bendzin was occupied by Prussia. They gave away the Zamek, the Castle, to one of the Hohenzollers, including all that belonged to the Zamek and again brought it to a complete collapse. There was no care taker for the Zamek and it fell into ruins.

In 1807 Bendzin is annexed to the Warsaw Kingdom that belonged that time to the Napoleonic Marshal J. Lanues de Montebello, who, two years later, fell in the war at Wagram and all his possessions were confiscated in 1913 by the authorities of the Warsaw Kingdom, after the decision was taken by the Vienna Congress. A lot of credit is given to Bendzin for the organizing of the new Administration. Within the limits of the Province Administration of the Kingdom, with the capital in Miechow, a new Parish was created, Olkusz-Siewierz, with the new government seat in Dombrowa Gornicza. This was one of the largest parishes with fifteen villages which occupied the largest part of the later Zaglembie Dombrowskie. Right at the beginning of the nineteenth century, many coal mines were opened and five industrial colonies were created.

Even towards the end of the Napoleonic war in 1813 the Tsar's armies came to Bendzin to plunder. Not until 1826 did Bendzin start to come up again when a Huta Cynku (Zinc-Works) of 500 mufflers opened up in cooperation with the coal mines "Ksawery" near Slawkow. That year when the Miners Administration took over the leadership under Stanislaw Stasic, did the commerce start to blossom in Bendzin and surroundings.

In 1875 a new coal mine opens up, named "Redeny" by the Coal Miners Administration.

In 1833 the Bank Polski is taking over the coal industry and this gave the industry the lift it needed. Since before the take over it was very disorganized, and with this again Bendzin and Dombrowa Gornicza is getting richer through commerce and a well known merchant by the name of Spiro is becoming leader in all their needs in the Mine Administration in Dombrowa Gornicza. The Miners Administration is ordering uniforms for all the miners which are being made by the tailors in Bendzin.

In the 1830s a hospital is built for the miners, a druggist from Bendzin is opening up a drug store near the hospital. In the same time there are problems in Bendzin with the Zamek, the Castle, all those years that the Zamek was neglected is showing now. The walls surrounding the Castle are falling apart and after an incident where a person is killed by the falling debris from the walls in 1825, the commission is ordering the complete destruction of the Castle. Luckily by that time, all of Europe took interest in preserving and rebuilding all antiquity.

Already in 1816 an architect by the name of Feliks Radwanski is taking an interest in the rebuilding of the Castle, since by that time the main artery of commerce from the miners was in Bendzin. A decision was taken to rebuild and to save the Castle, and to build a school for the miners right inside the Gardens of the Castle. This project failed and instead a House of Prayer for the miners brought to Dombrowa from other towns, was built. Those miners were brought in 1838 mostly from Saxony.

After new roads were built from Bendzin to the zinc works in Dombrowa Gornicza, horse drawn wagons are being used to transport the zinc not only from Slawkow and Olkusz but from the completely new mines in Zychlice and Bobrownik that did not come till now when new machinery is being brought in, realizing how important it is to the coal miners and the zinc industry.

Not far from the coal mine Ksawery, a new zinc works is built, the third in the country. No special name was she given but it is described in documents as "Huta Cynku pod Bendzinem," the zinc works near Bendzin. This Huta was equal to the Huta Constanty, which was built a bit earlier heaving 500 mufflers, four ovens to heat the Gallomine and two fire ovens.

In 1829, when there was a recession in that industry, only 185 workers were employed and this was a lot by these standards, since there were no other industries that employed more than 200 workers.

A new road was built to Warpie, because there were stone quarries and this was the main material used for building homes and factories. For that, money was paid to the owners of the grounds where the roads were built. For that road to the Warpie alone, 98 property owners had to be paid for or exchanged for other properties. A lot of the grounds were given to the miners as their own, primarily on the Bendzin-Dombrowa road. Most of it, however, belonged to the State.

In 1879 a theater is opened for the miners. Most of the actors were from Bendzin.

In 1832 a new section was built to Ksawcry near Bendzin and it had twenty homes. In 1882 that colony on the same road Bendzin-Dombrowa had 116 homes with 613 workers living there.

In 1858 "Direkcja Towarzystwa Drog Zelaznych Warszawsko-Wiedenskie" (the company to build roads) started buying out ground to lay Rail-Road-Tracts from Zabkowice to Sosnowiec. This was the first railroad in the Polish Kingdom. It was built from 1845 to 1848 and was called the Warsaw-Vienna-Train.

In 1859 the railroad station in Sosnowiec was inaugurated. This was the border station. Near the station a Duty Office was built. In the same time a new railroad station was built in Bendzin. This one opened up new inroads for the social economic development in that region.

In 1878, 29 coal mines produced 55 million pudd (?) of coal. These mines were all around Bendzin-Sosnowiec-Dombrowa and villages like Wojkowice Koscielne, Strzyzowice, Lagisza, Golaniec, Strzemieszyce and Slawkowiec. In conjunction with the growth of the population of Bendzin, the city started getting bigger. In 1673, there were 40 houses and 346 inhabitants but in 1789 there were already 279 houses and 1,200 inhabitants.

The account books show that in 1823 Bendzin had three stone buildings other than the Castle and the church, as well as a few city buildings. One was the house where the Wojt (Administrator) lived, the city hall near the Old Market (Stary Rynek), The Mill on the Czarna Przemsza River, 256 wooden houses and 2,254 people, but in 1856, there were already 361 houses of which 120 were of stone and there was a population of 4,140.

In the 1880s it was obvious that all the homes where the miners lived are falling apart and the "Towarzystwo," the Administration which owned the coal mines, was forced to buy those homes and demolish all of them. This was the end of the first Colony "Ksawery" as well as "Mydlice" and also the mine "Nowa" which was located outside Dombrowa that grew partially out of "Radocha" (later part of Dombrowa) and part of the Plebania (the Church) in Bendzin. (Again an incident where the church had more money than even the Miners Administration that went broke with buying out the homes.) It encompassed the terrain from Bendzin to Dombrowa (the homes demolished). That (Towarzystwo) Administration started building a new colony on the terrain of both sides of the road from Bendzin to Dombrowa and that colony was named Koszelew now belonging to Bendzin.

In 1899 on the outskirts of Bendzin (Walcownia Blachy Cynkowej) a zinc plate mill was built, which was in operation until World War II when the Germans demolished it.

In 1923, near the same place, a new factory arose (Fabryka Przetworow Cynkowych) for the manufacture of zinc products that was called (Polskie Zaklady Przemyslu Cynkowego).

Since Bendzin has now a main railroad station, Warsaw-Vienna, the economy grew by lib and pounds, and so did the population.

It is interesting to notice how much the population of Bendzin grew.

Year	**Estimated Population**
1789	1,200
1827	2,254
1835	2,500
1852	3,334
1858	4,140
1880	5,424

The whole district in 1872 had 92,764 population and in 1980 171,098. The main revenue for the people around Bendzin, was the coal industry.

In 1823 the first houses were on Modrzejowska and Slawkowa streets. The Second World War from 1939 to 1945 has changed the city of Bendzin a lot in its looks and shape. The Jewish quarters were burned down to the grounds and never rebuilt, the Old Market (Stary Rynek) was destroyed and used as a highway cutting through the old city leading to the (Huta) Iron-Works in Katowice. It was said, this was "a crime committed to the Old City of Bendzin."

The most characteristic buildings were preserved on the Zamkowa street and Czeladzka. Those were one story houses. A most interesting picture was found after the war, showing the houses of the Old City, and this is a part of Plebanska street with highly interesting buildings where the destruction of the Jewish quarters was in 1939. It is interesting to note, that outside the Old City a very important building is still standing. This is the building of the Jewish "Kehila" (Administration), built in 1838, near the Czarna Przemsza River, corner of Podzamcze and Bozniczna streets. Jews belonged to the "Kehila" in Bendzin, from eight different towns and villages.

As I mentioned before, there was a synagogue, a school for Jewish children, a Jewish cemetery and a Jewish hospital. I have to mention here, too, that in the nineteenth and the twentieth centuries, Jews were in the majority in Bendzin. For instance, in 1880 out of the entire population of 6,090, 1,403 were Christians and 4,687 were Jewish on a terrain that involved eighteen parishes: Bobrownik, Choron, Dombrowa, Grzichow, Kozieglowy, Kromolow, Losien, Niegowa, Olkusz-Siewierz, Ozarnowice, Pinczyce, Poreba-Mszyglodzka, Rokitno-Szlacheckie, Rudnik, Sulikow, Wlodiwice, Wojkowice-Koscielne and Zarki. Those were places that counted 134,717 heads. In that number there were 121,339 Catholics, 107 Orthodox, 235 Protestants and 13,036 Jews.

Among the other houses in Bendzin, we have to mention also the City Hospital. The first one was built in 1790, and it is assumed that it has been located at the same place where there is now the hospital, on the Malachowsiego street.

Other public objects little known about, supposedly right on the bridge of the Czarna Przemsza River, is a house known as "Komora Celna," the Duty Building, which at the end of the nineteenth century had one mounted guard unit in Czeladz, Kuzmierce, Mlynek, Modrzejow and Wesola.

The tradition of a building on the bridge was kept since the middle-ages until the destruction of it by the Germans when they overran Bendzin in September of 1939.

In that whole view of Bendzin, a great part was played by the commerce, from the end of the nineteenth century. In that region, there were 29 coal mines, eight iron foundries, eleven coal establishments, eleven brick factories, nine factories of mortar and cement, one tenner, three power mills, and 54 water powered mills, twelve weaving factories, one cotton factory, one vinegar factory, one oil factory, one distillery, five breweries, and nine alcohol distilleries.

Bendzin in the twentieth century was seen as a city planing town, with a mixed population because of the migration from other cities to Bendzin.

Year	Population
1901	35,320
1902	31,654
1903	33,690
1904	35,320
1905	36,112
1906	38,870
1908	42,381
1909	47,791
1910	50,500
1911	50,000
1914	36,010
1918	30,259 after World War I

In 1903 Bendzin proper had three iron-works, three coal-mines, seven large factories, three electric and water powered mills, two breweries, two (Tartaks) sawmills, eight brick factories and 506 different commercial factories, numerous commercial institutions (establishments).

In 1930, 42 factories employed 5,500 workers, there were 2,156 commercial establishments.

In the year when the First World War broke out, Bendzin built a new electric company (Okregowa Elektrownia Zaglembia Dombrowskiego). The same year, the Russians left Bendzin after their occupation and the Germans in turn occupied Bendzin. The German occupation lasted until the 11th of November (Armistice day) 1918, when Bendzin again became Polish.

At the end of the nineteenth century, and the beginning of the twentieth century, is a time of class distinction in Bendzin. Political parties become known and grow and so do strikes. The city of Bendzin is going outside the walls. The city grows without a plan. Along the streets of Kollontaja, Malachowskiego and Kosciuszki new modern and expensive homes are coming up. Chaotic in the beginning then somehow more planned. On the outskirts of the city new homes are being built, like in Gzichow Malobadz, Warpie, Ksawera, Koszelow, Syberka and New Bendzin.

Now Syberka is an all new masterpiece. As it can be traced the building of the city had a good impact on its culture.

Bendzin has a great history going back to the eleventh century as recorded. The Jewish population of Bendzin has a great history but now Bendzin is "Judenrein," free of Jews. Last time I was in Bendzin in 1990 there was only ONE Jew left, Mr. Szwarc. His wife who was a cousin of mine died in 1990. In 1988 when I was there, the first time since 1945, my cousin was still alive.

Poland will never be the same without the Jews, and the Polish Jews will never return to Poland. Anti-Semitism in Poland is as virulent as it ever was. Even the new generation that grew up without Jews is very anti-Semitic. The Polish Church as before the war is still preaching anti-Semitism. Polish Jews may go to Poland for a visit, only for a visit, but I do not think that they could ever live there. We the survivors of the Holocaust go back only to visit the graves or the concentration camps that in my opinion are the graves of our parents and families. Again in my opinion all of Poland is a Jewish cemetery. The earth of Poland is soaked through with Jewish blood. More Jewish blood was lost there than in all of Europe put together.

There were five extermination camps and they were all on Polish territory. Not by chance, by design.

We, the Polish Jews, the survivors of those Concentration Camps, can never forgive nor will we forget.

The caliber of the Jew that we lost in World War II will never be reproduced again. Nowhere in the world.

The 1.2 million children that we lost in the war of annihilation was our future. This left a black spot on all of humanity. The world may hang its head in shame.

Bendzin the former New Market renamed. Plac 3-go Maja with the monument for the "Unknown Soldier" of the First World War, was destroyed by the Germans at the beginning of the occupation of Bendzin 1939. (My brother Bernard and I were watching as the Germans dismantled the monument.)

Bendzin. The Halle. (Before the old market)

Dowbrowa Gornicza, Coal Miners School.

Bendzin. A small street "Oifn Berg" on the hill.

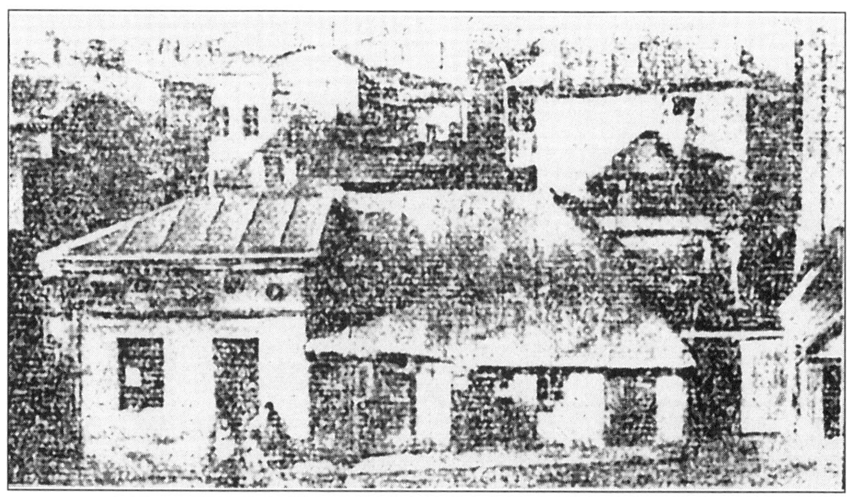

Rybna street, "Jatke Gass."

Bendzin Kollontaja street.

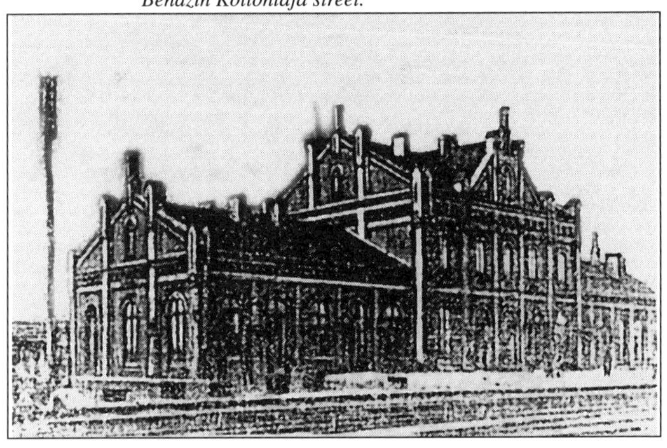

Train station at Warsaw-Vienna lines. Photo 1945.

The Mikveh Jewish Ritual Baths, built in 1838 at the corner of Podzamcze and Bozniezna streets. The street is now named "Heroes of the Warsaw Ghetto."

Bendzin. Pilsudski street.

Bendzin. Malachowska street.

The new Railway Station in Bendzin.

The Train Station in the Old City of Bendzin. Built 1848-1859. On that place a new station was built in 1915.

Modzejowska street in the Bendzin Ghetto.

Bendzin, the outlet of the Zamkowa street now Czeladzka street. Picture from 1906 showing the conditions and the character of the buildings in Bendzin in the XIX century.

The building of the "Wojt" Mayor of the City of Bendzin. Corners: Czeladzka and Stary Rynck.

Bendzin, Zawale street. Photo around 1930. From the Archives in the "Zaglembie Dombrowskie Museum" in Bendzin.

Bendzin, "The Warpie" section, with mud huts. Picture before 1939. Photo by: L. Balcerowski.

A visit by the "Gerer Rebe" in Bendzin.

"Hechalutz" from the "Poaley-Agudas-Israel" in Bendzin.

"Tarbut" in Dombrowa 1925 with the representative of the "Saim." Dr. Szlomo Wajnzuiher, seated in the center.

Chaim Nachman Bialik in Kalsbad 1930 with a group of friends from Bendzin, seated from left: Bialik, Hirszaj from "Hajnt" and S.Z. Ickan. Standing: Avrum Hampel, Wajnsztock, Wachtel and Halprin.

Bendzin. The "Kehila" Pres. Rubenlicht, Ferenz and Manela. With Jewish soldiers, just before the war.

Icchak Grinboim in Bendzin at the opening of the Sport Stadium "Hakoach." Among others seated from right: Ptasznik, Dr. Rechtszaft, Lajb Goldsztajn, Avrum Liwer, Dr. Wajnziher, I. Grinboim, Helena and Szymon Firstenberg and Szloimo Frenkel.

Chaim Nachman Bialkik in the orphanage 1930.

Bendzin. The Orphanage. All children were deported to Auschwitz.

From the Stenographic Report of Deliberations on the Jewish Question Headed by Fieldmarshal Göring at the Department of Aviation of the Reich, on November 12, 1938, 11:00 hours

Goebbels: Synagogues were burned in almost all the cities of Germany. Opportunities have now opened up for the manifold utilization of those plots where synagogues stood. Some want to turn them into parking-lots, others wish to erect buildings on them.

Göring: How many synagogues were, in fact, burned?

Heydrich: A total of 101 synagogues were burned; 76 were dismantled. There are 7,500 destroyed shops throughout the Reich.

Goebbels: There must be some excuse for the destruction of synagogues. Those that are no longer intact must be evacuated by the Jews. The Jews should pay for this. Here, in Berlin, the Jews are willing. Synagogues that were burned were evacuated by the Jews themselves. Some can be turned into parking-lots, and on certain sites buildings can be erected. This, I think, must be published as a directive throughout the land. That is, the Jews themselves must dismantle damaged or burnt synagogues, and place the totally abandoned plots at the disposal of German societies.

I think it is now necessary to establish a regulation prohibiting Jews from attending theaters, cinemas and German circuses...the present situation of our theaters permits us to take this step. Theaters are packed full in any case, with hardly any room inside. It is unthinkable to permit Jews to sit alongside Germans in places of amusement, cinemas or theaters. Later on we can consider the possibility of allowing the Jews a cinema or two here in Berlin, where they can show Jewish films; there is nothing for them in German theaters.

I also think it mandatory to remove Jews from all areas of public life, where their presence is provocative. Thus, for example, it is still possible today for a Jew to share a sleeping compartment with a German. A directive must be issued by the Reich Minister of Transportation establishing special compartments for Jews only when all Germans have been seated; they must not be mixed together with Germans, and when there is no room – the Jews must remain standing in the corridor.

Göring: I think it is preferable to give them their own special compartments.

Goebbels: But not when the train is full to capacity.

Göring: Wait a minute! There is only one Jewish car. If it is taken, the others must remain at home...

Goebbels: ...And then there must be a directive prohibiting Jews from going to bath-houses, beaches, health-spas and German vacation sites....

Göring: They can be given their own special ones.

Goebbels: We can consider whether to give them their own, or whether to make German ones available to them, but not the nicest ones. And let it be stated that the Jews may go for convalescence to these baths. We must consider whether or not it is necessary to prohibit Jews entry into German forests. Today Jews come in droves to the Grunewald forest; this is a constant provocation and there are often incidents. What the Jews do is so annoying and provocative, that matters always wind up with altercations.

Göring: Let us, then, set aside a portion of the forest for Jewish use....

Goebbels: ...And furthermore, Jews should not be permitted to sit in German public parks. I refer to the whispering campaign of Jewish women at the installations of the Fehrbelliner Platz. Some Jews don't even look so Jewish. They sit down near Jewish mothers and their children and begin to complain.

Göring: And don't even claim to be Jewish.

Goebbels:

I see this as particularly dangerous. It is necessary to supply Jews with their own fixtures – not particularly nice – and to declare: Jews may sit on these benches. They will be specially designated, with "For Jews only" written on them. As for the rest – they have nothing to look for in German park-installations. Lastly, the following point must be raised. In practice Jewish children still attend German schools. This is unacceptable to my mind. It is unthinkable that my son sit near a Jew in a German high school during a lesson on German history. Jews must be removed from German schools; they can look after education in their own community.

The Jewish Newspaper Our Telephone *of October 1913 announcing the death of the Bendiner Rabbi J.B. Graubart who held that position in Bendzin for the last 20 years prior to his death.*

The "Zaglembie Zajtung" of 1922.

Chapter Three

By 1933 the problem of Jewish survival in Poland was seriously complicated as a high powered, carefully nurtured program of Fascist anti-Semitism was added to the economic disaster of the Depression.

"The Course of Modern Jewish History"

Bendzin in My Times

Bendzin is located in the south central part of Poland, the industrial part of Upper Silesia. The region is called Zaglembie. It is very rich in coal mines. We were literally 'sitting' on the coal mines.

In 1939, when the war broke out, Bendzin was counting over 35,000 Jews, this was about 70% of the whole population of the city. Poland was a Catholic state where the structure of society classes was very much visible in the Jewish as well as the non-Jewish society. The Jewish population in Bendzin was active in every phase of industry, as well as trade. After all, the first Jews that came to Bendzin, as early as the eleventh century, were the working class in the needle trade as well as other trades, but businesses as small as they were, flourished when they were run by Jews.

Even in my times, the 1920s and 1930s, there were some very wealthy Jewish industrialists like the Firstenbergs. (Firstenberg's house during the war became the headquarters for the Gestapo. There was a large painting of Mr. Firstenberg in the house that was removed and a lifesize painting of Hitler was hung instead.) Also Jankele Gutman, Cesia (Cirele) Szajn in iron, whose beautiful house too was occupied by the Germans and is now "The House of Polish Culture," the Szwajcers in zinc, the Gambrinus brewery and so many other industries that employed hundreds of people in their factories. Firstenberg's factory was still in use in 1990 when I was last in Poland and, believe it or not, the machinery is still in use that was left when the Germans came in and confiscated the Jewish possessions. These wealthy Jews helped Jewish as well as non-Jewish institutions. For instance, Cirele Szajn saw to it that less fortunate youngsters in the Zionist movement, like the Hanoar-Hazioni, could spend time in summer camp. I was one of those youngsters.

Szymon Firstenberg

Helena Firstenberg

The "Firstenberg Gimnazium" (University) named after and supported by the Firstenbergs.

Mansion built in the XIX century in Bendzin, it belonged to the Cirele Szajn family. Now, The House of Culture for Youngsters and Children.

Cesia Szajn. "Cerele"

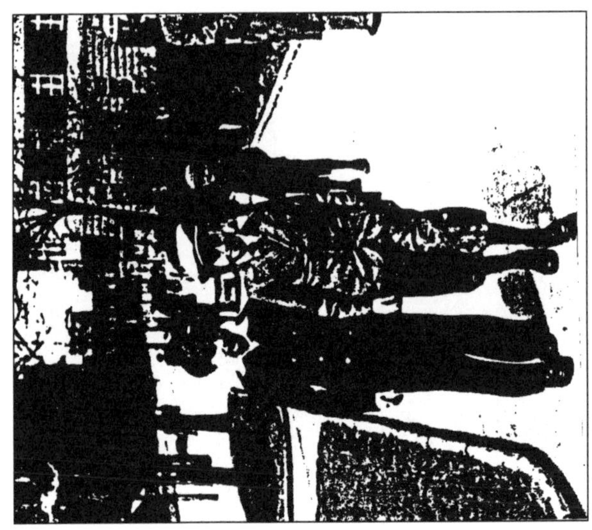

Arnold and Bernard Shay, 1936.

Arnold and Bernard Shay, summer camp early 30s.

Fela Frydman and Arnold Shay (Abram Szyjowicz)

„A"

RZECZPOSPOLITA POLSKA

Województwo Śląsko-Dąbrowskie
Powiat Będziński

Urząd Stanu Cywilnego w Będzinie
Nr. 36 / 1922

WYCIĄG AKTU URODZENIA

Zaświadczam że, Abram Lejzor Szyjowicz

syn — córka Sandela i Sury z Druchów

małżonków Szyjowiczów urodził się w Będzinie

dnia 16 lutego

tysiąc dziewięćset dwudziestego drugiego 1922 roku

Będzin, dnia 22. 10. 1948 r.

Urzędnik Stanu Cywilnego

z 666.

10 ZŁ 10 OPŁATA STEMPLOWA

Regierungsbezirk Dombrowa-O.S.
Polen

Copy of the Birth Certificate of Arnold L. Shay. a.s.k.
Abram Lejzor Szyjowicz

We state that Abram Lejzor Szyjowicz son of Sandel and Sara
nee Druch married couple Szyjowicz, was born in Bendzin the
16th of February Nineteen Hundred an Twenty Two 1922.

Bendzin 22.10. 1948.
Office for Civil Matters
signed; Stanislaw Czekaj

Zivilamt in Bendzin

Die Richtigkeit der Abs...
Goslar, den 21. ... 1949
Der Standesbeamte

Standesamt Goslar

Bendzin. The "Ohel" of Rabbi Graubart.

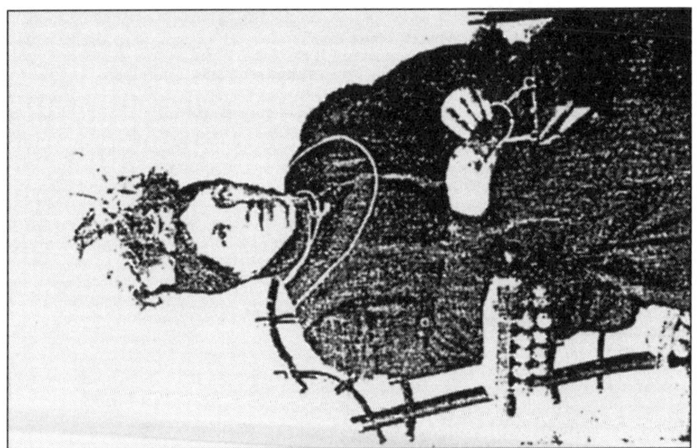

Mrs. Dvora Graubart, the Rabbi's wife.

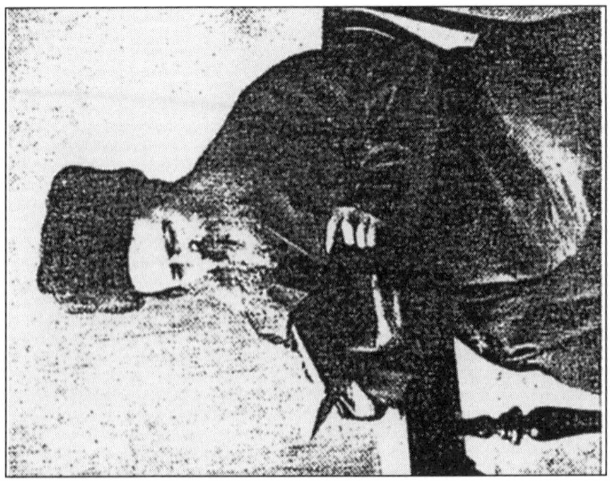

Rabbi I. Berisz Graubart

The Hebrew School "Jesod Hatorah" in Bendzin.

Bendzin. The old Jewish Cemetery on Zawale street.

Podwale street.

To the left an old stone building typical of the Old City of Bendzin in the XIXth century Modrzejowska street. The iron fence is around the Jewish cemetery which is now completely raised, as well as all the other Jewish cemeteries in Bendzin. Picture was taken in the 1930s. On this cemetery I witnessed many hanging of Jews by the Germans.

"Stary Rynek" the old market about 1900.

Bendzin.

Al and Lily Zimberknopf. Katowice 1934. President of Woolworth Co. in Bendzin.

The orchestra of the Jewish school, Powszechna Szkola #IV imieniem Henryka Sienkiewicza in Bendzin. The conductor Symcha Lustig seated third from left.

The Greeting Committee for the Bishop from Kielce in Dombrowa 1910. Standing from right: Sender Rajchman, not recognized, Szlomo Rechnic, Gerszon Szpilberg, Josek Szwimer, Lajzer Frochcwajg. Seated: David Josef Grinbaum, Felczer, Moisze Mitelman, Karpensztajn, David Ber Bergrajch and Mojsze Nower.

The Committee of "The Businessman Organization" in Sosnowiec. Pictured in the anti-Semitic German paper Der Sturmer, *the caption reads: "When Jews Got Rich."*

The Jewish Weekly.

Jews wearing the badge in the Bendzin ghetto.

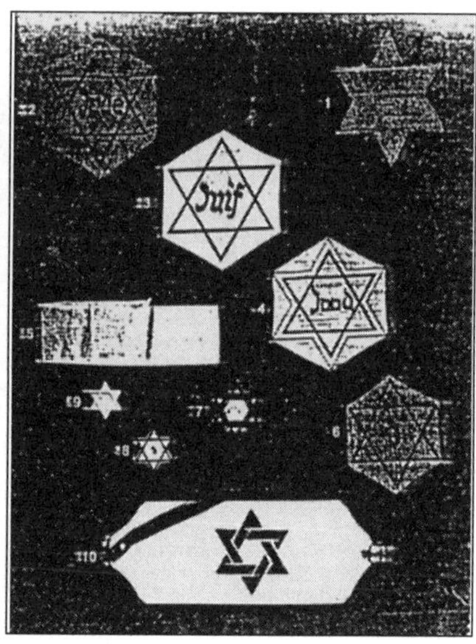

Jewish badges decreed by the Nazis.

Hanoar-Hazioni 1937. Arnold Shay front left.

Hanoar-Hazioni in the ghetto 1942.

Dr. Salomon Israel Weinzieher
Nur zur ärztlichen Behandlung von Juden berechtigt

Bendsburg 24.1.1943

Lieber Herr Alf! Von Ihnen habe ich schon lange Zeit keinen Brief erhalten. Hoffe dass Sie gesund sind und dass der Frau und Kindern recht gut geht. Meine Hoffnung ist völlig begründet, weil ich öfters Ihre Verwandten sehe. Ihre Schwägerin war etwas unwohl, ist aber schon völlig hergestellt. Meine Schwägerin, Estera Fader, die ältere Schwester meiner Frau, welche mit uns, wie Sie es wissen, schon viele Jahre lebt, war ziemlich schwer krank, was meine Frau stark bekümmerte, ist jetzt aber auch schon gesund, obwohl sie noch nicht gut aussieht. Ich übersende Ihnen zum Beweis ihr Lichtbild. Es wird mich sehr freuen, wenn Sie mich in paar Zeilen benachrichtigen, wie es Ihnen geht.

Best Grüsse von mir und meiner Frau an Sie und Ihre Familie.

Ihr ergebener
Dr Weinzieher

Bendsburg 24.1.43.

Dear Mr. Alf.
I did not get from you any letter for the longest time. I hope that you are well and that your wife and children are well. My hope is ment very well since I do see your family (relatives) often.

Your sister in law did not feel too well but, by now she is fine. my sister in-law, Ester Fader, the oldest sister of my wife, which, as you well know, is now many years alive, was dying, very sick, which my gave my wife many worries, is now however well, even though she does not look too good.

I am sending to you as proof her picture. It will give me much pleasure if you would send her a few lines how you are doing.

Best wishes from me and my wife
to you and your wife.
Yours.
Dr. Weinziher.

Letter from a Bendsburg M.D. whose name is stamped in the upper left corner. Below his name is the added notation "medical practice restricted to Jews only." The letter is dated January 24, 1943.

Jakub Gutman

Rachel Zaks. Bendzin 19. XII, 1929.

Stanislaw Wigodzki. A Jewish poet and writer.

Dr. Solomon Wajnziher.

The Jewish population of Bendzin, was always the leading community of Zaglembie, that boasted over 100,000 Jews. We had Jewish libraries, Jewish theater like the "Muza" and "Hazmir," Jewish sport clubs like the "Hakoach, Makabbi, Rzeznia, Gwiazda" (with some non-Jews too) and others.

Jewish Schools of Learning, like Javneh, Firstenberg's, Bojarska, and the school for boys that my brothers and I attended, "SZKOLA POWSZECHNA MESKA #2 IM. HENRYKA SIENKIEWICZA," the public school for boys, School Number 2, named after the famous Polish writer, Henryk Sienkiewicz. (When I was in the sixth grade, that school became coeducational. When I was in the seventh grade I attended the coed class.)

Zionist organizations, from the extreme right to the extreme left, to mention a few, Hanoar-Hazioni, Hashomer-Hazair, Tarbut, Poaley-Zion Left and Right wings, Hitachtud, Freiheit, Gordonia, Hashachar, Witkinia, Poaley-Agudat-Israel, Bund, Betar, and even the Kibbutz Boruchov. Jewish Self Help-Institutions like, Linas-Hacholim, Achnusath-Orchim, Achnusath-Kalah, Chevrah-Kedusha, and others now impossible to remember.

We had Juedish newspapers that were published in Zaglembie and distributed over the entire Province.

We had a most colorful youth, active in all sports, knowledgeable in all aspects of life and politics in the world. Almost all the clubs were Zionist oriented. The first group to enter Erez-Israel in the Alija, was the Bendzin group consisting of six Chalutzim. They left Poland in the summer of 1918 and made their way via Odessa and Constantinopole, timely reaching Jaffa on December 5, 1918.

Jews in Bendzin and the General Population

Year	General Population	Jews	%
1789	1,200	300	25
1835	2,500	1,200	48.6
1855	3,350	2.240	68.0
1897	13,550	10,839	80.0
1921	30,000	18,210	60.0
1931	50,000	24,000	44.0
1939	60,000	27,000	45.0

The Jewish population was estimated to have grown to almost 50,000 by September of 1939, in the first few weeks of the German occupation of Bendzin, with the Jews running from the smaller villages.

Bendzin is the oldest city in Zaglembie.

On page 43 in the book *The Jews of Poland* the author writes "...arguments conducted between the Jews and the Burghers of Bendzin 1757 which is appended to the privilege of the community of that town." In it the Burgher's representative declares "We also receive AD INCOLATUM in this town the entire congregation (i.e. the Jewish community) and each several one (Jew) individually; we grant permission for the pardon of property and permit those freedoms which we enjoy."

A very important, and a main emphasis in the privileges is in the economical sphere, enabling the Jews to earn a living in various branches of trade and craft.

POLIN. The Hebrew word for POLAND was obviously derived from the German POLEN. But its etymology was also explained as deriving from the Hebrew PO-LIN, which means; THERE FIND REST (or HAVEN) now in a book in Poland Chairman Abramski, Maciej Javchymny and Polanski. (I can assure you that it is not appreciated by most of the Poles that it has something to do with the Jews.)

Then came Hitler, the war, and the destruction of everything the Jews in Poland had worked for hundreds of years.

Hans Frank was appointed by Hitler as the General Governor for Poland. On September 8, 1939, Hans Frank published an order for all the Jews "to display in their stores the Star of David starting the following day." The Jews were also forced to make large 'contributions' of money, gold, silver and jewelry.

The decree by Hitler on October 8 and 12, 1939, provided to include in the Reich the Regierungsbezirk Kattowitz or unofficially Ost-Oberschlesien (east Upper-Silesia) which included Bendzin and Sosnowiec Chrzanow and Zawiercie counties as well as parts of Olkusz and Zywiec counties.

The war broke out on September 1, 1939. I remember how some of my friends ran towards the train station, from where the Germans were supposed to come into our city, with broomsticks or plain 2x2s to beat up those Germans. To their surprise those Germans arrived in a motorcade that was something unbelievable, we were never used to seeing the Polish soldier that well organized even when they were in a parade. The boys fast turned around and went home.

Oh yes! you could see the dust on their uniforms, as a witness that they must have been on the road for some time.

This was already Monday the fourth of September. But a week before that the Polish army set themselves in, in some Jewish homes, in our streets expecting the Germans to come from the side of Czeladz which was exactly the other end of the city that they came in. I remember how the Polish soldiers ripped out a wall (a few houses away from our home) in the Pik house on the second floor right above their grocery, and after dragging up the stairs a machine-gun placed it towards Czeladz to shoot on the Germans.

The Germans never came this way, they came from the side of Sosnowiec. In the same week before the Germans arrived to Bendzin the Polish soldiers even blew up a bridge on the Przemsza River on Czeladzka street (this was after fortifying the whole section). My kid brother Bernard who was only 15 years of age, was sent there to place the dynamite to destroy the bridge. What a joke. You could cross that river on foot.

I also remember how that same week, the Polish soldiers were stationed in Bendzin and they were expecting a shipment of ammunition and when the shipment arrived they opened the crates and found a shipment of boots. Hours before the Germans arrived into our city the Polish soldiers were in disarray. Some took off their uniforms and asked for civilian clothing and just left.

That same week before the Germans arrived, Polish-Germans were spotted on the Castle grounds wearing Swastikas ready to receive the expected German soldiers. Here, too, my kid brother Bernard was the one to spot them and reported to thc Polish Police but nothing ever happened.

We just were in tears when the Germans arrived and the Poles stood in the streets greeting them while the Polish girls went over to kiss them, the occupiers, with flowers in their hands. As the motorized columns passed through the streets of Bendzin, they went straight to the city hall. It seemed that they knew exactly where everything was. They stopped in front of the city hall and dropped off the Commandant with his staff and momentarily took over the city, naturally with the help of the former employees of the city hall. This was the "Magistrate" of the city of Bendzin on Kollontaja street.

The next day a notice appeared of the laws and edicts to the Jewish population. It was written in German and Jewish. It read:

"To All the Jews"

"All the Jews of all ages, both men and women, are required to register immediately with the Jewish Council. The Jews failing to obey this order will be refused ration cards, and will be prosecuted.

The Jewish text was signed by Moniek Merin and the German text by the German mayor.

Most of the Jews registered because it would have been just impossible to get along without the "Ration Cards."

The chief aim of the Gestapo was to make the Jews themselves be the party to their criminal activities. And for that the "Judenrat" was created and was supposed to serve their purpose. This in itself gave Moniek Merin the power he wished for.

The head of the Gestapo in Ost-Ober Schlesien was Alfred Dreier. His activities were centered at what we called "Department Yot," which means department "J" for "Jude" Jew.

Moniek Merin had invited the former dignitaries of Jewish prewar "Kehila" and nobody showed up. This ignorance infuriated him. There was not much that he could do but to report all this to the Gestapo. And report he did.

At the gate of the "Judenrat" a notice was posted that read: "A general assembly will take place at 10 A.M. at the square of the 'Judenrat.' The presence of all is required. The head of the 'Judenrat' will speak."

At the time posted, 10 A.M., a huge crowd had assembled at the square. This was the largest gathering of people ever. This is the speech he delivered:

"During the last three days I have invited you repeatedly to come here, but you despised me. I am putting myself in danger for your sakes, risking my own life as well as the lives of my nearest! I am going to die for you! Because of your contempt for me and for what I tell you. But now I decided differently. The whole of the Jewish community must not suffer, and shall not suffer, because of the few who disregard my directions. As for these last, I shall use the severest means at my disposal against them. And now I am making my last effort: I require of a group of people to come to me to a conference at twelve o'clock at noon. Those who should fail to appear, let their families not look here for help afterwards!" And he disappeared from the balcony.

This address was taken from the writing of the "Katzetnik." I want to mention here, that I, too, have heard the "King" Merin deliver speeches to the Jews in the Bendzin Ghetto on the "Kamionki."

This is the second address Merin delivered at 12 noon to the Jews waiting in silence:

"I have been ordered to hand over to the Gestapo five kilograms of gold and the set time limit is twenty-four hours. The danger is great; you surely know and recognize it as I do. There is only one holy aim before us: to save our lives from the fire burning around us, for we are enclosed in a death-ring. Let us ransom ourselves with our gold. Let our money atone for our lives. We are fortunate in that we can still do it, that we are able to ransom our souls. But the time is short. Each one of you will leave now in order to go round the town and collect gold according to especially made list. Do not pass over any Jewish home. I declare and announce here that this is not just a gold collecting action; this is a ransom action. You are not to eat or sleep until the needed amount is collected. I am now the first to remove my ring from my finger and to hand it over to you."

He removed his ring from the finger, put it on the table and left. The gold was collected as the Gestapo ordered, but this was not the end.

September 9, 1939, Saturday evening, the synagogue in Sosnowiec on Dekerta street number 14 is set on fire. So is the synagogue in Bendzin, on Bozniczna street.

(Later in this book I will give a complete account of that night in Bendzin.)

The Wehrmacht arrests and murders 44 Jews in Bendzin where 25,000 Jews live in the Jewish quarters alone. The old marketplace and the Jewish quarters are set on fire where 56 Jewish homes are burned to the ground, and several hundred Jews are burned alive when the German soldiers and S.S. men hindered the Jews from putting out the fires or from escaping it.

This was Plebanska street where I was born and raised. I knew all of the people that died there. Some I went to school with, some I played with. It was estimated that with the Jews that came to Bendzin from Germany and with the Jews from other towns that came to Bendzin to hide, Bendzin had about 42,000 Jews at that time.

Many of the Jews tried to flee, but the Germans beat them to it. Poland was occupied within 27 days. Germany and Russia sliced up Poland. Jews tried to flee to Russia, and here I have to mention some of my recollection of those days.

I remember when some Jews from Bendzin were caught in Slawkow, they all were killed by the Germans while crossing the bridge in Slawkow. The Jews were pushed into the water and drowned. One name especially stands out in my mind, that is Kaplan, the Cantor of the synagogue in Bendzin. Some Jews from Bendzin made it across Poland and saved their lives in Russia.

We always listen for news and news did get to us, sometimes distorted but most of the times true. Once those Jews arrived to Przemysl they just had to cross the San river and they were on the Russian side. Many of my friends from school, from the Zionist movement and even from the street where I lived went, but some friends names stick out more than others and one of the names is Icek Preszow, my closest friend from school and from the neighborhood. We were always together. He used to get his allowance from his parents and it was for both of us, as my parents could not give me an allowance and his parents knew it because they were friends of my parents.

His home was my home, in his home I had another home, in his home I had enough to eat, in his home I had a second set of parents, and I loved their concerts they used to give in their home, the whole family played violins. We were friends even before we started school but in school we were together from the first to the seventh grade and until he left for Russia. In Russia he joined the Air Force and was shot down over Germany about 1944. His memory will always be dear to me.

I have to go back now to the year 1939. Just before the war broke out. In July of that year like a few years before that I went to summer camp from the Zionist movement, Hanoar-Hazioni, with a group of boys and girls. This time I think we went to Jelesnia in the Karpatien mountains. A month late when I came back there was already scary talk about Germany. This was already the sixth year of Hitler's reign.

Let me go back one more year, to 1938. When the Germans occupied Czechoslovakia, Za-Olzie, the other side of the river Olza was "gifted" by the Germans to Poland, after the Germans raped Czechoslovakia. This was called "Slask Czesinski," the Czech-Sielesia. One incident of that time that I will never forget about Za-Olzie I have to mention here. This fact will show the short-sightedness of Poland.

Poland was in a state of drunken extra galactic. As if they won a war. I was that time at a special school where I took business courses in the evenings. See, after I finished seven years public school and had not the means to go to a private high school (even though my parents had tried but could not afford it financially) I went to a school supported by the state.

The classes were conducted in the evenings and even though I was working the boss had to give me off a couple hours earlier so I could attend school. There were only a few Jews in that class. I was the only Jew in my class and distinguished myself in all fields even in P.V. (Przysposobienie Wojskowe) which is like here in the states the ROTC. I will not go into details of what I had to endure as a Jew in that school (my other co-religionists had probably to endure the same), but as I started out I have to mention that one incident.

The head master of that school was Professor Ocoszynski, who during the German occupation of Poland was a Nazi collaborator and, after the war when the Russians were in Poland, he collaborated with the Russians (according to a Polish friend of mine whom I believe 100%).

One evening, after Poland got that gift of Za-Olzie from the Germans, Professor Ocoszynski called a meeting of the P.V. to deliver a speech to us. I was there. The speech that still sticks to my mind, was where he announced with tears streaming down his cheeks, "After so many years Zaolzie is ours," and the Hip-Hip-Hurrah went on for a few minutes without stopping. In that same speech he thanked Germany for "that most magnificent gift." I was then only 16 years old, but I cannot forget the impact that speech had on me. I remember when I came home and told my father about it and Dad tried to calm me down. I asked my father "don't they understand that this is not the end?" And it was not.

Now going back to the fleeing of the Jews from Bendzin. The Poles took advantage of the situation and many robbed the Jewish houses of all their possessions. The Germans naturally did not take kindly to it and a lot of the Poles when caught were hanged in the public square. Those incidents were reported all over Poland. Then it started right next day.

Food. The stores run out of food and there were no deliveries of food to the Jewish owned stores.

The store owners were forced to sell out all they had. Lines formed in the middle of the night to wait in front of the bakery or grocery, or dairy product. And here again our Polish neighbors showed their anti-Semitic cooperation with the Germans and their hatred for the Jews, even though the Germans were our common enemy.

Many of the Poles would point out the Jews in the lines to the Germans "on Jude, on Jude" pointing that we are Jews and the German soldier would beat the Jew pointed at with his rifle butt and chase him from the lines to the delight and laughter of the other Poles. The German could not recognize a Jew from a Pole but the Poles were very helpful in that respect and very willing and delighted to cooperate with the Germans.

Jewish businesses were confiscated and handed over to the German "Treuhander" trustee. Sometimes a German would come into a Jewish store, look around and give the Jewish owner one or two hours to clear out and he would take over. The same would happen to Jewish owned homes or apartments. A German would come into a Jewish home that he had picked for himself beforehand, ask the Jewish family to take with them whatever they can carry of their belongings and leave within an hours time. Yes, and the Jews had to clean the home for the German to make it ready to move in. This became a daily occurrence, never knowing who would be next.

As I mentioned before, Dreier was the head of the Gestapo and the "Department J" Moniek Merin was called to the Gestapo. Moniek Merin did not speak German so he took with him his private secretary Felicia Schwartz or as we remember her, Fanny Charna. She was about twenty-five years old, black eyes, black hair, just beautiful, and a brain.

Dreier delivered a lengthy speech to them about the restrictions concerning the Jews which had to be followed and he, Moniek Merin, as the head of the "Judenrat" is responsible for enforcing those laws immediately.

Dreier made Moniek Merin accountable for all this stating that otherwise heads will be rolling including his own (Moniek Merin).

The first order was to deliver five kilo of gold and Moniek Merin and Fanny Charna were given documents by the secret state police stating that they not be harmed since they represent the Jewish Council.

Naturally they called immediately all the rich men and dignitary to a meeting that was supposed to be held the next day at noon. They called the people the second and the third time and nobody showed up.

Moniek Merin was afraid for his own life. But Fanny Charna was more relaxed. Her mind was working.

On the third day Fanny Charna called the Gestapo. She asked to be connected with the head of "Department J" and asked to be seen by him right away for consultation. Dreier agreed. A half an hour later Fanny Charna was in his office and told him what happened with the meeting that Merin called.

Dreier stood up and invited Fanny to join him in his car and they drove off straight to the office of the "Judenrat." He asked for the list of the Jews. He took out a red pencil and told Moniek Merin to underline twenty of the richest Jews names with that red pencil.

Moniek Merin held that red pencil in his hand for the longest time, knowing that this will mark the death of the twenty people he underlines. Fanny Charna saw what was going on, grabbed that red pencil and without hesitation marked the twenty names. Dreier took the list and walked out.

Next morning the square of the house of the "Judenrat" was filled with people. Moniek Merin came out and spoke to the people. Explaining that he asked for assistance and nobody came, for that the community, not he, will pay the price.

He told the people too that his orders must be obeyed or the Jewish community will pay again and again. The gold was collected and the required amount was delivered to the Gestapo.

Then it started with confiscating from the Jews gold, silver, diamonds, furs and others like copper, steel, et cetera. Like the one I remember in February of 1940 when the Jews were ordered to deliver by 4 P.M., next day, 15 kilo of gold and 60 kilo of silver, or harsh measures will be taken against the Jewish community.

Dr. Weinziher, that time the head of the Jewish community, complied. The gold and silver was collected and delivered to the Germans, but individual Germans started blackmailing Jews for valuables and in order to scare us they would shoot a few Jews. And then came radios, electrical appliances…there was never an end to it.

Then came more severe "punishments," hangings of Jews for no reason at all, beatings, cutting of beards, taking Jews wherever they would be, loading them on trucks and taking them away. Sometimes they would come back but most of the time not. Grabbing Jews in the street to clean the streets, to clean the German homes and sometimes just for fun to scare those poor souls out of their wits.

Then the "Judenrat" was established in Bendzin and all other surrounding cities, Sosnowiec, Dombrowa, Zawiercie, and a few others that were run by Moniek Merin, who later ran all of Upper Silesia ghettos. In the same time that ghettos were established in other cities and all over the Zaglembie district.

Jaworzno "Judenrat" was run by Mr. Mehler.

The Chrzanow "Judenrat" was run by Mr. Zucker.

The "Judenrat" in Trzebinia was run by a Mr. Mandelbaum. But they all took orders from Moniek Merin. "THE SUPREME."

All this was done with one thought in mind, to make it easier for the

Germans to round up the Jews and to "liquidate" them. Those "Judenrats" did a splendid job. The Germans were very thankful to them. As long as they were needed, the Germans gave them a free hand. But they, too, met their maker and in the same way as the Jews before them.

Bendzin as a Judenrat wanted to run their own affairs, but Moniek Merin was threatened by it and would not allow it. Moniek Merin would not hesitate to liquidate anyone who would stand in his way or did not obey him. And there were many instances where he would show his power and punish his adversaries in the cruelest way and without regrets. He was the soul ruler of all the ghettos in Upper Silesia and ruled them with an iron fist.

Up to about the beginning of 1943 Merin had his own car, bragging about being the only Jew under the occupation who had a car. (It was exaggerated like everything else that Merin said or did.) To make sure that everything in Bendzin goes his way, he set up his brother Chaim Merin as the head of the Bendzin "Judenrat."

The central offices of all the "Judenrats" in the "East-Upper-Silesia" were located in Sosnowiec on Targowa 12. This was the most famous address in all the ghettos of Zaglembie.

Later on I will bring in of what had happened to the leaders of the "Judenrat" including Moniek Merin. (He was born 1908.)

With the help of civilian Germans all kinds of factories were set up in the ghettos. Thousands of Jews were employed in these so-called shops for very little pay, and most of the times no pay at all. I worked as a tailor in one of those tailor shops for the firma Rosner.

In Bendzin, Alfred Rosner ran a tailor shop with about 7,000 Jews.

In Sosnowiec, Mr. Held had a shop with about 2,000 Jews.

In Zawiercie was a shop with some 5,000 Jews.

There were other shops in Bendzin and Sosnowiec where, like the Hartmuth Loitzsch of "The Bendsburger Bekleidungs-Industrie Seiler-und-Sattlerwerk-statt" on Talstrasse 7 and 101, Wallstrasse 1 and Marktstrasse 42, they made shoes, purses, and so many other leather goods and thousands upon thousands of Jews worked there. But even all that hard work, very little pay, very little food did not satisfy the hungry German beast.

And how can we not mention that Saturday, September 9, 1939, just one week after the Germans march in into our city of Bendzin. We lived on Plebanska 14 just a few houses away from the church on Plebanska 2 and on the other side, just a few houses away from the big synagogue.

Chapter Four

Where is my street?
Where is my home?
Gone is the Jewish sector!
Gone is the laughter of the Jewish children!
Gone is the Jewish life!
Gone is every Jew of Bendzin.

Arnold L. Shay

World War Two

In his book *The Second World War: A Complete History* Martin Gilbert writes of that night that will live in infamy… "Behind the lines, the atrocities continued. At Bendzin on September 9, several hundred Jews were driven into a synagogue, which was then set on fire. Two hundred of the Jews burned to death. On the following day the Germans critically charged Poles with the crime, took a number of the hostages, and executed thirty of the hostages in one of the public squares. On September 10 General Holder noted in his diary that a group of S.S. men, having ordered fifty (50) Jews to work all day repairing a bridge, then had them pushed into a synagogue and shot.

Colonel Wagner wrote in his diary on September 11, "Nothing like the death sentence! There's no other way in the occupied territories!"

This writer (Arnold L. Shay) considers the above mentioned book by Martin Gilbert (as well as all his other books on World War II) to be the best works on the history of World War II. I, as a survivor of that period, can surely appreciate it.

So, at this time I want to add my personal experiences of that September 9th in Bendzin.

The following pages carry a complete account of my family's endurance of that night and the following days. Our loss of everything we owned. Our living hell going from place to place. Hunger, degradation and most of all of what it did to my parents.

I will remember that day until the day I die. That Sabbath day we lived in more fear than any day since the Germans had occupied that city of Bendzin, about four days before.

On that September 9, 1939, six of us in the family, mother, father, one sister and three of us brothers, slept in one bad, being afraid to separate. (One of my sisters, the oldest one was not at home that night.) This was not even our apartment. The windows of our apartment were facing the street, so we moved into our cousin's apartment (who was away at that time), the son of my mother's brother (Usher Selig Druch), who lived in the rear of that building.

We heard noises, there was no light anywhere, there was a curfew. My father had a pocket watch and wanted at one time to see what time it was, and asked me to look at the watch while he was lighting for one second the cigarette lighter, so I could see the time. I bent down to see the time and my hair caught fire. Nobody would even cry out for fear to be heard outside by the German, but my mother caught a towel and wrapped it around my head. Little did we know that a much bigger fire was raging outside.

The Germans had set our big synagogue on fire, with some of the Jews in it, as well as the main Jewish sector of Bendzin, from the synagogue on Buzniczna street all the way up through Plebanska to the church on the corner of Plebanska and Koscielna streets. All of a sudden we heard screams and the fire engines from the outside. By that time we could already smell the smoke that was all around us. Father opened the door from the apartment, which was on the first floor, and we saw that we were all locked in by the main heavy wooden gate in front of our building. That had to be closed at the 6 P.M. curfew.

Within minutes all of the tenants were in the courtyard, everyone trying to escape the fire. No one could get out. There was panic but no screams, not to attract the Germans. We heard shooting and screams coming from the outside in the streets. We had our night-wear on, our own apartment which was in front of the building and was the oldest part of the building, this was the wooden structure and was by that time all engulfed in flames.

Father grabbed a pair of pants, mother in her nightgown could not, or was just confused, find anything else, so she grabbed the tablecloth off the table, (it was Saturday night) we the children grabbed whatever we could wear that was laying near the bed. (Some of us never had taken the cloth off) and all of us started running towards the locked wooden gate in front of the building where, in the meantime, all of the other tenants have already gathered. I don't know how but we got the gate open. We thought that we were safe, but outside German soldiers were shooting everyone in sight.

My father who spoke a perfect German, called out to the German soldier not to shoot, he wants to talk to him. I can still see that German soldier how he put the rifle down leaning on it, and motioning with his head, to my father to come over. I still think that, the soldier thought that my father was not a Jew, or he was just caught by surprise with my father's German. I still don't know what my father told him, we never talked about it afterwards, but the soldier motioned to my father with his right hand to go to the right which was on the left of our house and towards the church.

I think he was trying to tell us that near or at the church we will be safe. As we ran out I in desperate fear looked around, I could see the houses, all of them in flame, the whole streets, up and down from where we were standing, as far as my eyes could see, were on fire, only fire. In front of us, in back of us, and all around us.

But one scene that I will never forget, that house, that house right across from our house, that house that I could see from our bedroom window each and every day, that beautiful house that was owned by the Zaks' family, David and Edith Zaks. That house was now completely in flame, that beautiful brick building with the balcony that I always admired, that house was now literally splitting in half like a toy house, and the fire just shooting upwards from the inside. I knew then that no one inside could survive.

As we were going towards the church I noticed that one house in our street had a huge picture of the Madonna and the Child hanging out the window and with a lot of lights all around it. This was the Chachulski house, a Christian, our neighbor on Plebanska 10. Now I can see that our Christian neighbors knew that the Germans will burn down our homes, or they would not and could not have been prepared with that picture. As a matter of fact, next to that Christian house, Plebanska 8 was a house owned by a Jewish family, the Gutmans, (where I learned the tailor trade, where I was for three years, day in and day out it was almost like my home) and it was spared in order not to endanger that next house.

The Gutman house is still standing, but now with a Christian Polish family living in it. (Last time I saw that house was 1990 at my last visit to Poland.)

As we were running, the German soldiers and S.S. men were shooting at us from all sides. A cousin of mine, Pesl Druch, who lived in the same house where we lived, one floor above us, who was holding in her arms while running, a little baby, was shot in the leg and as she was falling down, she fell on top of the baby squashing it to death. She picked the baby up and kept on running with that baby in her arms and bleeding from her leg. My family ran as fast as we could, constantly checking if we are still all of us, together. All of a sudden I called out to my father that my younger brother Bernard and my older sister Laja are not with us.

We all wanted to backtrack to look for them, but the Germans kept shooting at us and we had to run for our lives. Not until next morning did we find out what had happened to my brother and sister. My brother Bernard had fallen through a grate into a basement outside window and my sister Laja saw it and would not leave him but helped him to get out of that basement window.

Our ordeal was by no means over. The worries about Bernard and Laja if they are dead or alive were constantly with us and yet we could not even talk about it, we could not stop but keep on running with bullets flying all around us. My older brother Izaak, who was with us, worked before all that madness for a large toy firm (Jama) and had the keys to the store and their apartment above the store, in a plush neighborhood on Potocka street. Because they had fled Bendzin when the Germans came to our town, and had left the keys to the apartment and the toy store to my brother Izaak to check it from time to time until they were able to return, we thought that it would be best to go there for safety. And so we did.

As we approached that building, we noticed a big commotion and outside the building all the tenants were lined up in their night wear and some S.S. men were watching them. Father told us to pretend that we are not bothered by it and to go inside the house as if we belonged there, but, as we got closer to the building one S.S. man approached us and in a very friendly tone said to my father, who always was ahead of the column, to leave as fast as we can, that these people are going to be shot. Again I think that this S.S. man did not think that we were Jews. We did not know if to believe him or not, but father said we are leaving, that he thinks that this man is honest, that he probably means well. He may have thought that we are not Jews or he may have been a decent man, because next morning we found out all of these people in front of that building that night were shot.

We then started anew to look where and how we could save ourselves. Father suggested a friend of his who lived on Malachowska street, not far from the Polish police station, and we started towards that street. As we came to that house and knocked at the front door of the building which too was a heavy wooden gate, the caretaker, an old Polish man, came out.

He recognized my father but would not let us in. Father put his foot in the door and begged him to let us in, but his reply was that he would not let any Jew in, and he would not endanger his life for any Jew (not in such a friendly term). Naturally father was persistent and told him that he will make such a racket that the Germans will come over and he, too, will be in trouble. He had no other choice but to let us in. All of us were up all night worrying about what had happened to our brother Bernard and sister Laja. If they are safe, if they are still alive, if we are safe there, telling our friends what we saw and what we went through until we got to their house.

Next morning we went to see what had happened to our street. Well! Nothing was left standing from the three streets where most of the Jews of Bendzin lived, except the church, the Chachulski's house and the Gutman's house that was next to the Chachulski house. It is impossible to describe the sight we had in front of us. My parents just could not stop crying. All our possessions were gone. We thought that we may be able to salvage something from our apartment, but all was gone. All we could see were ashes of the burned out houses, especially the wooden structure that our apartment was in.

The only thing that I could see was my sister Sofia's burned out iron bed that she called her "golden bed" because every so often mother had to paint that bed with golden paint so it would not rust. As a matter of fact, in 1945 after the liberation when I went back to Poland to Bendzin because I heard that my sister Laja survived the camps, I went to look at the street where I lived and everything was the way I had seen it in 1939, nothing else but only that "golden bed" was still showing.

But as we started looking around, we saw that we were the lucky ones. Burned corpses were all over the streets. I found half a torso of one of our neighbors that lived right above us, Menashe Russ, the tailor. I found his head, chest and part of his right arm biting his fingers. This sight will be with me as long as I shall live. His beard was burned off but I still could recognize our neighbor Menashe Russ. Two houses away I found my friend Brat from Plebanska 12 who worked with me for Icio Gutman as a tailor. He was shot and probably thought that he could hide in a clothing closet but instead was burned there. All around corpses were laying.

After we made sure that nothing could be salvaged from our apartment we had to start thinking of a "new life" no matter what. We then went to my father's older brother "Joivele the Baker," who was not touched by the fire, where we stayed a few days. We had nowhere to go. My uncle had a full house of his children and grandchildren, about 40 people all together, not the nicest people to think of their relatives. Too selfish.

My family had no place to go, no money to buy food, no clothing on our backs, plain and simple — nothing to live for. Except we were all alive, we had one another, we would not let our parents die and our parents had to live for us. After much pleading, crying and begging, the Jewish community leaders finally got a room for us. It was not much but it was a place to put our heads down, it was in the former locale of the Zionist movement "Gordonia." We were happy, the family will be together and somehow we will make it.

We got one room for all seven of us. The room was less than 8x8 feet. In the beginning we had no beds or blankets or anything. After a couple of weeks we received a small oven that stood about two feet high, the top was about one foot by two feet with two small burners, one single bed and one military cot, two blankets, two pillows and one small closet for the clothing that we did not have. And this was called "LIFE." But we did not complain, we had nobody to complain to. We made a new life with whatever we had. After another few weeks we received some clothing but no shoes. Life was going from bad to worse.

The Germans crippled the whole Jewish economy, Jews lost their rights to work as doctors, lawyers or even artisans. They could only work for Jews. My father lost in the fire the only sewing machine that we owned. We had no money to buy food on the black market. On top of this that my father, as a Jew, could not work, that a family of seven we had but one pair of shoes given to us, by I don't even remember whom, because all of our possessions were gone with the fire, we had nowhere to live, we had no money to buy the most needed daily things.

When my brother Bernard and I would stay for hours in line to get some bread or groceries, there would always be a Pole who would point at us to the German soldiers that we are Jews, we would then be chased out of the line and most of the times catch a few hits with the rifle butt. I don't have enough paper nor do I have enough ink to describe those days after the fire.

I would steal a few potatoes from the train parked in the train station and watched by the Germans, so my mother could make a potato cake and I would stay at the corner of the street selling pieces of the potato cake to passersby and I was hungry but would not dare to eat one piece. I had to bring the money home so that the whole family would have something to eat.

I had no shoes so my feet were wrapped around with rags. I don't

1933-1943 TABLE OF ANTI-JEWISH LEGISLATION IN GERMANY—

DATE	SOURCE	TITLES OF LAWS, DECREES, AND ORDINANCES	ELIMINATION FROM: CIVIL SERVICE, PROFESSIONS, LABOR SERVICE, ARMY, INDUSTRY & COMMERCE
1933 April 7	RGBL., I, p. 175	Law for the Restoration of Professional Civil Service.	Exclusion of "non-Aryan"* civil servants; exceptions for "privileged non-Aryans."
April 7	RGBL., I, p. 188	Law Regarding Admission to Legal Profession.	Exclusion of "non-Aryan" lawyers: exceptions for "privileged non-Aryans."
April 22	RGBL., I, p. 222	Decree Regarding Physicians' Services with National Health Insurance.	Exclusion of "non-Aryan" physicians from panel practice; exceptions for "privileged non-Aryans."
April 25	RGBL., I, p. 225	Law against the Overcrowding of German Schools.	
July 14 July 26	RGBL., I, p. 480 RGBL., I, pp. 538/39	Law Regarding Revocation of Naturalization and Annulment of German Citizenship. Decree to Same Law.	
Sept. 22	RGBL., I, p. 661	Law Regarding Establishment of a Reich Chamber of Culture.†	
Sept. 29	RGBL., I, pp. 685 ff	Law Regulating Peasant Holdings.	Exclusion of "non-Aryans" from farm labor and ownership of land.
Oct. 4	RGBL., I, p. 713	Law Regarding Editors.	
1934 March 23	RGBL., I, p. 213	Law Regarding Expulsion from the Reich.†	
1935 May 21	RGBL., I, p. 609	Defense Law.†	Exclusion of "non-Aryans" from the Wehrmacht.
June 26	RGBL., I, p. 769	Reich Labor Service Law.†	Exclusion of "non-Aryans" from Labor Service.
Sept. 15	RGBL., I, p. 1146	Reich Law on Citizenship.	
Sept. 15	RGBL., I, pp. 1146/47	Law for the Protection of German Blood and Honor.	
Nov. 14	RGBL., I, pp. 1333/34	1st Decree Supplementing Reich Law on Citizenship.	Compulsory retirement of Jewish officials.
1936 1937		Minor decrees and ordinances supplementing earlier legislation issued during these two years.	
1938 March 28	RGBL., I, p. 338	Law on the Legal Status of Jewish Communities.	
April 22	RGBL., I, p. 404	Decree against Aiding in Concealment of Ownership of Jewish Enterprises.	
April 26	RGBL., I, p. 414	Decree Regarding Registration of Jewish *Property*.	
July 6	RGBL., I, p. 823	Law on Industrial Enterprises.†	Exclusion of Jews from industrial enterprises.
July 23	RGBL., I, p. 922	3rd Notice Regarding Identification Cards.	
July 25	RGBL., I, p. 969	4th Decree Supplementing Reich Law on Citizenship.	Cancellation of licenses for Jewish physicians with exceptions for care of Jewish patients.
Aug. 17	RGBL., I, p. 1044	2nd Decree Supplementing Law Regarding Change of Names.	

DATE	SOURCE	TITLES OF LAWS, DECREES, AND ORDINANCES
Sept. 27	RGBL., I, p. 1403	5th Decree Supplementing Reich Law on Citizenship.†
Nov. 12	RGBL., I, p. 1579	Decree Regarding Atonement Fine for Jews
Nov. 12	RGBL., I, p. 1580	Decree Regarding Elimination of Jews from German Economic Life.
Nov. 12	RGBL., I, p. 1581	Decree Regarding Restoration of Jewish Places of Business.
Nov. 15	V. B. Nov. 16, '38	Ordinance Regarding School Attendance of Jewish Children.
Nov. 28	RGBL., I, p. 1676	Police Decree Regarding Appearance of Jews in Public.
Dec. 3	RGBL., I, *pp. 1709 ff*	Decree Regarding Utilization of Jewish Property.
1939 Feb. 21	RGBL., I, p. 282	3rd Ordinance Regarding Registration of Jewish Property.
March 4	H. F. Mar. 4, '39	Decree Regarding Employment of Jews.
April 30	RGBL., I, *pp. 864 f*	Law Regarding Leases with Jews.
July 4	RGBL., I, pp. 1097 ff	10th Decree Supplementing Reich Law on Citizenship.
1940 Feb. 2	J. N., #10	Decree Regarding Emigration Tax for Jews.
Feb. 6	J. N., #11	Decree Regarding Clothes Rationing for Jews.
1941 Sept. 1	RGBL., I, p. 547	Police Decree Regarding Identification Badges for Jews.
Oct. 31	RGBL., I, *pp. 681 f*	Decree Regarding Employment of Jews.
Nov. 25	RGBL., I, pp. 722 ff	11th Decree Supplementing Reich Law on Citizenship.
1942 Apr. 17	J. N., #16	Ordinance Regarding Identification of Jewish Apartments.†
Apr. 17	J. N., #16	Decree Regarding Use of Public Conveyances.
May 15	J. N., #20	"Nuisance" Decree.
May 29	J. N., #22	"Nuisance" Decree.†
June 19	J. N., #25	Decree.†
Oct. 9	J. N., #41	"Nuisance" Decree.†
1943 July 1	RGBL., I, p. 372	13th Decree Supplementing Reich Law on Citizenship.
AFTER 1943		*No further legal material available.*

Abbreviations: RGBL., I — Reichsgesetzblatt, Teil I (Reich Law Gaz-
V.B. — Voelkischer Beobachter
H.F. — Hamburger Fremdenblatt
J.N. — Juedisches Nachrichtenblatt

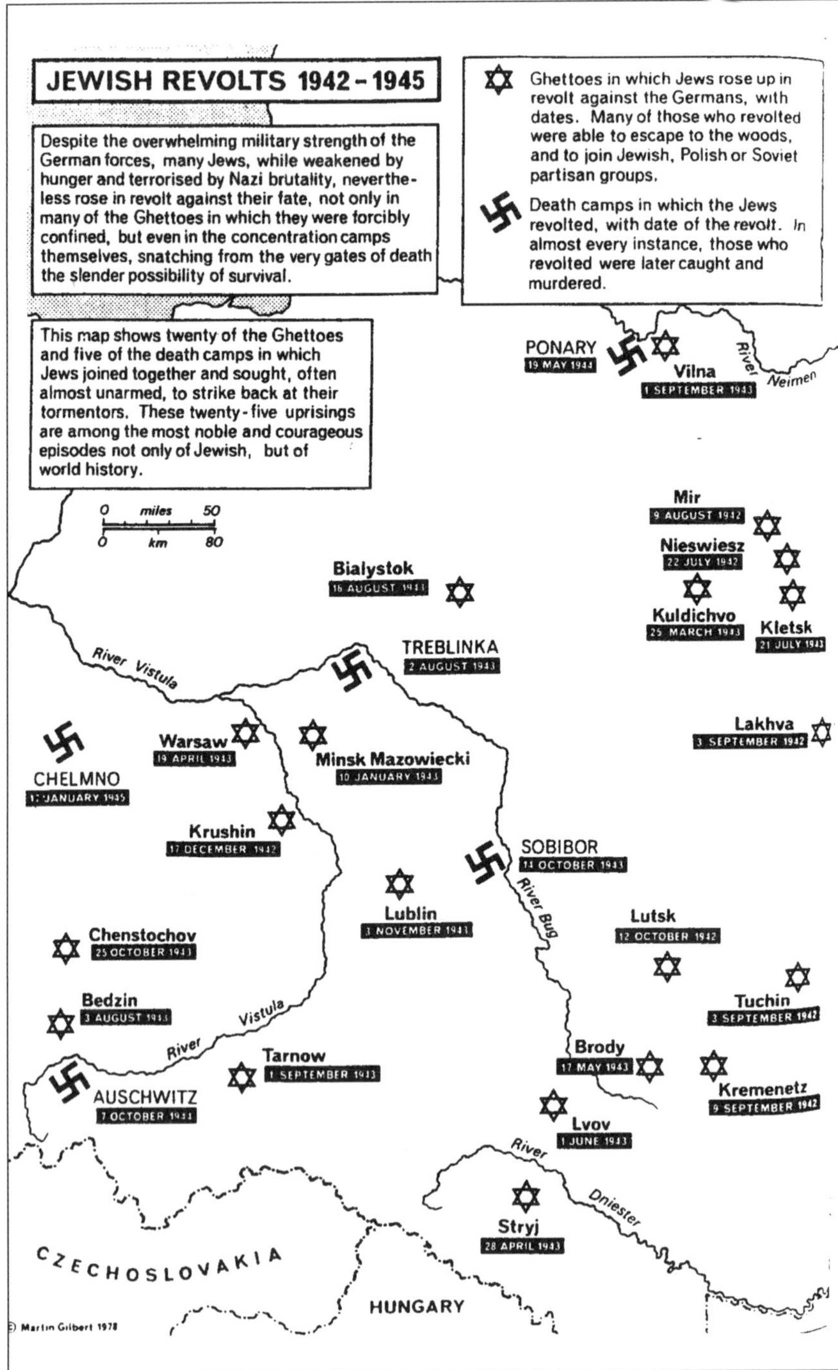
JEWISH REVOLTS 1942-1945
Despite the overwhelming military strength of the German forces, many Jews, while weakened by hunger and terrorised by Nazi brutality, nevertheless rose in revolt against their fate, not only in many of the Ghettoes in which they were forcibly confined, but even in the concentration camps themselves, snatching from the very gates of death the slender possibility of survival.
Ghettoes in which Jews rose up in revolt against the Germans, with dates. Many of those who revolted were able to escape to the woods, and to join Jewish, Polish or Soviet partisan groups.
Death camps in which the Jews revolted, with date of the revolt. In almost every instance, those who revolted were later caught and murdered.
This map shows twenty of the Ghettoes and five of the death camps in which Jews joined together and sought, often almost unarmed, to strike back at their tormentors. These twenty-five uprisings are among the most noble and courageous episodes not only of Jewish, but of world history.
0 miles 50
0 km 80
PONARY
19 MAY 1944
Vilna
1 SEPTEMBER 1943
River Neimen
Mir
9 AUGUST 1942
Nieswiesz
22 JULY 1942
Kuldichvo
25 MARCH 1943
Kletsk
21 JULY 1942
Bialystok
16 AUGUST 1943
TREBLINKA
2 AUGUST 1943
River Vistula
Lakhva
3 SEPTEMBER 1942
Warsaw
19 APRIL 1943
Minsk Mazowiecki
10 JANUARY 1943
CHELMNO
17 JANUARY 1945
Krushin
17 DECEMBER 1942
SOBIBOR
14 OCTOBER 1943
River Bug
Lublin
3 NOVEMBER 1943
Lutsk
12 OCTOBER 1942
Chenstochov
25 OCTOBER 1943
Tuchin
3 SEPTEMBER 1942
Bedzin
3 AUGUST 1943
River Vistula
Brody
17 MAY 1943
Tarnow
1 SEPTEMBER 1943
AUSCHWITZ
7 OCTOBER 1944
Kremenetz
9 SEPTEMBER 1942
Lvov
1 JUNE 1943
River Dniester
Stryj
28 APRIL 1943
CZECHOSLOVAKIA
HUNGARY
© Martin Gilbert 1978

Boys from the Bendzin Ghetto 1940-1941. From left: Suche-Berish Tauz, David Gitler, Zelkowicz and Israel Gitler.

NOTICE.

AS PER STATEMENT OF THIS ORDER ALL JEWISH INHABITANTS OF THE CITY OF ZAWIERCIE ARE REQUESTED TO PAY A

RM. 10 "HEAD TAX"

THE HEADS OF THE FAMILIES HAVE TO PRESENT THEMSELVES AT THE CASHIER AT THE JEWISH "GEMEINDE" IN ZAWIERCIE MALACHOWSKA ST. 10. TO PAY FOR THE WHOLE FAMILY.

AFTER PAYMENT IS MADE, EVERY PERSON WILL GET A RECEIT TO SERVE FOR THE AUTHORITIES..

THE CONTRARY WILL BE SEVERELY PUNISHED.

ZAWIERCIE 5. JANUARY 1940.

THE EALDERS OF THE JEWISH COMMUNITY
IN ZAWIERCIE

PS. ZAWIERCIE WAS IN UPPER SILESIA, AND ALL OTHER CITIES RECEIVED THE SAME NOTICE.

Bekanntmachung

Gemäss der Verordnung müssen alle jüdischen Einwohner der Stadt Zawiercie

RM 10.-

pro Kopf entrichten.

Die Familienvorstände haben innerhalb 3 Tagen vom Erscheinen dieser Bekanntmachung in die Kassa des AELTESTENRATS DER JÜD. GEMEINDE IN ZAWIERCIE, MARSCHAŁKOWSKASTR. 10, die von allen Familienmitgliedern Gesamtsumme einzahlen.

Jede einzelne Person wird nach Einzahlen der Gebühr eine namentliche Bescheinigung, welche als Beweis für die Behörden dienen wird, erhalten.

Zuwiderhandlungen dagegen werden strengst bestraft werden.

DER AELTESTENRAT
der Jüd. Kultusgemeinde
in Zawiercie

Zawiercie, den 5 Januar 1940.

Bendzin. 5 Jewish hostages taken by the Germans at the beginning of the war in 1939. In the center is my father Alexander Szyjowicz.

A Polish policeman identifying and ticketing a Jew for leaving the Ghetto.

think that any of you readers can understand the shame I felt standing there on the street corner like a beggar. I don't think that anyone can understand my hurt. I just wanted to die, but I could not. I had to think of my family, my parents, and you just don't die when you want to.

Two months later, around November of 1939, all Jews were ordered to wear a white armband with a blue Star of David on it. The punishment for not wearing the armband was severe. Then all Jews were ordered to pay "Kopfsteuer," a head-tax (only two Marks), that had many reasons for the Germans. Some of these reasons were the census. The Germans did not know how many Jews they inherited, and this was a perfect way to get a count of the Jews. Oh, yes, you could maybe get away with not registering, some did get away with it, I did.

But the repercussions were too high to take chances. As a matter of fact, since I did not have any work I got the job of writing out the applications for the "Kopfsteuer" for which I received one groszen a piece and later on I even got to deliver these applications and got paid two groszen a piece. See, nobody wanted that job for many reasons, it did not pay much and to deliver them it was too cold, it was winter and a very harsh one. But I was hungry and so was my family.

And about two months after that the Yellow Star with the word "Jude" on it would replace the former. There were different Yellow Stars for some countries (see photo on page 60). Somehow to us this was not a badge of shame as the Germans intended. We wore this Star with pride. I wore a pin with the Star of David in my lapel all my life.

The atrocities that the Germans committed in the Jewish sections are impossible to enumerate. Every German, military or civilian, had a right, or if you want a privilege, to do with a Jew whatever he pleased. They would stop a Jew in the street and take all his money, all his jewelry or just simply shoot him for no reason at all.

I, too, tried to run to the Russian side. I did not tell anybody, I got about 15-20km. I stopped and said to myself "what am I doing, even if I was successful, what would happen to my parents?" Well, I got so seized with that thought and came back embarrassed that I had only myself in mind. And many Jews had parishes for that reason that we just could not leave our parents.

The European Jew was too much family oriented. You just would not leave your parents. We were brought up that way. I loved and respected my parents too much. I thought about it many times. I happened to survive but how many youngsters did not, just for that reason, that they

The A. Rossner tailor shop in Bendzin, which supplied uniforms for the Germans (March 4, 1941).

Israel Justman, a prominent Jew in Bendzin at slave labor.

Jews are being transported off to camps.

The Germans watched and enjoyed their (Jewish) victims suffer. This time the victims were Jewish children.

The German "Master" watches how his victims agonize before their death.

Bendzin. Jews transported for slave labor.

Bendzin. Jews at forced labor.

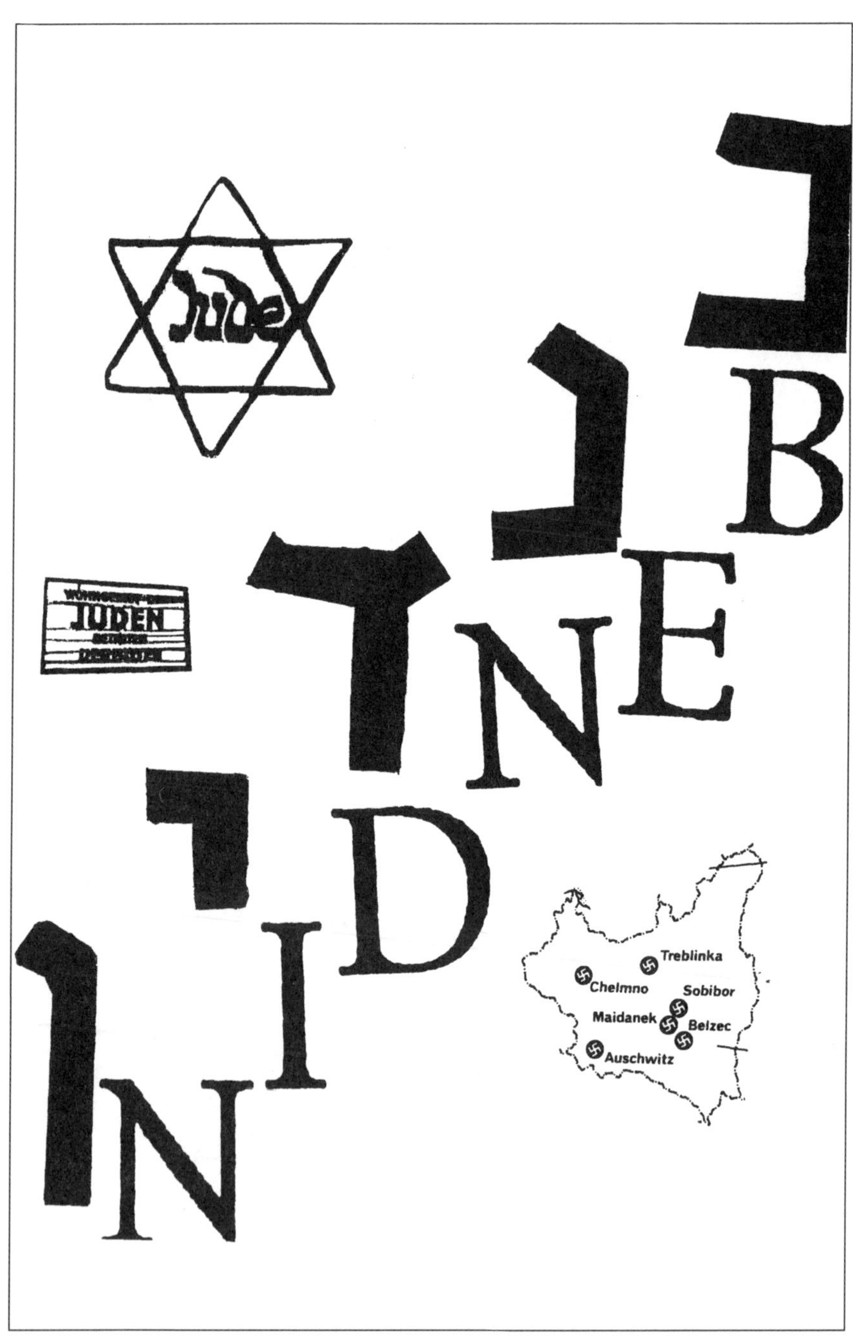

Collage by Arnold Shay.

would not leave their parents, they would not break up the family. I am sure, now in hindsight, that those parents would have preferred their children to leave and survive. But those were different times, different circumstances.

About 1940, a German by the name of Alfred Rosner, wounded in World War I, with special preferences, opened up a tailor shop to work for the German industry, specifically on German uniforms. It became right away a big business for many people. People paid a lot of money to get in. Everybody knew that if you work for Rosner, I will not go to a Slave Labor Camp or Concentration Camp, or even be caught in the street by a German for work. You would have the best "Sonder" (protection) when you are with the Rosner shop.

I would like here to explain as much as I can about the "Sonder." Sonder was the abbreviation of "DER SONDERBEAUFTRAGTER der BESETZTEN GEBIETE in OST-OBERSCHLESIEN." They were our masters. We were their slaves. Theirs was the decision of who shall go to a Slave Labor Camp or who shall live or die in a Concentration Camp. They were the masters of our destiny. I even remember the names of some of those murderers because, as a tailor in the special section for the custom tailors, I did work on their clothing. I remember Knoll, Ludwig, Lindner…there were so many of them I cannot even think of them now. (Better not or I just get sick.) But there was a catch to it. You needed your own sewing machine. I had no money and no sewing machine,

My father went to work on the only thing we retrieved from the fire, a burned out sewing machine, only the head of the machine, the table was gone. My father worked day and night with my help on that machine. We took the "head" from the machine apart, piece by piece and soaked it in oil and after about two weeks the head was assembled. I don't even know if it worked. But with all that it was not easy to get into the "Rosner shop."

People started making money from our misery, rich people bought sewing machines and with heavy bribes got into the shop. People that could not even sew on a button and the poor tailor was left out in the cold. The tailor shop started out with a few hundred and last count was between 7,000 and 9,000 tailors. Yes, I remember those big shots in Rosner's shop. I remember the Smietana's, the Krzesiwo's, the Ferleger's, Siegel and many others that got rich on our misery.

They became the aristocracy in town. Everybody wanted to be their friend. For lots of money, boys and girls were brought back even from slave labor camps and got into the Rosner shop, or other shops. They did not have to be tailors or other mechanics as long as they had money. It became almost impossible to get into the shop for a poor guy like me without money. With the help of my father's friends I got into the shop. I had no money. This was the only way for me. Then my brother Bernard and I started making some money. My brother as an electrician and a damn good one and, if I may say so, I as a tailor.

Through friends of my father I got a job in the Rosner's custom tailor shop where I worked during the day, and from the shop I would not go home but to the Gutman brothers that had before the war a top notch tailor clientele, and I would work there on the clothing that Motek Gutman would prepare for me during the day, before he would go to the Rosner tailor shop where he worked the night shift. We worked on different shifts and this was perfect for both of us. We both could make an extra few zlotys at home.

And somehow we managed to bring home some money for food. Father, even if he would have had his sewing machine, could not work or get a job to work for somebody else. Most people had no money for clothing and the ones who had a few zloty would worry more of how and where to get a loaf of bread or a few potatoes than about clothing.

Chapter Five

Today I am going to play the prophet
If international Jewry should succeed
in...plunging Europe into a world war,
the result shall not be...a victory of Judaism
but the annihilation of the Jews of Europe.

Adolf Hitler

Happy to work

I was very happy that I was busy. Mrs. Gucia Gutman, the wife of Motek Gutman, was very good to me. She knew my parents for one thing, she appreciated my helping out her husband, and most of all that someone was in the house while her husband was away at night. My parents did not appreciate it very much, but I brought home the money for food. I tried to be home weekends with my parents.

In 1941, my sister Laja was taken to a slave labor camp in Czechoslovakia. To Gabersdorf Kreis Trautenau Sudetengau. This finished off my parents. By that time my older sister Sofia and older brother Izaak were already away, and all this was too much for my parents to bear.

Then another German by the name of Michatz opened up a big shop, and this became a new business for my brother Bernard, as an electrician. This shop became a money maker for him. He got the job to bring electricity to the Michatz shop.

The Judenrat started moving the richer Jews into a section that was always considered as having the lowest class of people in Bendzin, and this became "the place" for the rich. The section was "Unter dejm Berg," Under the Mountain. This section never had any electricity and my brother was working day and night to bring electricity to the rich.

Then a shoe factory opened up and it got a bit easier for many Jews. For our household too it got easier when Bernard and I started making some money.

But this, too, did not last too long. April 1942 Bernard was sent to a Slave Labor Camp. Two weeks later my father got killed by the Germans.

Then four months later, on August 12, 1942, there was a general "resettlement" which meant shipping off to a Concentration Camp or plainly, liquidation, and my mother with 2,000 other Bendzin Jews, was shipped off on the 16th of that month (after four days of agony, waiting to be released) to Auschwitz, where that whole transport was sent to the gas chambers.

Here, I have to detail my sister Laja's sending off to a slave labor camp, then my brother Bernard's shipping off to another slave labor camp, my father's death and my mother's last journey to Auschwitz.

One day, (guess it was about April) in 1941, we heard that there is going to be a "snatching" of young girls for compulsory labor, and my parents were very much afraid that they will take my sister Laja. When it got dark, we did not put on any lights in the room and kept very quiet, then all of a sudden we heard noises and after this shouts of commands that we could not make out, but my parents went right-a-way to bed and put Laja near the wall and mother on top of her, always thinking that she may shield her with her body.

All of a sudden our door is kicked open and two Jewish militiamen burst in shouting, "where is Laja Schyiowitz?" They had a list in their hands, and knew where to look for their victims. They ransacked the room while the German soldiers were standing right outside in the yard. See, the Germans would not dirty their hands so to speak in rounding up the Jews, besides, they knew that they can depend on their helpers to do their dirty deeds. See, every militiaman wanted to be the best in catching their victims and to please their masters. I had no great love for either of them then, nor do I want to hear their excuses now.

They were collaborators and they ruined many a Jewish life. I don't buy any excuses for their deeds. I condemn the militia. They are guilty in our misery as much as the Germans. The Germans would never have found so many Jewish hiding places, as their collaborators the militia did. The German mentality was different than ours. I accuse all those in the militia uniforms, without exception, and the "Judenrat" in collaborating with the enemy, the Germans, in all of their heinous crimes.

One militia man (of whom I have a picture in my archives and is shown in this book), went over to the bed without saying a word, grabbed my father first since he was on the outside of the cot, then grabbed my mother, and forced her rudely out of bed and let out a scream, "where is Laja?" In all that haranguing with the militia, Laja made her way somehow, to get under the cot. Well, they were not satisfied and turned the cot over to find Laja.

I will never forget my sister's face at that moment. I have never seen anybody till then, being that scared, that afraid. As long as I shall live that picture will be in front of me. Her face was completely twisted in agony. Her eyes wide open and just looking at the distant as if begging please help me. My parents started begging, pleading, crying, nothing helped. As the milicjant as we called them, was forcing Laja out the door, my mother made a last attempt to save her daughter.

I don't think it was as much an attempt to save Laja as it was the cry of defeat, of helplessness. I have never seen my mother losing control of herself, I never knew the moment when my mother was not the perfect lady. At that moment when the milicjant forced Laja out the door into the German's hands, mother launched at him hitting him and screaming with all her strength. I could not bear it and the same time was powerless since all that time, while all that was happening, I was on the floor and one militia man had his foot on my throat so I could not move.

I don't even remember why he did that. I don't know how and why I wound up on the floor, all I can remember now is that when the militia man came in, asking for my sister, I said she is not home and I was hit with the police stick over the head.

Very few militia men survived the war. As far as I am concerned, one is too many, but anyone that is still alive, if there is a God, I hope that they never have a moment of peace in their life, and that their children will know what their fathers did and hate their fathers as much as we who suffered from their hands do.

Bernard's ordeal was a bit different, although not much, but painful nonetheless. Bernard was making already good money, he had a good profession, and was good at it. We all lived with our parents in that one room apartment, all I mean is mother, father, Bernard and I. The family was getting smaller every time. All the other children were already in different camps by then and we did not even know where. We still tried to make life bearable. Then another calamity.

As if all that was not enough. Bernard is next in line. How much can my parents take. Where in heaven is God. My parents were the most wonderful people. Do they have to be hurt that much? They never hurt anybody. God fearing people. Always ready to help, even though we had not much. Why? Why? I keep asking.

By that time we had already left the locale of the Gordonia. All Jews had to leave the city limits and move out to the "suburbs" of Bendzin. Please, do not get the illusion that the suburbs was that beautiful peaceful place you were dreaming of to move one day. The suburbs were by no means what we know as suburbs to be. The suburbs of Bendzin were just on the outskirts of the city, where primarily the poor Polish

Bendzin. Transporting the belongings to the Ghetto.

Jewish militia in the streets of the Sosnowiec Ghetto.

Bendzin Ghetto. Jews living in the street.

farmers or coal miners lived. There were a few nice homes but most of them were old, dilapidated homes. Those Poles from "suburbia" were as unhappy as us.

They, too, were chased out of their homes and made to move. All Jews living still in the city, were evacuated to the suburbs. The Jews took whatever meager possessions they still had and moved to "suburbia." Some had horse-wagons but they were the horses, since Jews were not allowed to own horses (except the Judenrat had horses to move different stuff from one place to another), others just moved by hand or on their backs whatever they could. Sometimes you were lucky enough to be able to rent a wagon.

We were allotted a certain time and we had to be out of our apartment by that time, or our possessions would be thrown out in the yard by Jews who were caught in the streets especially for that purpose. The Germans had fun with all that and I think they gave us so little time to move so that we could not do it in time. They were standing there with cameras and taking pictures of our miseries.

All those pictures of that period enclosed in that book were taken mostly by the Germans. We were not allowed to own cameras. Owning a camera was punishable with death. They wanted their superiors to see what a good job they were doing. And a lot of those pictures were sent home to their families to join in the fun. Within two weeks the city was free of Jews and "resettled." We, my family, again got allotted a one room apartment in a basement because by then we were only four in the family. No more seven. Our "apartment" was on Wolfberg strasse 6, the section was called "Kamionka," this became our city. Life again was under the most miserable conditions as before.

When I found out that Bernard is being sent away to a slave labor camp, I just went out of my mind. I happened to be at work that time at the "Rosner Tailor Shop." (This was just at the end of our Passover holidays.) I left the shop as I did many times before, (naturally taking a big chance of being caught and sent off to a camp).

I remember that I came just in time when he was getting on the trolley car to be taken to the railroad station and shipped off to camp. I was delighted and felt relieved when I saw that the guard on that car where Bernard was, was watched by a cousin of ours, Srul, who was a bigwig in the militia. He was "Erster Revier Ordner" in the militia. I got through to Bernard with sign language, to jump car and run with me to freedom.

I did not wear that time the "Yellow" Star of David that we were forced to wear, in order not to be recognized as a Jew, since getting out of the Rosner Shop, I had to go through streets not designated for Jews. But I did not know that the milicjant Srul, was not going to let Bernard jump the car. He stood with his foot across, blocking the door opening, not allowing anybody near the door.

I don't think that I am able to describe my disappointment and heart-break when I had to go home without my brother. And how can I tell my parents that another one of their children has been taken away? But I had to tell them that Bernard is not coming home. I know Bernard's heart and feeling that moment when he knew that he is going for slave labor. But I don't think that he or anyone could understand the way I felt at that time.

That night we spent crying and praying. Nobody said a single word. I knew that I am next in line, and I knew that my parents thought the same thing. We could read one another's mind. But at that moment I promised myself that I am going to disappoint the Germans. I will do all in my power to be with my parents as long as they are around. I did just that.

From time to time I had to disappear from the ghetto. My parents did not like it, but I had to do it. I would not come home from my work in the shop but leave to the "Aryan" side, to "organize" some food. From then on going in columns in the morning to work in the Rosner Shop, I would deviate a bit and wind up on the "Aryan" side to see my "contacts" who were not Jewish but could help me.

My parents started suspecting of how dangerous those excursions were and care for it a bit. I remember when one night my mother said she wanted to talk to me. I had to listen to her, she worried why I am taking chances with my life and that she cannot afford to lose me too. It was very hard to explain it to my parents, especially when my father was already very bad after the beating he got from the Germans and we knew that his life is at the end.

About four days later, after they took Bernard away, one morning about 11 A.M., the 28th of April 1942, a man came to the "Rosner Shop" to see me. He came over to the machine where I was working and kept looking at me. From his looks I knew that there is something wrong. I asked him what he wants and he said that he had bad news for me and that he didn't know if he should tell me that I could not help the situation either way. After me insisting that he tell me, he said that he just came from inside the ghetto and that he was told that I should come home, that my father is dying, but there is no use since there is no way I can leave the shop.

To get out of the shop I had to have a pass. My mind started working. I knew that if I am going to ask for a pass to leave work just on somebody's say so, I will not get it. And if I don't get the pass, then for sure I will not be able to leave. I decided to take matters in my own hands. Going downstairs was easy, (I worked on the third floor on uniforms for the "Wehrmacht"). I looked around and saw nobody, I opened the front door that was never locked because nobody would dare leave the shop that was outside the ghetto, and just walked out, first taking off the Yellow Star that could give me away that I am a Jew. I started walking towards the ghetto as if I was in no danger.

I did get home without an incident. As soon as I got close to the house where I lived, I could hear my mother cry. I was only praying that I am not too late. I wanted to see daddy alive. I went inside the apartment and saw a few strange men inside, while my mother was outside the room in the little foyer that divided our room from the bins for stuff to put away for the tenants. Among the men in the apartment I recognized was one Mr. Shulim Plawes who at that time was the head of the "Chevrah-Kedushah," which were the men who performed the last rights. Mr. Plawes told me that my father is dying but that he probably waited for me.

I went over to my father and sat down on the cot and talked to him. He could not answer, but I noticed that every time my mother would cry outside the door, father would turn his head towards the door as if trying to listen to mother. Mr. Plawes noticed it too, and he came over to me and told me to go out and ask mother not to cry, to be quiet so that father could close his eyes. Father was in agony. As long as he could hear mother, he could not die in peace. I went out of the room and told mother to stop crying for a moment. Mother stopped, I think Mother knew that father will not and cannot close his eyes as long as he can hear mother.

I went back to the room and went over to my father placing my hand in his. He closed his eyes, foam came out of his mouth, father squeezed my hand and gave a long sigh. Father was dead. I did not know what to do. I did not go back to the shop that day, I stayed until my father was given the last rights. With prayers by the men that were there, they washed him and I took a sheet and made the "Tachrichem," the suit a Jew is buried in according to the Jewish laws and customs.

I helped put father on the floor with the feet towards the door, again as the Jewish custom is, and covered daddy for the last time with a blanket, the only one we possessed. Mother and I spent that night in the dark holding hands and not being able to talk. We were both still, motionless, the whole night.

My mind was working overtime. I started thinking back of the happenings that brought on my father's death. My mother was not too well since they took away Laja, neither was my father too well since then, not being able to work, constantly looking on how the family suffers. No food or clothing and he is not able to provide for us as he did for so many years.

Plenty or meager, but father was always the provider for the family while my mother took care of the children five and the household. Father was getting progressively worse. By that time father was in his mid-forty's. Then about two or three days after Bernard was sent away, two German soldiers came in the apartment with two militia men, under the pretense that a light was showing through the shades. No lights were allowed to show through and we used the only blanket that we had to cover that one window in the apartment as long as we had a light on. Later we used the same blanket for us to cover ourselves.

They asked my father to get dressed and go with them. Mother and I were in the house that time. My father first started pleading with them that he is not well and cannot leave the apartment. By that time the militia man jumped in and started to get rough with my father trying to force him out of bed. Daddy said to them, that there is no use, that he will not go with them, that he knows what his end is going to be and that if he has to die he rather die on his own bed.

By that time one of the soldiers walked over to my father pushing aside the militia man, constantly holding his rifle in his hand, and said with a smile on his face to my father, "you want to die on your own bed? This can be easily arranged." He turned the rifle around and with the rifle butt hit my father in the chest real hard. This I could not take anymore and I jumped in to protect my father from another blow. What happened next I do not remember. All I know is that when I came to, I was on the floor and my mother standing over me and crying "the last one is dead" and kept on repeating it even when I stood up and took her hand.

I had a large bump on my forehead and mother told me that I got hit on the head with the rifle. (That bump got as big as a walnut and stayed with me until 1953 when it was removed by Dr. Ulin at the University of Pennsylvania in Philadelphia.) I asked about father and mother told me that when he started spitting blood they left him for dead. Mother told me that she does not know what to do with father. How to stop the spitting of blood. With my last strength I went over to father, he did not seem to be alive at all. See, father was always a very petite man, but now he looked like a little kid. If it was not for his mustache and beard he would look like an emaciated little kid.

I knew right there and then that this is the end of my father. A much stronger man could not endure what my father went through, mentally, psychologically and now physically. All this was going through my mind and here I am powerless to help my father whom I loved so dearly and respected so much. I think that mother knew then what I was thinking.

Mother put her head on my shoulder and sobbed quietly. All I knew then was, that if it was not for me, mother would not want to live any longer. I will not even try to explain it, but I do not think that there ever was a greater love between two people than that of my parents. I was by that time 20 years old, but I had never heard my parents have an argument or even a misunderstanding. My father called mother Mama and mother called my father Daddy, and that is what we children always knew. My mind could not relax. All that happened in the last few weeks since Bernard got taken away, went through my mind like in a flash.

I remember how, one evening when I came home from work, my father pointed to me to sit down on the cot near him and he started out " I know that you will think that I lost my mind, but I was not even asleep when I saw it." He went on telling me how four men came to the house dressed in black and without saying a word took him away. The next day, the same thing happened, men dressed in black came and wanted to eat his flesh right off his body, he claimed that he saw them cut his flesh and eat it. Mother cried when he talked about it, but I sat there motionless realizing that this is the end.

After telling me the story he looked at me with his still so very beautiful big black eyes, now even larger than ever because of his so frail a body, and all he could say was, "I know my son that you don't believe me, but did you ever know me to lie to you?" I could read his dream, I knew what it all meant, but how can I make him understand that I know that this is his finale, this is thc end. After this I did not leave him the whole night.

On April 28th, 1942, my father's suffering came to an end. I know now as much as I knew then that he was finally at peace. No more pain, no more problems, no more worrying about his family and no more feeling guilty for failing his family, for which neither I nor anybody else in the family could or would blame father. I am sure that if there is a heaven, father is there. Where else would there be a place for so great a man as he was?

Much of that night, as father was laying on the floor, mother and I were quiet, we did not talk but our minds worked. I probably went through my father's whole history, of how when he was born, his mother died at birth, how his stepmother whom his father married after only a few weeks, tried to poison him because she did not want to bring up somebody else's child. How his older brother Jojvel, who was a baker, carried him in a basket to work, after a few attempts by the stepmother to poison him, and how, just being a youngster, his brother Jojvel dropped him off, at the boat to England to my father's oldest sister who lived there for many, many years.

How my father came back many years later to visit his family, he met my mother, fell in love and never went back to England but married my mother and settled in Poland, where he felt most uncomfortable. See, my father was even then, 50 years ahead of his times. He did not belong in Poland, he was too sophisticated.

Our house was always full of people. No food but wall to wall people. Day or night you could find people in our apartment. My father knew probably every language spoken. People used to come in any hour of the day for father to read a letter they received from abroad. If it was in English, Italian, German or any other language.

Next morning I had to make arrangements for father's funeral. It was not easy. I had to go to the "Judenrat" for a permit and wait for hours until they could see me, to drill me, to see how much money the "Judenrat" could get out of me. I had nothing and finally they decided to let me go and I got a permit to get out of the ghetto next morning and I could take only six people with me to the funeral, since our cemetery was outside the city in a small town of Czeladz. We walked to the cemetery with an escort of two militia men and two German soldiers. We were not allowed outside the city by ourselves.

At the cemetery there was another funeral, of a woman who committed suicide by jumping out of the third story window from the Jewish Orphanage that served as a transit place for Jews to be sent to Auschwitz. Her husband was not Jewish and as it got a bit uncomfortable to have a Jewish wife, her husband threw her out of the house and wanted no part of the Jews. She was not accepted by the Poles as a Christian so she had no other choice but to go into the ghetto and there she met the same fate as all the other Jews, and one day she was arrested and sent to the "Orphanage" from where all the Jews collected there would be sent to Auschwitz to be exterminated. Remember that there was no one at her funeral. No family, no friends, no Jews and no Poles.

Going back to my father's funeral, since I could take with me to the cemetery only six people, naturally, I took the closest to my father. I do remember everyone that was there, my father's two brothers, Yojvel and Dovid, as well as my father's two sisters, Krajndl and Ryvcia, my mother and I. All the others from my parents very large family were already killed or in different camps. (Concentration Camps or Slave Labor Camps.)

My father's brother Joske was still alive but both he and his wife were very sick and mother would not let me tell them about father's death. Mother said that this news would finish them off.

As soon as we arrived I asked the keeper who was not Jewish but set in to that position by the Nazi's where my fathers "plot" was and he took us there, showed us the place and left us to do our own digging. I have to inject here that all the way, which was at least six kilometers, from the ghetto on the "Kamionki" all through the city of Bendzin where we used to live to the town of Czeladz where the Jewish cemetery was, we had to carry the casket on our shoulders and we were watched by two German Schutzpolizei.

As we started digging the grave, the ground was still frozen from the strong winter that we had just days ago, we worked without stopping. Finally we had the grave ready and as we started lowering the casket the lid of the casket came off and revealed my father's face showing that the "Sharbens" pieces that cover the eyes of the dead according to the Jewish law or custom, came off and were laying at the side of the face. The "Sharbens" had to be put back on the eyes of my father after we closed his eyelids, but they would not stay on.

Yes, no one would volunteer to go down into the grave and I had to do it. I had the hardest time to put them back on my father's eyes. Every time I put the "Sharbens" on, father's eyes would open. This happened a few times and finally I was told to step out of the grave, we put back the lid on the casket and we covered the grave with dirt. After this, we all said "Kaddish" and marched back home with the same militia man and the German escort. All this ceremony took at least six hours.

As we came into our one room basement apartment, mother broke down crying, this was the first time since that whole ordeal. Oh, how I remember the first few words mother uttered through her heavy breath and eyes full of tears. "See my son," she said to me, "they all went home to their families as few as there is left of them, (meaning father's brothers and sisters) but we came home without our father." And this was so true. No matter how much they felt the loss, only we could and did feel the emptiness in the house.

Next morning mother set "shiveh" (set in mourning) and I had to go to work in the factory. (Compulsory work for the German industry, slave labor.) I wanted to stay home but mother insisted for me to go, she knew that if I did not show up for work I would be sent to a concentration camp.

That day after work I stopped in to order a marker for my father's grave. I did not know how long I would be around and I wanted my father to have a tombstone on his grave. At least some day, maybe if one from the family will survive, we may know where our father's remains are. I ordered a marker, but, by that time Jews were not allowed any more a stone marker but a marker made out of tin. This was a plain piece of tin of about 12x12 inches with father's name on it. No more, just the name. Sandel Szyjowicz. No more.

Two days later mother and I got a permit from the "Judische Kultus Gemeinde" and we went again to the cemetery, again with an escort, but this time with one militia man and only one German, and we placed the marker. It was already late in the evening when we came home. See, we did show up at the Gemeinde at 9 A.M. but our escort, the German, did not show up until about 2 P.M. and without him we could not leave.

Life for mother, or for that matter for me, too, was not the same. Now that it was only mother and I, the one room basement apartment became too big for us. Not that we sought so, but the Judenrat decided to give us another family to live with us. That other family, by the name of Czapa, consisted of an old lady with very bad manners, her son and his wife and a baby.

Not that I mind. I had to go to work, not only to bring some money home but to secure a position that I may stay in the ghetto and not to be sent to a concentration camp, and my mother did not have to be by herself all day while I was away at work. Little did I know that mother would have been better off by herself than this kind of company. And little did I know that four months later my own mother would be sent to the gas chambers in Auschwitz.

I have to bring in here the story of that family because if it was not that my mother and I had to live with it, it would have been good for a play, a comedy if you will.

The man of that household who was the son of that family, was a tailor by profession, not educated, and worked with me in the same tailor shop for the Germans, firma Rosner. I do not think that any one of them, mother or son could sign their names. They were rude, bad mannered, loud, lewd and just impossible to live with. On the other hand his wife was a perfect lady, petite, very pretty, well educated, from a highly respected family, a teacher by profession and very delicate like a china doll (that's what the war brought together).

Her husband did not treat her nice, which upset my mother very much. There were instances where he would make his wife get up to make a glass of tea for him while she was breast feeding the baby. We all knew that he was doing it only to show that he is the master of the house. But also his mother who was a very simple woman got into the act only to show that she gave her daughter-in-law such a "wonderful" husband.

For me this was very hard to bear nor could my mother take it, but as hard as it was we kept separate, since the day that my father died, mother could not sleep by herself. If I had to go to work on my other job at the Gutmans, mother would not go to bed but sit up all night in the dark. Mother was afraid of her own shadow.

Life in the ghetto went on. I was busy with the Zionist Movement that by that time was underground, and tried to do as much good as we could for the ghetto population and as much harm as we could to the German industry.

Chapter Six

The last wish of my life has
been fulfilled.
Jewish self-defense
has become a fact.
Jewish armed resistance and revenge have
become realities.

Mordchai Anielewicz,
Leader of the Warsaw
Jewish Combat Organization

Resistance

The following is the best account this author ever read on the resistance of the Bendzin and Sosnowiec ghettos. Some of it was translated by the author from the Polish book *Zycie I Walka Mlodziezy W Gettach W Okresie Occupacji Hitlerowskiej 1939-1944*, (The Life and Struggle of the Youth in the Ghettos during the Hitler Occupation 1939-1944) by Bernard Mark. Printed in Poland and published by Ikry, Warszawa 1961.

The author mentions on pages 62 and 63 about the fighting of the Zaglembie ghettos in Gorny Slask where the struggle against the Nazis took place, how dangerous it was for the Jews to hide in the woods where bands of the Polish NSZ murdered Jews that fled the ghettos.

On pages 68-69 the author states, and rightly so, and I as one of the victims of the Bendzin ghetto, can surely testify to it, that the youth from poor families were the first victims of "snatches" to forced labor camps. He also states that "in the ghettos of Zaglembie and Gorny Slask, a specific situation was present that required extra vigilance for the underground," when in the Warsaw and Krakow ghettos informers and confidants for the Gestapo, who kept track of the members of the resistance in Bendzin, Sosnowiec and surrounding cities and villages, the most distrusted by the underground was the "Judenrat" (Jewish Administration) with the collaborator Moniek Merin at the head.

Merin had contact with the youth from the Zionist movement from before the war and tried to conscript them to work with Jewish militia. The resisters he handed over to the Gestapo. (I, too, was one of the Judenrat victims.) The first act of the fighting youth was to expose Merin for what he really is, to show to the forces of Merin that we can and will fight him. "The struggle of the youth in the ghettos of Zaglembie and Gorny Slask, was the fight against work for the occupants (Germans), against the expulsion (of the Jews) and the tactics of the Judenrat in collaboration with the Germans and the enemy within, that wanted the destruction of the resistance. In that fight the organized youth came out with a mighty arm. On the other hand they had little success with the ghetto population. Merin, however, in the beginning was successful to deceive most of the Jewish population."

The fighting militant youth of Bendzin, Sosnowiec and surroundings, concentrated on two sections, the Communists and the Kibutzniks. They both acted separately and, even though, there are known attempts of collaboration against the common enemy.

From October 1940, in the active lines of the Communist youth groups there were many fighting heroes. The Zajdman brothers, Samuel Zacharjasz, Dubinski, Minc, Roza Lustig, Ber Graubart, and many others who vanished in the basements of the Gestapo or in Auschwitz.

In Spring of 1943, groups of the youth were already dissolved, so that at the liquidation of the ghetto, they were practically non-existent any more. It can be said that the main energy of the Communist youth group was used up in the years of 1941-1942, counting great losses and making it felt in the "field" of propaganda, fund raising and sabotage in the German production.

The second section of the fighting youth were the Kibbutz, members of the Hashomer-Hazair, Dror and members of the townspeople, the Democratic Zionists who in the beginning concentrated in the field of education, culture and saving the youth and the children, and for a long time dispensing advice on self-help, self-defense and self-rescue. Self-rescue has become the prospective, because of the proximity of the mountains and the Czech border. Through that road, many of the Jewish youth got through to Hungary, where the persecution of the Jews did not start until 1944 and was not as intense then as in the other countries that the Germans occupied. Some of these escapees got through to Slovakia and later were found in the lines of the Slovak and Russian Partisans. Some of these youngsters from the Kibbutz went via Hungary and Turkey to Palestine. They were the first messengers of the catastrophe that befell the Jews of Poland in 1942-1943.

That way, via the Bendzin ghetto, resistance camps, running through Slovak and Turki, a young member of the Kibbutz, Chaja Klinger, who died not long ago in a Kibbutz in Israel, came to Palestine. The startling memoirs of her life were published after her death.

Let's go back to the Bendzin ghetto, the center of the fighting Jewish youth in Zaglembie Dombrowskie where the character of the activities of the Kibbutz changed in the mid of 1942. Some form of resistance was active already before; for instance, from time to time flyers were sent to the German families in the city as well as outside our town. Those "flyers" were anti-Hitler and anti-war, they were primarily sent to families who lost sons on the East-front. The names and addresses were taken from the newspapers, from the obituaries and telephone books.

In mid 1942 under the influence of slogans that were brought to the ghetto youth by Mordchai Anilewicz, the hero of the Warsaw ghetto uprising as well as other messengers from the anti-Fascist groups from Warsaw, the Kibbutz youth changed into a fighting Jewish organization, (ZOB) "Zydowska Organizacja Bojowa," whose leaders were a former teacher Baruch Gettek, a member of the Kibbutz Dror, Hersz Szpringer and Zvi Brandes.

This started an intensified search for arms. A group of very young liaisons in who's minds was Miss Pejsach, a daughter of a veteran of the workers movement who was murdered by the Nazis. Renia Gelbart brought arms from Warsaw and wherever she could get it. During one of those "excursions" Miss Pejsach, who had great courage and was very well liked by the youth, fell. The impact was painful, but the hot preparations went on.

Trying to choke all those activities right from the start, Merin gave an order in February 1943 that the Kibbutz must send all their help (workers) to the Militia (Jewish police) which was preparing for a new round of "snatching" Jews for compulsory labor. The Kibbutz said NO! The youth came out of it in victory, the rounding up of Jews was called off. Merin was furious.

HERE THE END OF THE JUDENRAT

In August of 1943 the last liquidation of our ghetto takes place. The alarm of the youth group was not heeded by the people in the ghetto. The group realizing that Zaglembie will not change into a fighting ghetto like Warsaw, decided at least to fight alone for their honor. An armed self-protection group of young people occupied two bunkers. In an uneven fight with a large army of Germans, equipped to its teeth, the flower of ZOB in Bendzin and Sosnowiec sacrificed their lives for honor. They all fell. Among them the before mentioned leader, liaison and heroin from Warsaw, the beloved Frumka Plotnicka.

The German documents as well as witness accounts contain much evidence of the group and individual escapes of Jewish youth, from camps dispersed around all of Silesia. Some met with partisans groups and joined them, others died from hunger or fell prey to the Volksdeutschen, Naturalized Germans (Polish turn coats), and were handed over to the Germans.

After much fighting, the spirited youth of the Zaglembie ghettos in Silesia, a scantily amount of physically broken people remained, as stated by the activist and member of the KPP (Polish Communist Party) and the PPR (Polish Workers Party) and famous writer Stanislaw Wigodzki from Bendzin (whom this writer knows personally very well). Roza Lustig fell into the hands of the Gestapo with the two brothers Pinie and Josl Lubling, Izaak Kozlowski and others in Autumn of 1942. They were taken to Auschwitz together with the Pole Wawrzyniec Starycki liaison of the PPR with the Ghetto Kamrads.

They all disappeared in Auschwitz. Wigodzki published his book in 1961 in Poland, where it was approved by the Ministry of Culture to the libraries of Evidence of General Information for Fundamental Schools, Professional, Technical and Institutions to Educate Teachers.

A lot of these young people from Zaglembie also fled to the East and Russia where they joined partisan groups as well as the Russian armies, and came home much decorated. One of my very dear friends, Icek Preszow, fled to Russia, became a very much decorated pilot and was shot down and lost his life over Germany.

In the book *The Jewish Catastrophe in Europe*, published by The American Association for Jewish Education and edited by Judah Pilch, the following is written about the resistance movement in the Bendzin and Sosnowiec ghettos, "Jewish self-defense was organized in the ghettos of Bendzin and Sosnowiec, immediately after the news of wholesale massacre of Jews in Poland reached these Jewish Communities."

Jewish youth sought membership in nearby Polish partisan groups, but were told that anyone desiring to join had to possess a revolver of his own. Since there were never any firearms in the ghettos of Bendzin and Sosnowiec, the Jewish youth attacked German soldiers with bare hands and took possession of their weapons. Many young Jews were killed during these attacks, but some succeeded in meeting the arms requirement and joined the Polish guerrillas.

Here I (the author) have to add a note from my own experience with the Polish partisans. I did have a gun and 60 rounds of ammunition as was required, and met up with the Polish underground in the Karpatien Mountains in the village of Szczyrk in 1942, and even though I did meet all the requirements, I was not accepted. I toured all around the mountains with my companion, a young lady by the name of Fela Fridman, who, by the way, was instrumental in obtaining the arms and papers for us, where the Polish partisans were stationed, from Bielsko-Biala to Szczyrk, Jelesnia, Sucha, Zywiec, Morskie-Oko, Trzy-Korony, Zakopane and so many other small villages that I cannot even remember now. I don't even know now if I mentioned those villages in order. But I was there.

My meeting up with the Polish partisans, even so not unique, is worth mentioning. We met with Polish partisans in the mountains and were told by one that did not recognize me as a Jew (I don't know how he did not recognize me as a Jew or maybe he never met a Jew. See, the Poles had a nose that could smell a Jew from the farthest distance), that some of the Polish partisans big-wigs are in Szczyrk and that is where I and my companion, Fela Fridman, went. We arrived there at night, they gave us where to bed down, and we slept with our eyes open and mouth shut, we were afraid to utter even a good-night greeting.

That first day, next morning, I did not even wash, yet, I went to the latrine and one Pole lets out a scream "we have a Jew here." I was right-away taken to their leader, without even letting me tell my companion where I am going, and after heavy interrogation I was told that I cannot be with them. I was taken then to another room and again that man in a German uniform that questioned me before and sat with his back to me all the time, asked the two other man in German uniforms, to leave the room. He then turned around and faced me with a question "do you know who I am?" I said no and I truly did not know him, then he started in a very soft voice and said "if you are from Bendzin you have nothing to worry. You said," he said to me, "that you lived on Plebanska street, tell me who was the Pole that had a shoe store near the church?" and I told him that their name was Sowa. He laughed the first time and said "you have nothing to worry. I will see that you and your girlfriend get back to Bendzin. There is no place here for you," (in 1945 I met one of the Sowa's sons either in Oranienburg or Sachsenhausen concentration camp) and wished me good luck. I still think that he was a son of the Sowa family.

He turned around again with his back towards me and called in one of his adjutants and told him to drive us to Bendzin and to drop us off at the ghetto gate. And here is the saddest part of that whole incident. By that time it was already January of 1943, a very harsh winter. He drove a German car with two Nazi little flags on both front sides of the car. We were told to lay on the floor of the car. To make us feel relaxed he told us that if a German should stop him he will tell him that we are Jews and that we ran away from the Bendzin ghetto and he is taking us to the German Police Station in Bendzin, and he added "you better pray to your God that we are not stopped."

We were not stopped, but just before we hit the gates from the ghetto, he stopped the car and told me to take off my suit. I did, he took the suit and told us to get out of the car, as we got out he drove off leaving me standing in the bitter cold in my underwear. We stood there for a while trying to figure out how we can get inside the ghetto. I don't know how long we drove, but by that time it was already late at night. As we were hiding behind some trees we heard noises and we recognized that they were Jews returning from work.

Without being noticed by the guard we sneaked in with the crowd. The boys started clinging around me so I would not be noticed by the guards and nobody said a word. What I am still trying to figure out, is why he took my suit. I was a little guy, my suit could only fit a Polish kid. I will never forget that incident as long as I shall live. Oh, later on I had plenty of ribbing, the guys that shielded me wanted to know who stole my suit while I was out with a girl.

Chapter Seven

Not much will be left of the Jew…
the prophecy the Führer made about
them is beginning to come true in a most
terrible manner.

Joseph Goebels

The last report in the ghetto

The last report by the Commissioner of the Upper Silesia Ghettos sent to his superior. A copy of that letter with a notation(?) was delivcred to the few remaining bigwigs in thc Judenrat. First the notation, then the letter. All in translation by this writer from the German:

The Commissioner Dreier, our protector and a friend of the Leader of the ghettos, Moniek Merin and his assistant Fanni Czarna, delivered on the 4th of August 1943 to his superior the following short account;

"As of the day of the 3rd of August 1943, my region in the East Upper Silesia was completely Judenrein, "cleaned out of Jews." The liquidation of the Jewish possessions is in the hands of the Magistrates of Bendzin and Sosnowiec which have accepted those possessions as their proprietors."

Here is the author's note. I have to mention that when this letter was sent Moniek Merin and Fanni Czarna and the real bigwigs of the ghettos were already dead for close to two months. They were executed at Auschwitz on the 26 of June 1943, as I mentioned in one of my articles included in this book on page 202.

For information I want to call to the reader's attention, that in our region, there were in 1939 over 100,000 Jews, of which about 15,000 young people, men and women, were sent to "Arbeitseinsatz," slave labor camps, and the rest of about 80,000 were liquidated in the last fifteen months by "resettlement."

(Signed) Dreier mp
Commissar

Here is some noteworthy information on the few remaining Jews there. The conclusion of the ghettos of Upper Silesia has to be mentioned.

The last place where the Jews still remained in the Upper Silesia District of which the Commissar Dreier was proud was Zawiercie, but even there, in a short time all the rest of the remaining Jews were "Resettled." I remember when the Jews from Zawiercie arrived in Auschwitz. Icio Gutman, my neighbor, the man where I learned the needle trade, came with that transport and so did one of his brothers-in-law. His wife who was from Zawiercie, Jadzia Klasner, Icio told me was supposed to be in the woman camp. He never found her.

I have to mention here the story how I helped Icio in Auschwitz. He and his whole family were good to me and I wanted to repay him. I went to Wachmeister Kurbanik, for whom I did tailoring and stealing, and told him that he could use Icio Gutman as a custom tailor, and so it was. A week later Icio Gutman had his "own tailor shop" in the mid of death at Auschwitz.

It is now known that a very few Jews were still left in Bendzin working for the Germans until about the beginning of 1945, then they, too, were shipped off to camps. In the Underground (literally) of Srodula and Kamionki, where the ghettos of Bendzin and Sosnowiec were, 2,000 Jews were hiding after the complete liquidation of the ghettos. Some of them survived under the most inhumane conditions over six months, but tragically most of them sooner or later were caught and executed.

Isaiah Trunk in his book *Jewish Response To Nazi Persecution* makes a statement: "To begin with, there is a predilection in the general histography of WWII for investigating the crimes and motives for the criminals while avoiding the experiences of the victims in many instances. One result of this one-sided concern with the Nazis aspect of war and the Holocaust is the mistaken notice that within the immense bureaucracy and technology of genocide, the Jewish victims were passive objects of the "process" and therefore merit far less specialized study."

I also agree with Mr. Trunk that up till now the prime concern was Martyrologie, Resistance and the Nazi policy of extermination. And that there may have been some passiveness to resistance. Yes I am very happy that Mr. Trunk as a prolific writer, that has my greatest respect and admiration, he mentions farther in his book, the resistance and "the other side of the coin," and no! Jews did not go "to slaughter like sheep."

We, the survivors, do not owe anybody any apologies, no one who was not "there" will or can ever know what resistance really is. To live one more day in a ghetto or concentration camp was resistance to the

Germans. Let me just bring out a few ways of resistance that we had to think of and about it. Let's say that I have a gun and a German stops me in the street for my I.D. Nothing would probably give me greater pleasure than to take out my gun and shoot the…German on the spot. Yes. Some would probably consider me a hero for such an act. Oh, a dead hero for sure.

Now let's say that I would get a way with it!! But, again, let's consider the repercussions of such an act by a Jew against a German. (You saw what happened to the Jews on "Kristalnacht" because of Greenspan??) If a German was shot in the ghetto, in most ghettos, the ghetto was tenths, this means that every tenth Jew living in the ghetto would pay with his life because I wanted to be a hero. You had to weigh this in your mind in a split second, if you can or want to take that chance with other lives or even your own. Would you take such a chance?? I could not. Another instance of "going to slaughter." I was at the railroad station in Bendzin on that fateful day of August 15 or 16, 1942 when my mother, May She Rest In Peace, was being taken to Auschwitz. She knew where she was going and yet her only resistance was a prayer to God for me as the last of five children that was still "home."

Resistance, physical or otherwise, was impossible against those armed German murderers, she was too week, too exhausted, too resigned to death. Her only fear of me being harmed was greater than the fear of death. Can anyone understand this?? No! Not someone who was not there. Sometimes I feel that not even us that were there can understand it.

And yet, the Jews were the first ones to put up resistance in any and every way. Heydrich, shortly before he died of the wounds he received at the assassination, wrote to Hitler, I quote "I put the Jews in ghettos, no food, no water, no sanitary facilities and yet "they" refuse to die." What a recognition of resistance. That beast recognized the resistance of the Jews.

Yes! The Warsaw Ghetto Uprising will go down in history of all people especially the Jews. This was the first time in history of the Third Reich where the Germans had to leave their dead on the streets of the Warsaw Ghetto, that they so much hated, and retreat for reinforcement. This was the first time in the history of the Third Reich where they had to call in the Luftwaffe to help them set the whole ghetto on fire.

They had to destroy the whole ghetto to get to those young fighters, and even then, the ones that found their way out via the sewers, formed the mightiest underground that the Germans had to contend with. Some joined different underground groups or met with the Russian army. It took the Germans longer to subdue the Warsaw Ghetto Uprising than to overrun all of Poland.

But, in the same time, we forget the other heroes?! How about a youngster of seven or eight years of age who would leave the ghetto through the barbed wire to bring home a few potatoes or a piece of bread, to help the family to survive? How about the teacher who would teach the kids in the ghetto in a sub-basement, Hebrew Jidish or even a trade, so they, if they survive, should have some education. The teacher knew that if he is caught, death is the only thing he could look forward to.

There were so many acts of heroism by Jews in the ghettos, outside the ghettos or even the camps. But what bothers me most as a survivor, is that we the Jews are the only ones that are being asked why we did not resist. How about Czechoslovakia that was taken without as much as a shot being fired? How about Poland that was ripped apart in only 27 days? Where were their Armed Forces? How about France with their invincible Maginot Line that the Germans bypassed like a hip of trash? And all the other countries that fell under the German boot?

Oh yes! One little thing that I remember. Who watched that famous movie, *The Bridge Over The River Kwai*? Remember how those English officers built a bridge so that the enemy could win the war? Oh how helpless those English heroes looked, I did feel sorry for them. Well. Did anybody tell them that they went like sheep?? Did they??

But we the Jews, without an army, without a country, despised by so many, we are asked why we did not resist. And this by our own Jews, who would probably not last as long as we did. We are asked.

I remember 1944, while an inmate at Auschwitz, when they brought into the camp the Polish resistance fighters of Warsaw. They were lauded as heroes by the Poles. For the longest time Poland did not want to mention the Warsaw Ghetto Uprising, but called it the Warsaw Uprising. They were embarrassed that the Jews did a mightier uprising than them. Well. Without admitting it, the world knows better.

And while we are on the subject of resistance, how about the blowing up of the crematorium at Auschwitz?? Nobody but the Jewish underground did it. We paid a high price, but only the Jews did it. There was no help of the Polish underground that was supposed to help in the uprising. But this is a subject for another book.

The Jews of Bendzin had a history of good and bad. I am sorry to say that my generation in Bendzin knew only the bad times. My generation was the one that learned of anti-Semitism first hand. I do not think that any country in Europe suffered more from anti-Semitism than we the Jews of Poland. But the war was the worst that we had ever to contend with, every time new laws, new sufferings. It started right with the outbreak of World War II.

Chapter Eight

Their synagogues should be set on fire…
Their homes should likewise be broken
Down and destroyed…Let us drive them out of
the country for all time.

Martin Luther 1542

Dates to remember

September 1, 1939. A day to remember. Germany invades Poland, but this was a war against the Jews. The "Sicherheitsdienst," Secret Service (or S.D. as they were called), started its activities in Poland, as soon as they occupied a city.

September 2, 1939. The Germans occupy Zawiercie, Katowice District, Poland, where 7,000 Jews live. All Jewish men, between the ages of 17 and 50, are ordered to gather in the marketplace, where they are detained and tortured for nine days.

September 4, 1939. The Germans occupy Sosnowiec and a few hours later Bendzin. This was the province of Katowice in Southern Poland. At that time, the outbreak of the war, 28,000 Jews lived in Sosnowiec and about 35,000 Jews in Bendzin proper, not counting the Jews that lived in the vicinity of Bendzin or Sosnowiec.

That same day thirteen Jews are murdered in Sosnowiec and an unknown number of Jews are murdered in Bendzin.

September 5, 1939, a day I will never forget either. All Jewish men have to report on German orders in front of the City Hall. Whoever fails to report will be shot. We all reported, we did not know yet what to expect. I and my brothers were let go but my father was kept as a hostage. The Germans claimed that the Jews are killing Germans and they have to keep hostages. If a German will be killed the hostages will pay with their lives.

I do not have to describe how we, the children, felt coming home without our father. What were we to tell mother that father did not come home with us. Father was kept there for a few days with a few of the wealthiest Jews in our town. When father returned home half of his beard and half of his mustache was missing. Anything to degrade the Jews. Father had to report that way every day to the police for many days.

The other Jews were subjected to much cruelty and kept for a few days without food or water.

September 9, 1939. The synagogue on Dekerta street #14, Sosnowiec, is burned down. The Wehrmacht arrested and murdered 44 Jews in Bendzin, where 25,000 are living in the Jewish quarters alone. The old market place is set on fire, including 56 houses and the big synagogue on Buzniczna street. Several hundred were living in the Jewish quarters alone. It started about seven o'clock in the evening.

Several hundred Jews are burned alive when the German soldiers and the S.S. hindered anyone from putting out the fire or trying to escape it. This was Plebanska street that was set on fire too. I lived on Plebanska 14 where I was born and raised. Earlier in the book I give the whole story of that night. I knew most of the people there, I grew up with them, I went to school and Chejder with them, I played with them, I saw them dead.

The Jewish quarters and the surroundings of Bendzin were estimated to have had about 42,000 Jews living there at the outbreak of the war. After the war only 150 Jews of Bendzin survived.

September 20, 1939. A decree is issued by Reinhard Heydrich to all Gestapo divisions, which employed the code word "Special Treatment," meaning the actual physical destruction of the Jews to be carried out.

October 12, 1939. Following a decree by Hitler, the Nazis order that, in areas of Poland occupied by the Germans, a Jewish Council has to be established to serve as liaison between the Germans and the Jews. So the Councils for Bendzin and Sosnowiec were set up. (Later on more towns were included in that region.) Moniek Merin became the Eldest of the Councils for all of the Eastern part of Upper Silesia.

October 28, 1939. Bendzin, Sosnowiec and surroundings belonging to East Upper Silesia are ordered to wear white armbands with a blue Star of David on it to distinguish the Jews from the rest of the population.

November 23, 1939. The wearing of the Yellow Star becomes obligatory for the Jews in Poland.

December 12, 1939. The Germans order that all Jewish men between the ages of 14 and 60 have to do two years of forced labor. Labor camps are set up in the general government in Poland, Upper Silesia and Warthegau. In the beginning, most of the internees died of the cruel treatment and physical exhaustion.

April 15, 1940. The German Ministry of Interior decree that Jewish hospitals situated in the Nazi Administrated area have to be incorporated in the Euthanasia program.

Bendzin. Beth Hamedrosh inside. The artwork by: S. Cygler.

Bendzin. The "Beth Hamedrosh," the small Synagogue before it was burned down by the Germans September 8, 1939.

The Ark of the Law in the Great Synagogue in Bendzin, Poland. Photo: Israel Museum Archives, Jerusalem.

Bendzin. The exit door from the Synagogue. Metal and plastic by Chaim Hanft.

Wall painting in the Big Synagogue, by Cygler.

Part of the paintings in the Big Synagogue by Apelbaum and Cygler.

A section of the paintings in the Big Synagogue, by Apelbaum and Cygler.

A fragment of the wall painting in the Big Synagogue by Cygler.

September 9/10, 1939 the Germans did the most heinous deed chasing the Jews from Bendzin into the Synagogue and setting the whole place afire. This picture was taken by an unknown person (probably a German soldier). In the fore of the Castle are shown soldiers of the Wehrmacht and Gestapo man to make sure that the Jewish Sector is completely destroyed.

Part of the Plebanska street in the old City of Bendzin. In the background is the Church Sw. Trojcy, (where this writer lived for 17 years until the destruction of the whole Jewish Quarters in 1939). Picture taken 1939.

Bendzin. Workers are cleaning the rubble near the Castle after the destruction of the homes from the XIXth and XXth century. The man shown here is one of the most trusted watchmen of the Castle, Stanislaw Wach.

The Jewish Sector with the Synagogue after the burning in September 1939. People looking the next day for whatever they could find to salvage from the fire. "I may be among them."

Bendzin. The Big Synagogue in flames.

Homes that the Germans burned down and formed the first Ghetto in Bendzin on Podzamcze. Picture taken in secret by an unknown patriot 1942.

Tauntung of the Big Synagogue 1910.

A group of Jews in the Bendzin ghetto with their German guards, taken away for slave labor.

A group of Jews caught in the streets of Bendzin, taken for slave labor.

April 27, 1940. Heinrich Himmler, the head of the German Police and the Gestapo, orders the "Foundation of the Auschwitz Concentration and Extermination Camp in Poland." Auschwitz will play an infamous role in the history of Jewish Martyrdom. The number of people murdered in this camp is between 2½ and 3½ million. These victims are mainly Jews. But Gypsies and people from other nations in Europe are among them.

Many Jews from Bendzin perished in Auschwitz. The Jews from Bendzin were also very much in the forefront of the Auschwitz resistance and paid with their lives. Two of my friends from Bendzin will always be remembered, they lost their lives during the uprising in the Crematorium where they worked. One is Szaje (Lapo) Goldstein and Baumgarten.

April 29, 1940. In Warsaw, Poland, the Germans started surrounding one quarter with a wall. This quarter is destined to become the future ghetto. It encompasses 840 acres. It is intended not only for the Jews of Warsaw, but also for the Jews from the provinces. Many of the Jews from Warsaw fled to other towns and some arrive in Bendzin, where they are later caught in the same dilemma. From them we knew what to expect from our masters.

May 10, 1940. From the Polish Region of Zaolzie, 600 Jews are deported to a ghetto in the town of Zawiercie in the Province of Katowice that belongs to our Judenrat. A lot of these Jews are later brought to the ghettos of Bendzin and Sosnowiec.

June 4, 1940. The German Police shoot 29 persons, most of them Jews, in the village of Celiny, Bendzin District, Poland.

In April of 1941, 5,000 Jews from Oswiecim (later to be named Auschwitz) were resettled in Bendzin and Sosnowiec. The Jews of those two cities did an exemplary job in relocating the Jews from Oswiecim, the hospitals, the aged, and all other Jewish institutions. It is stated that "the refugees (from Oswiecim) were received with extraordinary warmth and affection."

September 1, 1941. All Jews after the age of six living in the German Reich are ordered to wear the "Judenstern," the Yellow Star, whenever they are out of the house. It was a yellow background with the word "JUDE" (Jew) in black in the center of the star. (Upper Silesia was annexed into the Third Reich.) The spelling "JUDE" comes in different languages according to the language of the country.

October 26, 1941, after the failed Evian Conference, the Nazis saw the reluctance of the word in helping the Jews, they decided to stop the emi-

"Hanoar Hazioni" 1941 in the Bendzin Ghetto. Standing from right: Jadzia Malach, Guta Gutman, Arje Hasenberg and Miriam Tencer. Seated: Szlamek Goldcwajg, Alexander Gutman and Izaak Gold.

"Hanoar Hazioni." Standing from right: N. Bialko, Rozia Zborowska, Srulek Gelbard, Zisio Urbach, Berek Gutman, Frymka Tuchsznajder, Berek Fontak, Josek Kerner, Szlamek Hercberg, Israel Diament, Israel Groswald. Seated: Chaskiel Kerner, Chawa Wekselman, Genia Torenhajm, Moszek Rubin, Bala Epsztajn, Sryja Kaminski, Malka Gutensztajn, Basia Szyf.

Zaglembie summer camp from "Hanoar-Hazioni" in Milowka, 1932.

The orchestra of the "Poale-Zion" in Bendzin at the first of May 1933 celebration. Symcha Lustig conductor.

gration of the Jews, announcing a general prohibition on emigration.

This made the Final Solution a fact and Eichmann was in his glory. This was what he dreamed of.

January 1, 1942. A ghetto is set up for the Jews of Bendzin, in Kamionka which is a suburb of Bendzin. The Jews are there interned to await deportation to the Extermination Camps. Until summer of 1943 numerous small deportations to Auschwitz take place.

March 5, 1942. Three Jews are hanged in a public viewing in the Olkusz ghetto on the charge of having left the ghetto to look for food. The same time a lot of Jews fled to Bendzin from there, which is not too far. The German Police forced other Jews to set up the gallows and carry out the execution.

May 5, 1942. 630 Jews from Dombrowa Gornicza, near Bendzin, are deported to the Auschwitz Extermination Camp, where they were all murdered. In the same time many of the Jews from Dombrowa Gornicza are transferred to the Bendzin Ghetto.

May 9, 1942. 8,000 Jews from the Bendzin ghetto are deported to the Auschwitz Concentration Camp and within hours are exterminated. Many of these Jews originally came from the city of Auschwitz, and fled or were deported to Bendzin.

May 10, 1942. 1,500 Jews from Sosnowiec are deported to the Auschwitz Extermination Camp. They, too, are gassed within hours of their arrival, the same as their neighbors from Bendzin just one day earlier.

May 11, 1942. The Gestapo hangs two Jews in Bendzin on the old Jewish Cemetery grounds. All Jews of Bendzin had to assemble and witness the hanging as if it was a party.

May 12, 1942. 1,500 Jews are deported from the Sosnowiec ghetto to the Auschwitz Extermination Camp.

May 17, 1942. From the Zawiercie ghetto, near Bendzin, 2,000 Jews are deported to the Auschwitz Extermination Camp.

May 21, 1942. 1,000 Jews from Olkusz, near Bendzin, are deported to the Auschwitz Extermination Camp. Smaller groups have already been deported to various concentration and labor camps as well as to the Bendzin ghetto.

June 7, 1942. 600 Jews from Szczakowa, near Bendzin, are deported to the Auschwitz Extermination Camp.

June 12, 1942. 2,000 Jews from the ghetto of Sosnowiec are deported to the Auschwitz Extermination Camp.

June 29, 1942. The 200 remaining Jews of the ghetto Olkusz, near

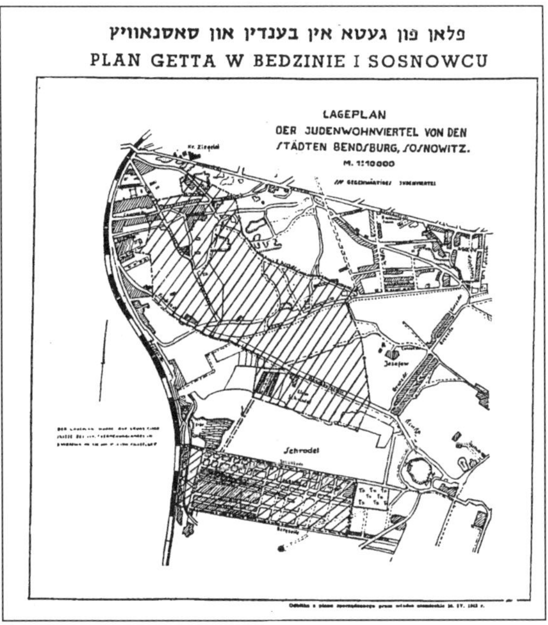

The plan of the Ghetto Dendsburg/Sosnowitz. (Former Bendzin/Sosnowiec)

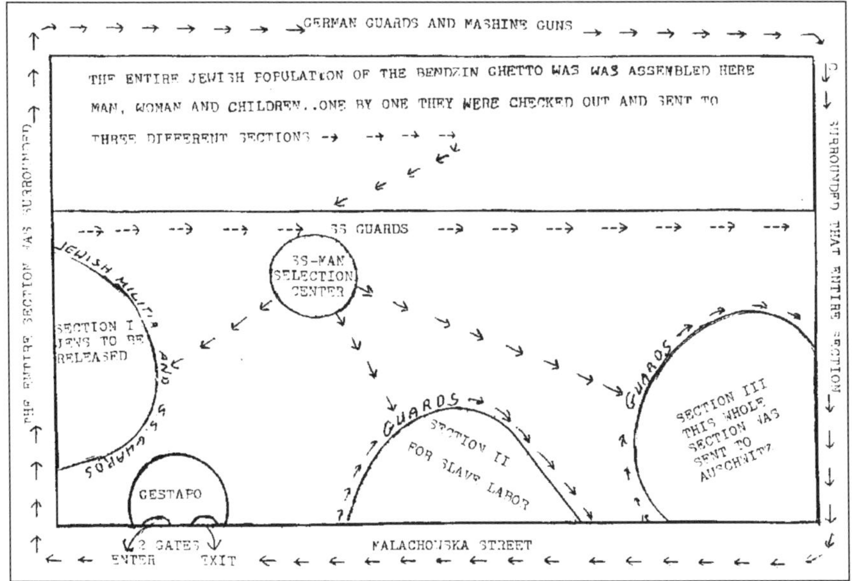

Bendzin Ghetto. The Jews were ordered to assemble on the "Hakoach" Sport Stadium, on Malachowskiego street on August 12, 1942, from there most of the Jews went to Auschwitz. According to the German Records at Auschwitz that whole transport upon arrival went straight to the Gas Chambers. My mother Sara Szyjowicz was in that transport.

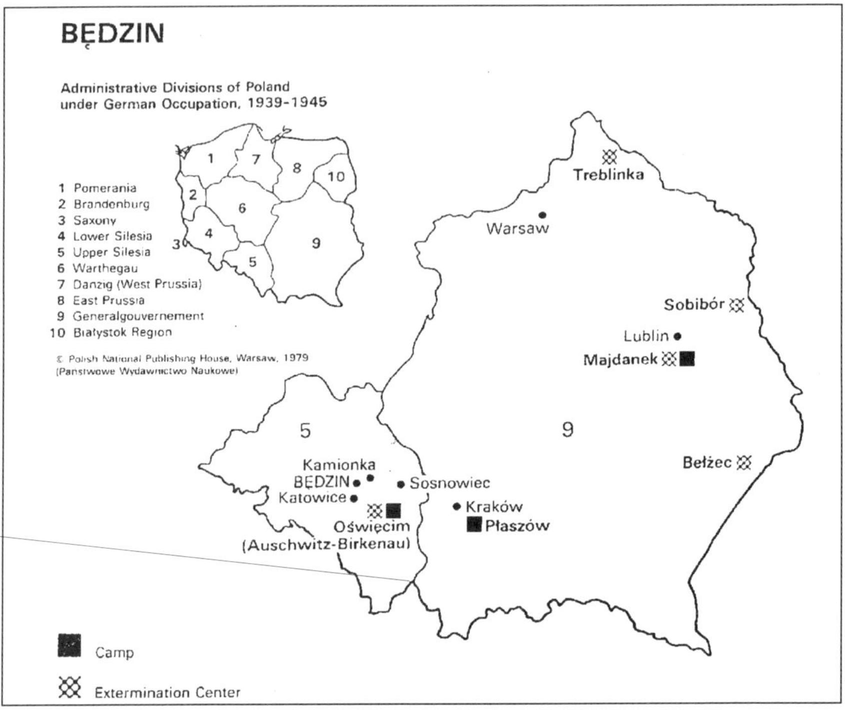

BĘDZIN
Administrative Divisions of Poland
under German Occupation, 1939-1945
1 Pomerania
2 Brandenburg
3 Saxony
4 Lower Silesia
5 Upper Silesia
6 Warthegau
7 Danzig (West Prussia)
8 East Prussia
9 Generalgouvernement
10 Białystok Region
© Polish National Publishing House, Warsaw, 1979
(Panstwowe Wydawnictwo Naukowe)
Treblinka
Warsaw
Sobibór
Lublin
Majdanek
5
9
Bełżec
Kamionka
BĘDZIN
Sosnowiec
Katowice
Kraków
Oświęcim
(Auschwitz-Birkenau)
Płaszów
Camp
Extermination Center

THE CASTLE
RIVER
CHURCH
KOŁŁATAJA
MARKET
CITY CENTRE PLACE
SACZEWSKA
בענדין
BĘDZIN
PLAN OF BENDZIN DRAWN
BY ARTHUR WIENER.

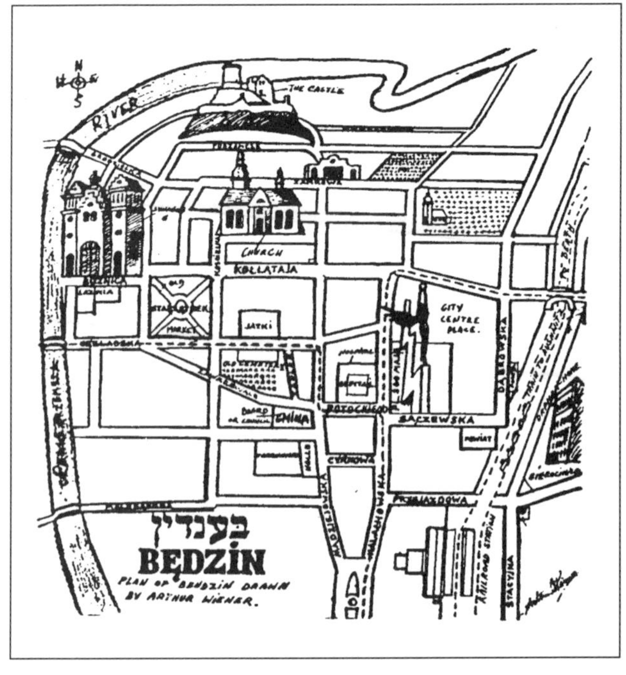

Sara and Alexander Szyjowicz, parents of Arnold Shay.

The Judenrat and the Medical Personnel in the Ghetto. 1) Moniek Merin, 2) Fany Czarna, 3) Chaim Moldczadski, 4) Chaim Merin, 5) Dr. Liberman, 6) Dr. Wajnziher, 7) Lewkowicz.

Szrodula 1942 Ghetto Bendzin.

Bendzin, are deported to the Auschwitz Extermination Camp. Only 20 Jews were left behind for the clean up of the Jewish properties, and they were shot when the job was done.

July 26, 1942. 6,000 Jews from Dombrowa Gornicza, near Bendzin, were deported to the Auschwitz Extermination Camp.

August 1, 1942. 5,000 Jews from Bendzin are deported in the second large scale transport to the Auschwitz Extermination Camp.

August 12, 1942. During a six day action, 8,000 Jews from the Sosnowiec suburb of Srodula, which is the Sosnowiec ghetto, and about the same number from the Bendzin ghetto in Kamionki and from Dombrowa Gornicza 550 Jews were sent to the Auschwitz Extermination Camp, where they were gassed upon arrival. (This author's mother was in that transport.)

The Jews were held there for four days without food or water before they were shipped off to Auschwitz.

August 18, 1942. Now the Germans officially establish a ghetto in Srodula, the suburb of Sosnowiec, which was adjacent to Kamionka the ghetto of Bendzin.

September 16, 1942. From Jedziejow, Kielce province, 6,000 Jews are sent to the Treblinka Extermination Camp, and only 200 Jews remained in the ghetto.

April 10, 1943. Heinrich Himmler, the head of the S.S., the German Police and the Gestapo, forbade the use of the code word "Sonderbehandlung," special treatment, in connection with the murder of the Jews. Instead, he recommends the term "Durchschleusung," a sort of transportation to the other world, in the language of the murderers.

May 12, 1943. Szmul Zygielbojm, member of the Polish National Council in exile in London, commits suicide as a protest against the indifference of the Allies to the fate of the Jews in Poland, who fight against the Nazis in the ghettos.

June 23, 1943. 1,800 Jews are deported by the S.S. from Strzemieszyce near Sosnowiec, to the Auschwitz Extermination Camp.

June 26, 1943. The ghetto of Dombrowa Gornicza, near Bendzin, is liquidated, and about 2,000 Jews are deported to the ghetto of Srodula, a suburb of Sosnowiec, and then on to Auschwitz for Extermination.

August 1, 1943. On the anniversary of the second deportation of the Jews from the ghetto in Kamionka, a suburb of Bendzin. This action takes two weeks due to the Jewish Resistance Movement of Bendzin that started in 1940 and has contact with the Resistance Movement in the

Warsaw ghetto.

The Gestapo shoots 600 Jews during the deportation from Srodula, the Sosnowiec ghetto.

August 3, 1943. Members of the "ZOB" Jewish Resistance Movement in Bendzin oppose the deportation to Auschwitz, by taking up arms and fighting the Germans. Many of them are killed and others managed to flee to the forest. Only 150 of the 50,000 Jews who lived in the Jewish quarters in Bendzin will survive.

During a three day "Action" 4,000 Jews from Dombrowa Gornicza, are deported to Auschwitz.

August 4, 1943. The deportation of Jews from Sosnowiec and Bendzin ghettos to Auschwitz takes place.

August 16, 1943. All Jewish inhabitants of the ghetto of Sosnowiec, with the exception of 1,000 Jews, are deported to Auschwitz.

August 26, 1943. The ghetto of Zawiercie near Bendzin-Sosnowiec is liquidated and the Jews are sent to Auschwitz. For passive resistance 100 Jews are shot and 500 Jews remain in a labor camp.

On the eve of the Jewish High Holiday, the new year, another transport arrived from Bendzin. There were already thousands of Jews from Bendzin, Sosnowiec and surrounding cities here, especially on the Jewish holidays the Germans wanted to show how powerful they are, and they surely were. I think that our God gave in to them. Maybe He was even powerless against the Germans.

All has been taken away from us. Our name. Our possessions. Our will to fight back, and yes, our ability to think clearly. All we had to show for it was a number tattooed on our left forearm. My number was 135584.

That morning it was raining without stopping. But we were awakened at 5 A.M. anyway and we had ten minutes to do our duties and get washed, ready for work.

We had at that time about six thousand inmates on the Quarantine Camp where most of the Bendiner were. In the ten minutes allotted to us it was impossible to wash and go to the "latrine" so most of us were "done" before we reached the latrine. And who would want to waste the water on washing when this may be all the water for the whole day. So we rather stick our tongues out and catch a few drops of that precious water.

All of my friends went out for work under the screams and whips of the vicious guards who hated the rain as much as we did. But, they could take it out on us. And they did with venom.

I did not go to work. I worked in the kitchen and was exempt. I remember that when we were counted, I always had to run right after roll call to the kitchen or even most of the time when the counting was late I had to go to the kitchen and stay in front of the kitchen and was counted there.

A week later, Yom-Kippur. And naturally, since it was a Jewish holiday, Yom Kippur, Day of Atonement, there would be a selection too. That day again, right after washing in the morning, we had to assemble in front of the barracks, and as always I had to go down to the kitchen in front of our camp to go to work and to be counted in front of the kitchen.

While running to work I noticed already the S.S. coming into the camp and that's when I realized that there is going to be a selection. We lost that day to the crematories almost half of the inmates of our camp the Quarantine. Not that it was any better in the other camps in Auschwitz-Birkenau that day. I will never forget that Day of Atonement, not that we had anything to atone for. We had committed no crime. Our only crime was to be born Jewish.

October 17, 1943. The remaining 500 Jews of Zawiercie interned in a Forced Labor Camp, are murdered by the S.S.

February 26, 1944. A transport of 54 Jews from Sosnowiec arrives at Auschwitz. The deportees are murdered immediately after their arrival. Those were the Jews left after the liquidation of the ghetto in August of 1943. They were left to clean out the ghetto.

April 14, 1944. German Task Forces arrest 150 men of the Jewish Community of Baja on the Danube, Hungary, and deport them. About 2,000 Jews are living in Baja at this time. Not included are the Jews from Bendzin-Sosnowiec who live in Baja in a Transit Camp. Baja in Hungary was one of the Transit Camps for Jews with foreign passports. Most of those Jews survived the war. The only known deaths are from natural causes. A lot of mail from these people exists from Baja as well as other similar internment camps in Hungary or Switzerland. I have a lot of that correspondence from those camps in my collection.

October 7, 1944. In the course of the uprising in Auschwitz, the Jewish Special Detachment "Sonderkommando" burns down a crematorium, kills a number of S.S. men, cuts through the barbed wire. Almost all were killed. Many from Bendzin.

Zalman Gradowski, after sixteen months in the Sonderkommando, writes in *A Chronicle of Auschwitz Sonderkommando* published in the book "The Literature of Destruction, edited by David G. Roskies," about two incidents he remembers. A courageous young man from a Bialystok transport had attacked some guards with knives, wounded several of them severely and was shot trying to flee.

The other exception, before which I bow my head in deep respect, was the incident of the "Warsaw transport." This was a group of Jews from Warsaw, who had become American citizens, some of them American born. All were to be sent to a German internment camp in Switzerland, where they would be put under the protection of the Swiss Red Cross; however, the "civilized" authorities brought these American citizens not to Switzerland but to the fires of the crematorium.

And then something heroic happened; a splendid young woman, a dancer from Warsaw, snatched a revolver from (Walter) Quackernack, the Oberscharfuhrer of the "Political Section" in Auschwitz, and shot the Referat-fuhrer, the notorious Unterscharfuhrer (Josef) Schillinger. Her deed bolstered the courage of other brave women, who in turn, slapped and threw vials and other such things into the faces of those vicious, uniformed beasts — the S.S.

Here I have to add what I know about that incident, since I was there at that time. (Josef Schillinger was shot in October 1943.) This celebrated case is widely documented. The version we heard then from the underground was the same as above with a bit different story about those women. They were from Warsaw but from the Pawiak where they interned to be sent to an internment camp in Switzerland or Hungary. The people were from different places, and that particular lady that shot Schillinger was one of those with a foreign passport and supposedly was from Bendzin. In that particular jail, the Pawiak, there were a few people from Bendzin with foreign passports (see page 173).

January 18, 1945. Evacuation of the prisoners in Auschwitz to different camps is on. Among the prisoners are many from the Zaglembie Region, Bendzin, Sosnowiec and surroundings. (This writer was among the evacuees on that day.) Many are shot and many died on the way.

Filip Muller, in his book *Eyewitness Auschwitz,* on page 68 writes about the transports from Bendzin and Sosnowiec that was the closing of those ghettos "Judenrein" free of Jews and what was the end of the people from these cities. Muller was one of those who worked in the "Sonderkommando" in the gas chambers of Auschwitz. The liquidation of the ghettos of Sosnowiec and Bendzin which began in August 1943 was one of a number of particularly brutal measures carried out in Birkenau at that time. Umpteen thousands were gassed within a period of ten days. This is an account of how it began:

One evening as we marched out on night shift hundreds of armed S.S. men were lined up along the street. Because of the comparative closeness of the two towns in Upper Silesia the S.S. were afraid that the local population as well as the Jews in the ghettos might have come to know about the atrocities perpetrated in Birkenau. For this reason several hundred S.S. men were ordered to action stations before the start of the campaign.

One more paragraph from Mullers book I would like to mention,

(I wish that book was read by every person in the world; because those few paragraphs that I am bringing out here from his book are only because of Bendzin that is my hometown.) These are his words: "Towards the end of the summer of 1943 a workshop for melting gold was set up in crematorium 3. It must have been unique in the way in which it obtained supplies. Two Jewish dental technicians were transferred to Birkenau from the dental hospital in Auschwitz. Their new place of employment was on the ground floor of crematorium 3.

Thirty-eight inch golden chain and associated golden maltese cross believed to be an authentic World War II relic. Made up of hundreds of pre-1945, European gold fillings, its origin has been associated with a Nazi extermination camp.

"A board outside their door announced 'No admission' to prisoners and S.S. men alike. For it was behind this door that the boxes of gold teeth were opened. These were teeth pulled from the jaws of Jews murdered in the gas chambers before their cremation. The teeth were soaked for a few hours in hydrochloric acid in order to clean off remnants of flesh and bone. Then they were melted in graphite molds with the help of a blow-lamp and formed into bars.

"At intervals of about a fortnight the gold was collected by ambulance and taken to Auschwitz. I was told by one of the technicians that frequently they melted down between five and ten kilograms a day. After the war it was learned that this gold went into the strong rooms of the Reichsbank."

On the previous page I wrote the account by Zalman Gradowski who too was working in the "Sonderkommando," about the shooting of Josef Schillinger inside the changing rooms (this was where the people got undressed before going into the gas chambers) but now I want to give Mueller's account of that shooting since Muller was inside the gas chambers at that time when the shooting occurred. Here Muller gives his account which is almost exactly but with more details…

"Surreptitiously S.S.-unterfuhrer Quackernack, Hustek, Voss, Boger, Schillinger, Gorges, Emmerich, Kirsch's Ackermann and others left the changing room one by one, returning after a short time armed with sticks. No doubt Lagerfuhrer Schwarz Hubert had given them the green light to deal with these people in the usual way. Instead of their earlier marked courtesy and lying talk there was now terse requests of 'Get undressed! Hurry up! Get ready for the bath! Come on! Come on!' The people did not respond, but simply kept standing about doing nothing. It was not surprising therefore that the S.S. men grew nervous.

"In order to demonstrate that they meant business, they shifted their holsters round to the front and opened the flaps. Then they came closer to the crowd and, assuming a menacing attitude, began to shout. When this had no effect either, they started to strike blindly at the crowd with their sticks. The S.S. increased their furious, merciless beatings. By now many people were bleeding profusely from blows they had received. And at long last the rest realized that resistance was useless. There was no way out. They began to undress, whereupon the S.S. men stopped beating them. Why we were still standing by the wall holding our boards no one knew.

"It was obvious that the S.S. felt themselves once more to be masters of the situation. Quackernack and Schillinger were strutting back and forth in front of the humiliated crowd with a self-important swagger. Suddenly they stopped in their tracks, attracted by a strikingly handsome woman with blue-black hair who was taking off her right shoe. The woman, as soon as she noticed that the two men were ogling her, launched into what appeared to be a titillating and seductive strip-tease act. She lifted her skirt to allow a glimpse of thigh and suspender. Slowly she undid her stocking and peeled it off her foot. From out of the corner of her eye she carefully observed what was going on round her. The two S.S. men were fascinated by her performance and paid no attention to anything else. They were standing there with arms akimbo, their whips dangling from their wrists, and their eyes firmly glued on the woman.

"She had taken off her blouse and was standing in front of her lecherous audience in her brassiere. Then she steadied herself against a concrete pillar with her left arm and bent down, slightly lifting her foot, in order to take off her shoe. What happened next took place with lightning speed; quick as a flash she grabbed her shoe and slammed its heel violently against Quackernack's forehead. He winced with pain and covered his face with both hands.

"At this moment the young woman flung herself at him and made a quick grab for his pistol. Then there was a shot. Schillinger cried out and fell to the ground. Seconds later there was a second shot aimed at Quackerneck which narrowly missed him.

"A panic broke out in the changing room. The young woman had disappeared in the crowd. Any moment she might appear somewhere else and aim her pistol at another of her executioners. The S.S. men realized this danger. One by one they crept outside. The wounded Schillinger was still lying unattended on the floor.

"After a while a few S.S. men came in and dragged him hastily to the door. Then a third shot was fired; one of the S.S. men pulling Schillinger let go of him and started to limp to the door as fast as he could. Then the light went out. Simultaneously the door was bolted from the outside. We, too, were now caught inside the pitch dark room.

"The people who had lost their bearing in the dark were running about in confusion. I, too, was afraid that this might be the end for all of us. I began to grope my way along the wall towards the exit. When I finally reached it I found nearly all of my companions, but also many of the others who instinctively had made for the door. A man who was standing near us had noticed that we did not belong to their group. He spoke to us in the dark and wanted to know from where we came. ‘From the death factory,’ one of my companions replied tersely.

“Suddenly the door was flung open. I was blinded by the glare of several searchlights. Then I heard Voss shouting; ‘All members of the Sonderkommando, come out.’ Greatly relieved we dashed outside and ran up the stairs and into the yard. Outside the door to the changing room two machine guns had been set up, and behind them several searchlights. Steel-helmeted S.S. men were lying ready to operate the machine guns. A horde of armed S.S. men were milling about in the yard.

“I was on my way to cremation when a car drew up and Lagerkommandant Hoess climbed out. Then there was a rattle of machine guns. A terrible blood-bath was wrought about the people caught in the changing room. A very few who had managed to hide behind pillars were later seized and shot. In the meantime, the ‘disinfecting’ officers had thrown their deadly ‘Zyklon B’ gas into the gas chamber, where the credulous, placing their trust in Hossler’s deceitful words, had gone less than an hour earlier.

“Next morning we learned that Schillinger had died on the way to the hospital, while Unterscharfuhrer Emmerich had been wounded. The news (of Schillinger’s death) was received with satisfaction by many camp inmates; for in section B2d Schillinger had been regarded as an extremely brutal and capricious sadist.

“The body of the young dancer was laid out in the dissecting room of crematorium 2. S.S. men went there to look at her corpse before incineration. Perhaps the sight of her was to be a warning as well, as an illustration of the dire consequences one moment’s lack of vigilance might have for an S.S. man.

“As for us, these events had taught us once again that there simply was no chance of escape once a person entered the crematorium; by then it was too late.”

Chapter Nine

This is a glorious page in our history
That has never been written
And never shall be written.

Heinrich Himmler

Appendum

The lawlessness that existed during World War II under the German occupation is beyond comprehension. It was seen with the civil population and in particular with the Jewish population.

Isaiah Trunk, in his book *Judenrat*, was a great source of information for me about Bendzin. I have given credit to a lot of writers in this book, but Isaiah Trunk has the most information about life in the ghettos and, particularly, information about life in the Bendzin ghetto that I have witnessed and never found so much information about. Thank you Mr. Trunk for the wealth of information on my home town Bendzin.

On the 21st of September, a little over two weeks after the occupation of Poland, Heydrich, the chief of the "Security Police," sent a letter which was a decree called "Schnellbrief," to all the heads of the "Einsatzgruppen" Task forces, in the occupied Polish territory.

The parts in this letter, "Councils of Jewish Elders," which deals specifically with the establishment of local representatives for the Jewish population and the letter are below in translation:

Berlin, 21 September 1939

The chief of the Security Police. PP (II0-288/39 secret)
Special Delivery Letter
To The Chiefs of all task forces (Einsatzgruppen) of the Security Police.
Concerning: The Jewish problem in the occupied zone.

I refer to the conference held in Berlin today, and again point out that the planned joint measures (i.e, the ultimate goal) are to be kept strictly secret.

Distinction must be made between

(1) the ultimate goal (which requires a prolonged period of time) and

(2) the sector leading to fulfillment of the ultimate goal (each of which will be carried out in a short term)

The planned measures require thorough preparation both in technique and in economic aspect.

Obviously the task at hand cannot be laid down in detail from here. The following instructions and directives serve at the same time for the purpose of urging chiefs of the task forces to practical consideration of problems.

COUNCIL OF JEWISH ELDERS

(1) In each Jewish community, a Council of Jewish Elders is to be set up which, as far as possible, is to be composed of the remaining influential personalities and rabbis. The Council is to be composed of 24 male Jews (depending on the size of the Jewish community).

It is to be made fully responsible (in the literal sense of the word) for the exact execution according to terms of all instructions released or yet to be released.

(2) In case of sabotage of such instructions, the Councils are to be warned of severest measures.

(3) The Jewish Councils are to take an improvised census of the Jews of their area, possibly divided into generations (according to age)

a. up to 16 years of age

b. from 16 to 20 years of age, and

c. those above and also according to the principal vocations — and they are to report the results in the shortest possible time.

(4) The Councils of the Elders are to be made acquainted with the time and date of evacuation, the evacuation possibilities, and finally the evacuation routes. They are, then, to be made personally responsible for the evacuation of the Jews from the country. The reasons to be given for the concentration of the Jews to the cities is that Jews have most decisively participated in sniper attacks and plundering.

(5) The Councils of Elders of the concentration centers are to be made responsible for the proper housing of the Jews to be brought in from the country. The concentration of Jews in the cities for general reasons of security will probably bring about orders to forbid Jews to enter certain wards of the cities altogether, and that in consideration of economic necessity they cannot, for instance, leave the ghetto, they cannot go out after a designated evening hour, etc.

(6) The Councils of Elders are also to be made responsible for the adequate maintenance of the Jews on the transport to the cities. No scruples are to be voiced if the migrating Jews take with them all their movable

possessions, as far as that is technically at all possible.

(7) Jews who do not comply with the order to move into cities are to be given a short additional period of grace when there is good reason. They are to be warned of strictest penalty if they should not comply by the appointed time.

(I am giving here only the first decree that is pertinent to my book and to my story of Bendzin. There were other such decrees.)

There were other factors that brought the council to life, of which there was no small measure of Jewish participation. The Germans would try to bring in Jews from other parts of the country or even other countries to work with the Judenrat, the council, Jews that had no idea of the city or its Jews.

There was and only for a short time, a council in Bendzin even before Moniek Merin entered the picture.

In Sosnowiec, a group of Jews was seized in the street. A German stepped out and asked the group (after they were held for 24 hours) who among them was on the prewar council. Mr. Lejzerowicz, the president of the prewar council, was not in the group so Moniek Merin who was in that group stepped out and offered his services. That's how the infamous Moniek Merin became the Leader of the Elders of the Judenrat in Sosnowiec and later on the Leader of the Central Office of the Jewish Councils of the Elders in Ost-Oberschlesien (East Upper Silesia).

The Germans have created an administrative entity. In Ost-Oberschlesien made up of a part from the Wojewodztwo Krakowskie, the Krakow province and the part of the Polish Silesia. Moniek Merin who became chairman of the Judenrat in Sosnowiec (about November-December of 1939), was appointed to form the Judenrats in the Regirungsbezirk Kattowitz. In the beginning of January 1940, "DIE ZENTRALE DER AELTESTENRAETE DER JUDISCHEN KULTUSGEMEINDEN IN OSTOBERSCHLESIEN" was born. (A federation like of Jewish Cultural Agencies in Eastern Upper Silesia.)

One year later, March 1941, there were 32 communities from ten counties in the "ZENTRALE" of the Regierungsbezirk of which the largest were two cities, Bendzin and Sosnowiec, with a Jewish population of 100,000. From all those communities, the largest was Bendzin, with 25,171 Jews.

The by-laws as printed in the Gazeta Zydowska, the Zentrale had the jurisdiction over all the local councils. The Leiter, Moniek Merin, represented all those councils in German matters. He appointed, fired and even arrested members of the councils in Ost-Oberschlesien at his will, in different counties even in Bendzin he put in charge his own man, his brother Chaim Merin.

He set up "Inspectors" for the local councils acting as liaison men to the "Zentrale" through nine different departments. (The department to deal with emigration existed only until 1940.) Those departments were authorized by the German authorities:

1) A legal department to act on behalf of the community or even a single individual.

2) A food department for the distribution of food to the Jews in the entire area of Ost-Oberschlesien. To purchase food products from private sources and, yes, to provide food for the soup kitchens.

3) A labor department to get Jews for the forced labor duty, to collect bribes from the ones that were released from those duties, and even punish the ones that did not show up for the forced labor.

4) A welfare department, to decide on relief and how it should be distributed.

5) A health department to confer with the physicians and provide medical facilities for them in the small communities and in general to supervise those institutions.

6) A finance department, the council supervised the financial activities, to estimate their monthly expenses and to check on the disbursement of those allocations. Their duty was also to help out financially the former owners of businesses that were confiscated by the Germans.

Moneies, too, were coming in from the outside from different Jewish organizations like; TOZ, Joint Distribution Committee, Red Cross and many others.

7) A department of education, that tried as much as possible to give some education to the youngsters that worried more about how to find a piece of bread.

8) A department of statistics, that help the Germans unintentionally more than the Jews in the ghetto by getting the census, the head tax (Kopfsteuer), distribute the armbands and collecting a fee for them as well as the distribution of the ration cards. (All this made it easy for the Germans to know how many Jews there were in the ghetto and where to find them.)

9) A department dealing with the archives, this department was primarily under the supervision of Moniek Merin and Fanny Czarna. There

HURTOWNIA GALANTERII

TELEFON Nr. 613-53.

Depesze: OSTRY, SOSNOWIEC.

P. K. O. w Katowicach Nr. 302.439.

F. OSTRY, SOSNOWIE

SOSNOWIEC, d. 30. Juni

ul. Modrzejowska 12.

An Fräulein

Bala Zajonz

in Firma Ostry

Auf Veranlassung der Treuhandstelle"Ost" mus jüdisc
gegen arisches Personal ausgewechselt werden.

Aus diesem Grunde kündigen wir Ihnen per 30. Juli 1
und beurlauben Sie ab sofort für den gabzen Monat J

Das Gehalt für den Monat Juli erhalten Sie am 31.VI

F. OSTRY, S... O.S

Modrz...gasse ...

Behördlicher Leiter

J. Pietsch

When the Germans came to Poland, they took over all the Jewish business establishments. This is a letter sent by a German trustee, stating that a Jewish woman is fired because the personnel is being changed to Aryan personnel.

June 30. 1940.

Miss.
Bala Zajonz
in Fiorma Ostry

On orders of the "Treuhandstelle "Ost"" (Trostee for Jewish businesses) the Jewish personel must be e exchanged for "Aryen".

On these grounds you are being let go as of July 30, 1940. and will pay you as of now for the whole month of July.

The pay for the month you will receive on the 31st of July 1940.

Signed
J. Pietsch

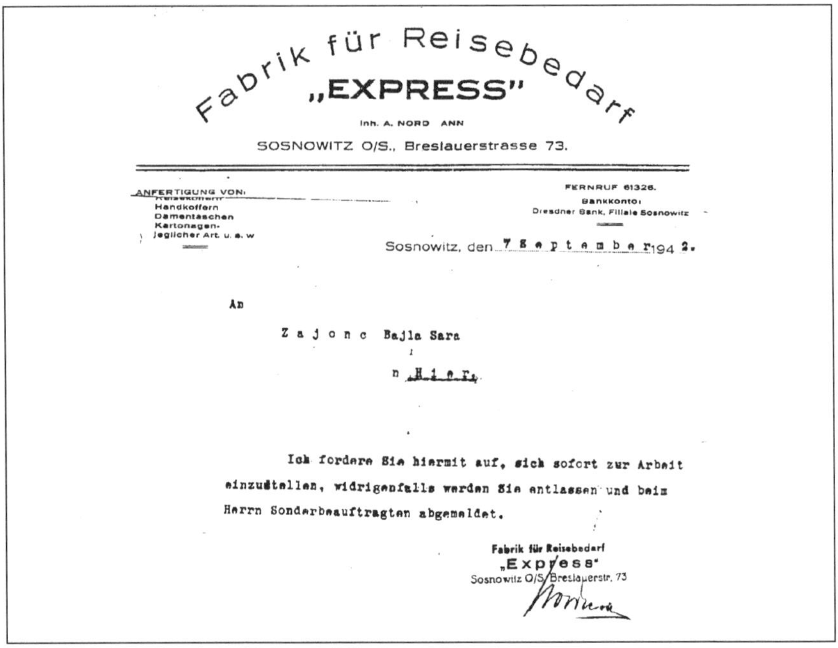

Fabrik für Reisebedarf
„EXPRESS"
Inh. A. NORD ANN
SOSNOWITZ O/S., Breslauerstrasse 73.

ANFERTIGUNG VON:
Handkoffern
Damentaschen
Kartonagen-
jeglicher Art. u. s. w

FERNRUF 61326.
Bankkonto:
Dresdner Bank, Filiale Sosnowitz

Sosnowitz, den 7 September 1942.

An

Zajonc Bajla Sara

Hier.

Ich fordere Sie hiermit auf, sich sofort zur Arbeit einzustellen, widrigenfalls werden Sie entlassen und beim Herrn Sonderbeauftragten abgemeldet.

Fabrik für Reisebedarf
„Express"
Sosnowitz O/S/Breslauerstr. 73

This is a letter from a German trustee stating that a Jewish girl is called back to work, two years after she was fired, while she was already in a slave labor camp.

September 7. 1942.

To

Zajonc Bajla Sara
Here

I am ordering you herewith to imidietly report for work Otherwise you will be let go and you will have to report to the "Sondrerbeauftragten.

Signed
???

A synagogue is used to collect and sortrensom money from the Jews in the ghettos.

Breaking down the Polish frontier September 1, 1939.

Collecting furs from the Jews.

Hans Frank General Governor Warsaw, September 1939.

German troops on their way by train to the Polish front. The slogan on their railway carriage reads: "To Poland, to thrash the Jews."

SECOND DECREE FOR THE IMPLEMENTATION OF THE LAW REGARDING CHANGES OF FAMILY NAMES, August 17, 1938.

Pursuant to § 13 of the Law of January 5, 1938, regarding changes of family names and given names (*Reichsgesetzblatt* I, p. 9), the following is decreed:

§ 1 (1) Jews may be given only such given names as are listed in the Guidelines on the Use of Given Names issued by the Reich Minister of the Interior.

(2) Paragraph 1 does not apply to Jews who are foreign subjects.

§ 2 (1) Insofar as Jews have other given names than those which may be given to Jews according to § 1, they are obligated, beginning January 1, 1939, to assume an additional given name, namely, the given name Israel in the case of males, and the given name Sara in the case of females.

(2) Whoever, according to Paragraph 1, must assume an additional given name is obligated to give written notice within a month from the date after which he is required to use the additional given name, both to the registrar with whom his birth and his marriage are recorded, and to the local police authorities in his place of residence or usual domicile.

(3) If the birth or marriage of the person required to give such notice is recorded by a German diplomatic representative or consul or in a German protectorate, the notice required for the registrar is to be directed to the registrar at the Registrar's Office No. 1 in Berlin. If the person required to give the notice resides or is usually domiciled abroad, the notice specified in Paragrah 2, Sentence 1, is to be given to the appropriate German consul in lieu of the local police authorities.

(4) In the case of incompetent persons and of persons of limited competence, the requirement to give notice rests with the legal representative.

§ 3 Insofar as it is customary to state names in legal and business transactions, Jews must always use at least one of their given names. If they are required under § 2 to assume an additional given name, this given name is also to be used. Regulations regarding the use of names of firms are not affected by this provision.

§ 4 (1) Whoever willfully violates the provision of § 3 will be punished by imprisonment up to six months. If the violation is due to negligence, the punishment will be imprisonment up to one month.

(2) Whoever willfully or negligently fails to give notice as provided in § 2 will be fined or punished by imprisonment up to one month.

The Reich Minister of the Interior
The Reich Minister of Justice

DECREE REGARDING THE UTILIZATION OF JEWISH PROPERTY

1 & 2. The owner of a Jewish enterprise may be requested to sell or liquidate the enterprise within a given period. A trustee may be put in charge of the temporary continuation or liquidation.

6. A Jew may be ordered to sell—in full or in part—within a given period, his agricultural or arboricultural property, his real estate or other property.

7. Jews cannot acquire real estate or real estate rights.

11. Within a week, Jews must deposit their securities, stocks and bonds with a recognized bank. A declaration must be filed stating that those papers already deposited belong to a Jew; all such papers must be identified as "Jewish."

12. Disposal of such papers requires the consent of the Reich Minister of Economics.

14. Jews are forbidden to buy, pawn or sell, except to public purchasing offices of the Reich, objects of gold, platinum and silver, precious stones and pearls, or other jewelry and art objects worth 1,000 Reichsmark or more. This provision does not apply to Jews of foreign nationality.

15. Permits for the sale of Jewish enterprises, real estate or other property may be granted conditionally. Such conditions may include fees to be paid to the Reich by the purchaser; or, instead of the whole or part of the price, the Jewish seller may be given promissory notes of the German Reich or entries of his claim into the *Reichsschuldbuch* (Reich Ledger of Claims).

was too much dirt and suspicion in that department to leave it open for others to see.

These departments were actually in service until April of 1940.

In December of 1940, the "Wohlfartsvereinigung" services organization was added to the "Centrale" in Sosnowiec. This organization was primarily established to take over The Joint Distribution activities in Ost-Oberschlesien that was not allowed to function in the incorporated provinces. The "Wohlfartsvereinigung" ended its activities in May of 1941.

Most of these activities of those departments were not supervised to the welfare of the ghetto population, and were only executed to the whims of our leader Moniek Merin the almighty crook. (I, who lived with these people until 1943, have very little [or nothing] good to say about the whole bunch of them.)

On September 29, 1939, the chief of the Army Ost ordered to take over all businesses with absentee ownership. This became the legal pretext to put in their own commissars. In the same time orders were issued to block Jewish bank accounts.

On November 1, 1939, Goering issued an order which had established the "Haupttreuhandstelle Ost." This made it legal to take over Jewish and Polish property in the occupied territories.

With the nomination of Hans Frank as Governor General, he established the "Treuhandstelle fur das General Government."

On January 24, 1940, the order "Beschlagnahmeordnung," Confiscation Order, made it legal to take over "Treuhandvervaltung" or the confiscation of properties, and they set up their "Treuhander" to run the Jewish businesses. Not that before this order Jewish businesses were not taken over by the Germans under different pretexts. Any German, civilian or uniformed, would take over a Jewish business without compensation to the owner.

October 26, 1939, it was "legalized" that Jews between the ages of fourteen and sixty were obligated to do slave labor. The Jewish councils had to deliver the slave laborers. Nothing was paid by the Germans for the slave labor. Any payment, as small as it was, was done by the Jewish Council not out of the goodness of their hearts, but primarily to get more workers. There was a special "Judenfond" set up by some of the local Mayors.

Slave labor was utilized not only inside the ghetto but thousands of young Jewish people were sent to labor camps in far off places. The young people from Upper Silesia were sent to many slave labor camps as early as 1940, never to come back home or to see their loved ones who were carted off to some concentration or liquidation camp.

My brothers and sisters never saw our parents again after they were shipped off to labor or other camps. Most of these youngsters were transferred from one labor camp to another, or from labor camps to concentration camps — if they survived at all. Some slave labor camps later on became annexed to concentration camps. The camp where my brother was, Labor Camp Blechhammer, was annexed to Auschwitz and the inmates were even tattooed with numbers from Auschwitz.

For some, life in the ghetto had to go on. We helped ourselves in any way possible. Black marketing and stealing from the trains some food or coals to heat up the house a bit became a daily routine.

When the different shops were created in the ghettos we found a way how to be employed in them. The shops were created by Germans and most of the time with Jewish participation. And it is understandable. The shops, as much as we worked only on military items, they served the individual German who opened the shop and also the Jewish population that was employed in those shops. To the Jews it gave a bit of security because the German looked on your employment to the German economy as a person who for now is still needed and worth living.

Anything to survive another day in the ghetto. Even farms were created. In Bendzin the farm was very profitable in many ways, it gave the young people a sense of pride as well as shelter and a chance for underground activities. On Srodula Dolna, where the Bendzin Jews were "resettled" from the city, there were a group of 34 Jewish boys and 27 Jewish girls. The farm provided food for the Jews.

In the small town of Strzemieszyce, not far from Bendzin and Sosnowiec, the Jews received permission from the "Burgermeister" to start a farm. In many smaller towns Jews planted their own little gardens. Again, it gave them pride and even some food for the table.

I remember too the "Dzialki" in Sosnowiec on Ostrogorska street. Even as late as 1942 we were still meeting there from the Hanoar Hazioni and different actions by the underground were undertaken there.

Different trade classes were organized in these places. In Sosnowiec courses of embroidery, corset making for girls and electricians for boys.

In Bendzin, there were courses in watchmaking, electromonters for boys and embroidery and corset making for girls.

In Dombrowa Jewish students were working as carpenters. They

The "Underground" working on a farm in the Bendzin Ghetto. From left: Enzel Fajerman, Szyja Erlich, Szmul Rajchman and Michal Dreksler.

In the Bendzin Ghetto on "The Kamionki" Enzel Fajerman, Szyja Erlich, Szmul Rajchman and Michal Dreksler.

Herszel Szpringer, "Dror," speaking to the "Resistance" group of "Hanoar-Hazioni" in Bendzin.

Szrodula 1942 Ghetto Bendzin.

Zionist movement was active even in the heart of Nazi Germany.

As time went on the amount of youth activity in the town increased. Young people who had been unattached joined up and new organizations were formed. The kevutzas, or cells, worked to capacity teaching their members the basics of Socialism, Zionism, and Jewish history, all of which were studied more seriously than they would have been in normal times. These groups offered their members a substitute for school; there was a healthy, home-like atmosphere and friendly instructors who were more like older brothers.

In the early spring of 1942 the Moazah took a census of the organized groups in Bendzin. The results were as follows:

Hanoar Hatzioni	500 members
Gordonia	300 members
Dror	250 members
Hashomer Hatzair	200 members
Hashomer Hadati	150 members

The size of each group was generally known to the others since the leaders of one organization would often take part in the meetings of another; kibbutz members in particular were invited to the larger assemblies. It should also be mentioned that the size of a group did not necessarily determine its effectiveness; Hashomer Hatzair and Dror, although smaller than some of the others, had extremely energetic organizers.

THE ORPHAN HOME — The last view of Bendzin for thousands and thousands. Next came Auschwitz and the gas chambers. Left: Inside the yard; right: from the street.

worked in two shifts. Trade courses were also organized in Olkusz, Slawkow and Strzemieszyce.

A lot of credit should go to different organizations that help in no small measure to ease the pains of hunger in the ghetto. Besides the J.D.C., which financed almost the entire relief work of the Jewish Councils, there were so many other Jewish Social Welfare organizations. (Some of them I mentioned in previous chapters). There were also the "Hauptrat fur Socialen Schutz," (Naczelna Rada Opiekuncza). Some assistance came from the "Reichsvereinigung der Juden in Deutschland," the International Red Cross in Geneva as well as the IRC in Poland.

Vaad ha'Hatzalah, the Israeli Rescue Committee, was posted in Turkey, which was at that time neutral. They stayed in touch with the Jews in the German occupied territories. They did the best they could in helping the Jews by sending food parcels and documents (legal or otherwise), as well as obtaining information.

Vaad ha'Hatzalah and other organizations spent lots of money to get information, but only one, a non-Jew, was successful in getting a message through to Poland.

That messenger arrived in the Bendzin Ghetto on the 16th of July 1943, and was personally delivered by the smuggler to the representatives of the Jewish Fighters Organization. The smuggler had the names of these representatives as well as money for them. After the delivery he went back to Turkey carrying with him a letter from the Jewish Fighters organization in Zaglembie.

The letter he delivered was in German and states as follows: "We were very happy to meet today your long awaited messenger with the letter from you. Unfortunately, your messenger came too late. For years we have been praying to find an opportunity to let you know about our lives and fight." They went on telling the story of the complete extermination of the Polish Jewry. They listed the towns and number of people killed.

The letter was signed by Frumka Plotnicka, Herszel Szpringer, Srulek Kozuch and Szlomo Lerner. They were all murdered, the only one to survive was Zwi Brandes.

They were telling of the Warsaw Ghetto uprising and that they too will be destroyed soon. They write: "In the few nearest weeks our area too will be 'Judenrein.' When you receive this letter, no living Jewish soul will be left here."

So on August 1, 1943, the liquidation of the Jews from Bendzin and Sosnowiec has begun.

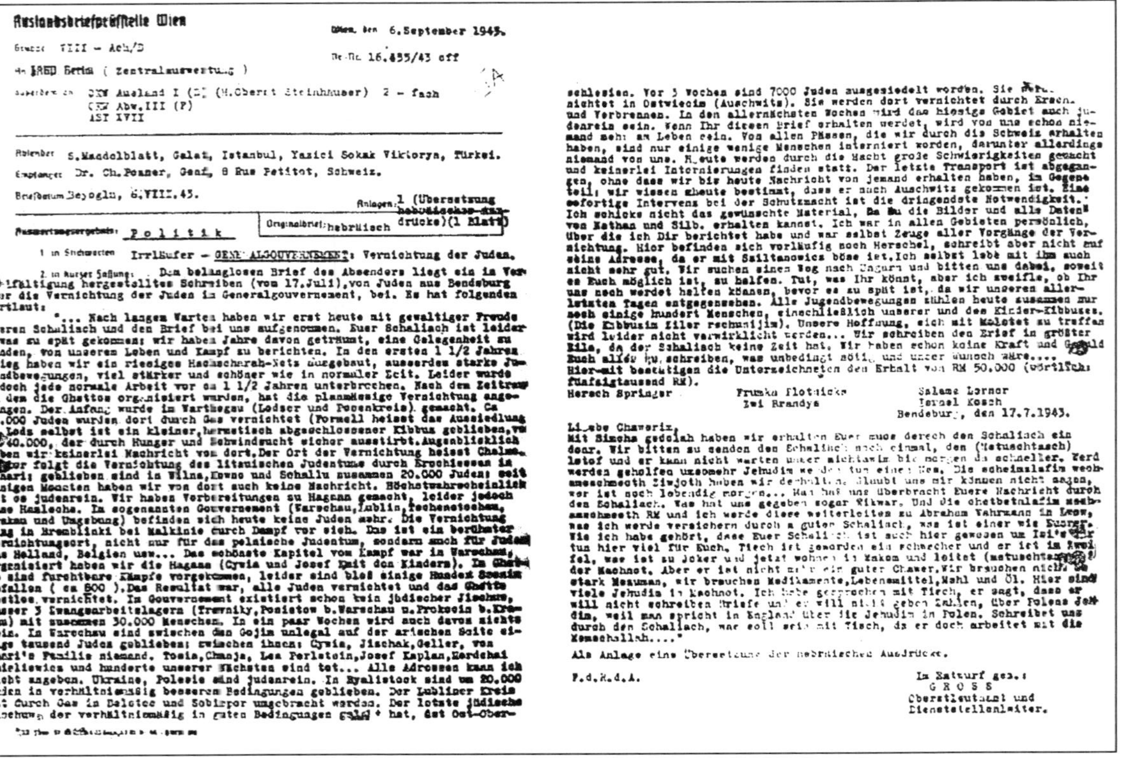

Auslandsbriefprüfstelle Wien

Wien, den 6. September 1943.

Gruppe: VIII – Ach/D

Br.-Nr. 16.455/43 off

An OKW Berlin (Zentralauswertung)

abschriften an: OKW Ausland I (Z) (M.Oberst Steinhäuser) 2 – fach
OKW Abw. III (F)
AST XVII

Absender: S. Mandelblatt, Galata, Istanbul, Yazici Sokak Viktorya, Türkei.

Empfänger: Dr. Ch. Posner, Genf, 8 Rue Petitot, Schweiz.

Briefdatum: Beyoglu, 6. VIII. 43.

Anlagen: 1 (Übersetzung ~~hebräischer Aus-~~ drücke) (1 Blatt)

Originalbrief: hebräisch

Auswertungsergebnis: P o l i t i k

1. in Stichworten: Irrläufer – GENERALGOUVERNEMENT: Vernichtung der Juden.

2. in kurzer Fassung: Dem belanglosen Brief des Absenders liegt ein in Vervielfältigung hergestelltes Schreiben (vom 17. Juli), von Juden aus Bendsburg über die Vernichtung der Juden im Generalgouvernement, bei. Es hat folgenden Wortlaut:

"... Nach langem Warten haben wir erst heute mit gewaltiger Freude Euren Schaliach und den Brief bei uns aufgenommen. Euer Schaliach ist leider etwas zu spät gekommen; wir haben Jahre davon geträumt, eine Gelegenheit zu finden, von unserem Leben und Kampf zu berichten. In den ersten 1 1/2 Jahren Krieg haben wir ein riesiges Hachscharah-Netz ausgebaut, ausserdem starke Jugendbewegungen, viel stärker und schöner wie in normaler Zeit. Leider wurde jedoch jede normale Arbeit vor ca 1 1/2 Jahren unterbrochen. Nach dem Zeitraum in dem die Ghettos organisiert wurden, hat die planmässige Vernichtung angefangen. Der Anfang wurde im Warthegau (Lodser und Posenkreis) gemacht. Ca 80.000 Juden wurden dort durch Gas vernichtet (Formell heisst das Aussiedlung). In Lods selbst ist ein kleiner, hermetisch abgeschlossener Kibbuz geblieben, von 40.000, der durch Hunger und Schwindsucht sicher ausstirbt. Augenblicklich haben wir keinerlei Nachricht von dort. Der Ort der Vernichtung heisst Chelmno. Später folgt die Vernichtung des litauischen Judentums durch Erschiessen in Ponari; geblieben sind in Wilna, Kowno und Schallu zusammen 20.000 Juden; seit einigen Monaten haben wir von dort auch keine Nachricht. Höchstwahrscheinlich ist es judenrein. Wir haben Vorbereitungen zu Hagana gemacht, leider jedoch ohne Hamleche. Im sogenannten Gouvernement (Warschau, Lublin, Tschenstochau, Krakau und Umgebung) befinden sich heute keine Juden mehr. Die Vernichtung ging in Kremblinki bei Malkinie durch Dampf vor sich. Das ist ein berühmter Vernichtungsort, nicht nur für das polnische Judentum, sondern auch für Juden aus Holland, Belgien usw... Das schönste Kapitel vom Kampf war in Warschau, organisiert haben wir die Hagana (Cywia und Josef mit den Kindern). Im Ghetto sind furchtbare Kämpfe vorgekommen, leider sind bloß einige Hundert Soanim gefallen (ca 800). Das Resultat war, alle Juden vernichtet und das Ghetto restlos vernichtet. Im Gouvernement existiert schon kein jüdischer Jischuw, ausser 3 Zwangsarbeitslagern (Trawniky, Poniatow b. Warschau u. Prokocin b. Krakau) mit zusammen 30.000 Menschen. In ein paar Wochen wird auch davon nichts sein. In Warschau sind zwischen den Gojim unlegal auf der arischen Seite einige tausend Juden geblieben; zwischen ihnen: Cywia, Jischak, Geller, von Jenri's Familie niemand. Tosia, Chanja, Lea Perlstein, Josef Kaplan, Mordchai Anielewicz und hunderte unserer Nächsten sind tot... Alle Adressen kann ich nicht angeben. Ukraine, Polesie sind judenrein. In Bialistock sind um 20.000 Juden in verhältnismässig besseren Bedingungen geblieben. Der Lubliner Kreis ist durch Gas in Belzec und Sobibor umgebracht worden. Der letzte jüdische Jischuw, der verhältnismäßig in guten Bedingungen gelebt hat, ist Ost-Oberschlesien. Vor 3 Wochen sind 7000 Juden ausgesiedelt worden. Sie sind vernichtet in Ostwiecim (Auschwitz). Sie werden dort vernichtet durch Ersticken und Verbrennen. In den allernächsten Wochen wird das hiesige Gebiet auch judenrein sein. Wenn Ihr diesen Brief erhalten werdet, wird von uns schon niemand mehr am Leben sein. Von allen Pässen, die wir durch die Schweiz erhalten haben, sind nur einige wenige Menschen interniert worden, darunter allerdings niemand von uns. Heute werden durch die Macht große Schwierigkeiten gemacht und keinerlei Internierungen finden statt. Der letzte Transport ist abgegangen, ohne dass wir bis heute Nachricht von jemand erhalten haben, im Gegenteil; wir wissen heute bestimmt, dass er nach Auschwitz gekommen ist. Eine sofortige Intervenz bei der Schutzmacht ist die dringendste Notwendigkeit. Ich schicke nicht das gewünschte Material, da Du die Bilder und alle Daten von Nathan und Silb. erhalten kannst. Ich war in allen Gebieten persönlich, über die ich Dir berichtet habe und war selbst Zeuge aller Vorgänge der Vernichtung. Hier befinden sich vorläufig noch Herschel, schreibt aber nicht auf seine Adresse, da er mit Sziltanowics böse ist. Ich selbst lebe mit ihm auch nicht sehr gut. Wir suchen einen Weg nach Ungarn und bitten uns dabei, soweit es Euch möglich ist, zu helfen. Tut, was Ihr könnt, aber ich zweifle, ob Ihr uns noch werdet helfen können, bevor es zu spät ist, da wir unseren allerletzten Tagen entgegensehen. Alle Jugendbewegungen zählen heute zusammen nur noch einige hundert Menschen, einschließlich unserer und des Kinder-Kibbuzes. (Die Kibbuzim Ziler rechunijim). Unsere Hoffnung, sich mit Molotet zu treffen wird leider nicht verwirklicht werden... Wir schreiben den Brief in größter Eile, da der Schaliach keine Zeit hat. Wir haben schon keine Kraft und Geduld Euch alles zu schreiben, was unbedingt nötig und unser Wunsch wäre....
Hiermit bestätigen die Unterzeichneten den Erhalt von RM 50.000 (wörtlich: fünfzigtausend RM).

Hersch Springer — Frumka Plotnicka — Zwi Brandys — Salame Lerner — Israel Kosch

Bendsburg, den 17.7.1943.

Liebe Chaverim,
Mit Simcha gedolah haben wir erhalten Euer muos derech den Schaliach ein doar. Wir bitten zu senden den Schaliach noch einmal, den (Metuschtasch) letof und er kann nicht warten unser michtawim bis morgen da schneller. Werd werden geholfen umsomehr Jehudim we... tun einen Nes. Die scheimslafim weohameschmeeth Ziwjoth haben wir dechalt... Glaubt uns wir können nicht sagen, wer ist noch lebendig morgen... Man hat uns überbracht Euere Nachricht durch den Schaliach. Was hat uns gegeben sogar Rikwar. Und die chetbetalafim weohameschmeeth RM und ich werde diese weiterleiten zu Abraham Wahrmann in Lwow, was ich werde versichern durch a guten Schaliach, was ist einer wie Zucker. Wie ich habe gehört, dass Euer Schaliach ist auch hier gewesen um Iai's ... tun hier viel für Euch. Tiech ist geworden ein schwacher und er ist im Zweifel, was ist zu Joker und jetzt wohnen in Makom und leitet (metuschtasch?) der Machnot. Aber er ist nicht mehr ein guter Chawer. Wir brauchen nicht so stark Meauman, wir brauchen Medikamente, Lebensmittel, Mehl und Öl. Hier sind viele Jehudim in Machnot. Ich habe gesprochen mit Tiech, er sagt, dass er will nicht schreiben Briefe und er will nicht geben Zahlen, über Polens Jehudim, weil man spricht in England über die Jehudim in Polen. Schreibet uns durch den Schaliach, was soll sein mit Tisch, da er doch arbeitet mit die Memschallah...."

Als Anlage eine Übersetzung der hebräischen Ausdrücke.

F.d.R.d.A.

Im Entwurf gez.:
G R O S S
Oberstleutnant und
Dienststellenleiter.

A copy of an official German document. The German foreign office intercepted a letter sent from Istanbul, Turkey to Switzerland. The two page letter was translated by the foreign office and sent to the O.K.W. "Oberkommando der Wehrmacht." The letter mentions the liquidation of the Jews in the General Government and naming Bendzin. The date is 6.9.1943.

PASSEPORT

AU NOM DE LA RÉPUBLIQUE DE PARAGUAY

LE CONSUL
DE LA RÉPUBLIQUE DE PARAGUAY
À BERNE

SIGNALEMENT

A Paraguay passport sent by Dr. Silberschein from Geneva in the beginning of 1943. Over 3,000 people who believed that these passports would save them were sent first to camps for foreign citizens and from there to annihilation in Auschwitz. Frumka Plotnicka (a leading member of the Hechalutz), the bearer of this passport, didn't use it, she stayed in Bendzin and died in the akzia in which the youth rose in self-defense.

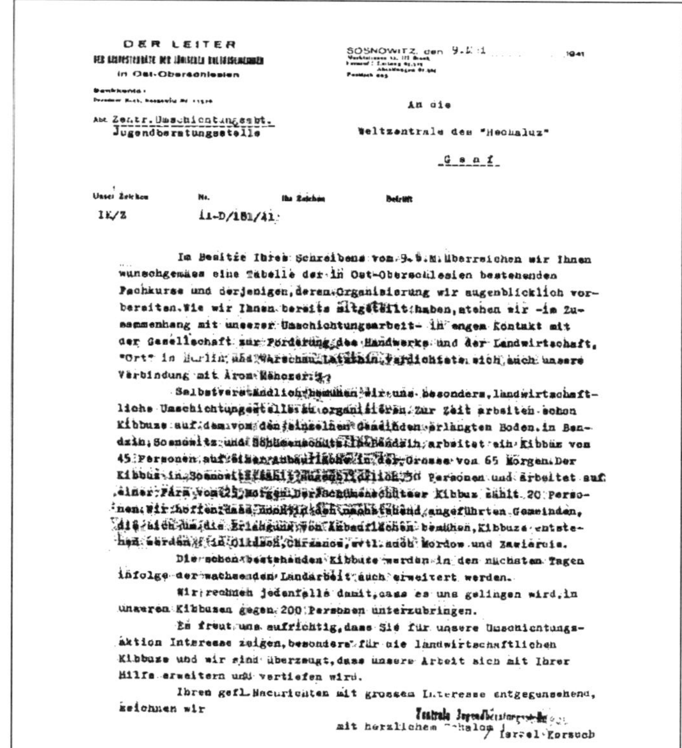

DER LEITER
[illegible]
in Ost-Oberschlesien

SOSNOWITZ, den 9.[illegible] 1941

Abt. Zentr. Umschichtungsabt.
Jugendberatungsstelle

An die
Weltzentrale des "Hechaluz"
Genf

Unser Zeichen IK/Z Nr. 11-D/181/41 Ihr Zeichen Betrifft

Im Besitze Ihres Schreibens vom 9.6.M. überreichen wir Ihnen wunschgemäss eine Tabelle der in Ost-Oberschlesien bestehenden Fachkurse und derjenigen, deren Organisierung wir augenblicklich vorbereiten. Wie wir Ihnen bereits mitgeteilt haben, stehen wir -im Zusammenhang mit unserer Umschichtungsarbeit- in engem Kontakt mit der Gesellschaft zur Förderung des Handwerks und der Landwirtschaft, "Ort" in Berlin und Warschau. [illegible] verdichtete sich auch unsere Verbindung mit Arom Mehozer[illegible]

Selbstverständlich bemühen wir uns besonders, landwirtschaftliche Umschichtungsstellen zu organisieren. Zur Zeit arbeiten schon Kibbuze auf dem von den einzelnen Gemeinden erlangten Boden. In Bendzin, Sosnowitz und [illegible] arbeitet ein Kibbuz von 45 Personen auf einer Anbaufläche in der Grösse von 65 Morgen. Der Kibbuz in Sosnowitz [illegible] 30 Personen und arbeitet auf einer Farm von 25 Morgen. Der [illegible] Kibbuz zählt 20 Personen. Wir hoffen, dass [illegible] den nachstehend angeführten Gemeinden, die sich um die Erlangung von Anbauflächen bemühen, Kibbuze entstehen werden: in Olkusch, Chrzanow, evtl. auch Modrow und Zawiercie.

Die schon bestehenden Kibbuze werden in den nächsten Tagen infolge der wachsenden Landarbeit auch erweitert werden.

Wir rechnen jedenfalls damit, dass es uns gelingen wird, in unseren Kibbusen gegen 200 Personen unterzubringen.

Es freut uns aufrichtig, dass Sie für unsere Umschichtungsaktion Interesse zeigen, besonders für die landwirtschaftlichen Kibbuze und wir sind überzeugt, dass unsere Arbeit sich mit Ihrer Hilfe erweitern und vertiefen wird.

Ihren gefl. Nachrichten mit grossem Interesse entgegensehend, zeichnen wir

mit herzlichem Schalom
Zentrale Jugendberatungsstelle
Israel Korsuch

A copy of a letter from Israel Kozuch on the official stationary of the "Judenrat" in Upper Silesia to the World Headquarters of the "Hechalutz."

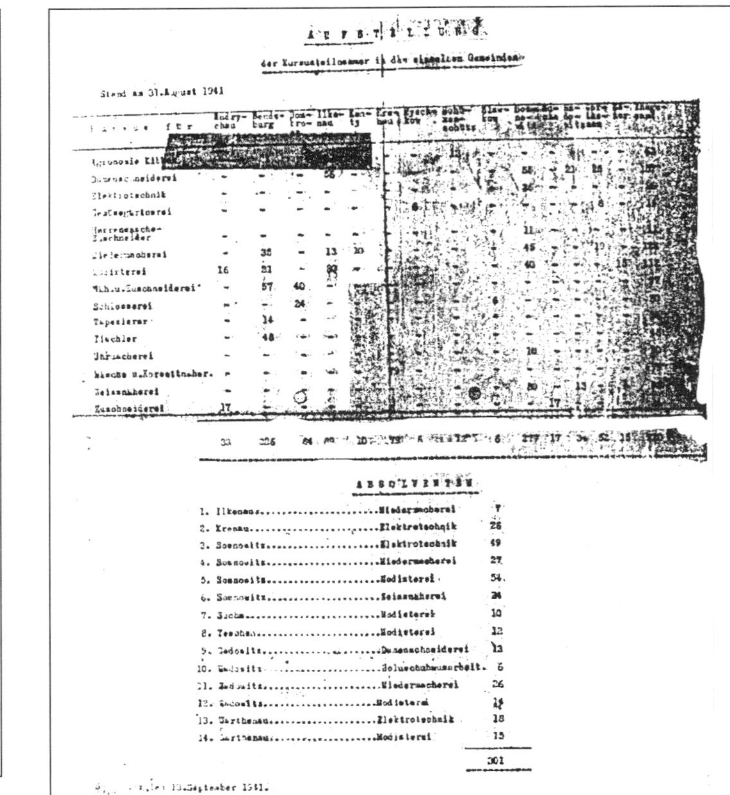

DER LEITER
DER ÄLTESTENRÄTE DER JÜDISCHEN KULTUSGEMEINDEN
in Ost-Oberschlesien

SOSNOWITZ, den 4. Oktober 1941

Abt. Umschichtung.
Jugendberatungsstelle.

Herrn
S. Schwalb
12, Bld. des Philosophes
in Genf Schweiz

Unser Zeichen: Z/. Nr. 11-D/501/41 Ihr Zeichen: Betrifft: Umschichtungsarbeit

Ihren Brief vom 15.VII.d.J. haben wir erhalten und bitten um Entschuldigung, dass wir ihn erst heute beantworten, wir waren jedoch von innern Arbeiten sehr in Anspruch genommen.

Nachstehend erlauben wir uns Ihnen einen kurzen Ueberblick über unsere Umschichtungsarbeit zu geben:

Die Tätigkeit wurde bereits ausgedehnt und wir beabsichtigen sie noch auszudehnen.

Die gegenwärtige Zahl der Kursenteilnehmer beträgt über 900 und 301 Personen haben bereits unsere Fachkurse absolviert. Die Ausdehnung der Tätigkeit der Fachkurse stösst zwar auf gewisse Schwierigkeiten, vor allem im Zusammenhang mit der Beschränkung der Kursenteilnehmer auf Jugendliche bis 16 Jahre einschl. Es ist uns jedoch gelungen, eine Genehmigung zur Errichtung von beruflichen Abendkursen für Personen über 17 Jahre zu erwirken. Dies wird uns die Möglichkeit geben, die von uns planierten Kurse für Männer, wie Ofensetzerei, Tischlerei, Schlosserei u.s.w. zu organisieren.

Gleichzeitig organisieren wir sog. Vorfachkurse für Jugendliche von 11 bis 14 Jahre, welche dem Aufwand von physischen Kräften auf den bisher bestehenden Kursen nicht nachkommen können. Es wird unsererseits besonderer Wert auf diese Kurse gelegt.

Es ist uns leider nicht gelungen, die Landwirtschaftliche Umschulung in der vergangenen Saison so zu fördern, wie wir beabsichtigt haben. Nur in Bendsburg und Schömenschütz bestehen Kibbuzim. In Sosnowitz arbeitete wie voriges Jahr eine Gruppe von Jugendlichen an der landwirtschaftlichen Farm. Ausserdem wurden in Zawiercie und Myschkow zwei kleine Gärtnereikurse geführt.

Wir beabsichtigen, für die kommende Saison die landwirtschaftliche Umschulung bedeutend auszudehnen. Es werden auf den einzelnen landwirtschaftlichen Farmen Treibhäuser errichtet, derer Bestehen sich auf die kommende Saison höchst vorteilhaft auswirken wird. Für den Kibbuz in Bendsburg organisieren wir einen theoretischen Agronomie-Kursus.

Zwecks näherer Orientierung überreichen wir Ihnen in der Anlage eine Tabelle der Kursenteilnehmer.

Indem wir Ihnen zum Jahreswechsel die allerherzlichsten Glückwünsche übermitteln, erwarten wir Ihrer werten Nachrichten und grüssen

mit herzlichem Schalom
Zentrale Jugendberatungsstelle
[signature]
Israel Korzuch

1 Beilage.-

A report by Israel Kozuch to Switzerlana dated 4-10-41. On official stationary of the Leiter of the Jewish Community in Upper Silesia.

AUFSTELLUNG
der Kursusteilnehmer in den einzelnen Gemeinden

Stand am 31. August 1941

Kurse für	Indrychau	Bendsburg	Dombrowa	Ilkenau	Kenty	[illegible]
Agronomie Kibbuz	[illegible]	[illegible]	[illegible]	[illegible]	[illegible]	[illegible]
Damenschneiderei	-	-	-	55	-	[illegible]
Elektrotechnik	-	-	-	-	-	[illegible]
[illegible]	-	-	-	-	-	[illegible]
Herrenwäsche-Zuschneider	-	-	-	-	-	[illegible]
Miedermacherei	-	35	-	13	10	[illegible]
Modisterei	16	21	-	80	-	[illegible]
Wäsche u. Zuschneiderei	-	57	40	-	[illegible]	[illegible]
Schlosserei	-	-	24	-	[illegible]	[illegible]
Tapezierer	-	14	-	-	[illegible]	[illegible]
Tischler	-	48	-	-	[illegible]	[illegible]
Uhrmacherei	-	-	-	-	[illegible]	[illegible]
Wäsche u. Korsettnäher.	-	-	-	-	[illegible]	[illegible]
Weissnäherei	-	-	-	-	[illegible]	[illegible]
Zuschneiderei	17	-	-	-	[illegible]	[illegible]
	33	226	64	[illegible]	[illegible]	[illegible]

ABSOLVENTEN

1. Ilkenau .... Miedermacherei 7
2. Krenau .... Elektrotechnik 26
3. Sosnowitz .... Elektrotechnik 49
4. Sosnowitz .... Miedermacherei 27
5. Sosnowitz .... Modisterei 54
6. Sosnowitz .... Weissnäherei 24
7. Jacha .... Modisterei 10
8. Teschen .... Modisterei 12
9. Bedzin .... Damenschneiderei 13
10. Bedzin .... Schuhmacherarbeit 6
11. Bedzin .... Miedermacherei 26
12. Bedzin .... Modisterei 14
13. Warthenau .... Elektrotechnik 18
14. Warthenau .... Modisterei 15

301

[illegible], den 13. September 1941.

Report to the letter of 4-10-41, as of the 31st of August 1941.

ZENTRALE UNSCHICHTUNGSABTEILUNG

Fachkurse-tabelle

STAND AM 5.4.1941

Lfd. Nr.	GEMEINDE	Zahl der jüdischen Bevölkerung.	Kursus für	Eröffnungs-Datum	Prüfungs-termin	Dauer	Teilnehmerzahl: Abiturienten	Teilnehmerzahl: Unterricht-empfänger	Teilnehmerzahl: in Aussicht stehende	Wöchentlich: Tage	Wöchentlich: Stunden	Be-merkung
1.	Bendzin	25.213	Agronomie	25. 4.41	25.10.41	6 Monate	-	-	100	6	60	
2.	"	"	Agronomie/Kibuz	1. 4.40	- -	dauernd	-	35	-	6	x	1
3.	"	"	Miedermacherinnen	20. 4.41	20. 7.41	3 Monate	-	-	30	5	15	
4.	"	"	Näh-u.Zuschneider	18. 3.41	18. 7.41	4 "	-	14	-	3	12	
5.	"	"	Ofensetzer	1. 5.41	1. 9.41	4 "	-	-	8	4	16	
6.	"	"	Tischler	21. 1.41	20. 7.41	6 "	-	32	-	6	30	2
7.	Chrzanow	7.894	Elektrotechnik	8.12.40	24. 3.41	3 1/2 Mon.	26	-	-	6	24	4/
8.	Dombrowa	5.390	Schlosser	11. 3.41	11. 6.41	3 Monate	-	34	-	6	36	3/
9.	Modrow	1.117	Elektrotechnik	20. 3.41	26. 6.41	3 "	-	25	-	4	16	
10.	"	"	Weissnäherei	20. 4.41	20. 8.41	4 "	-	-	25	4	16	
11.	Olkusch	2.940	Agronomie/Kibuz	25. 4.41	25.11.41	7 "	-	-	50	6	x	1/
12.	"	"	Damenschneiderinnen	15. 2.41	15. 5.41	3 "	-	25	-	4	16	2/
13.	"	"	Elektrotechnik	7. 1.41	7. 4.41	3 "	-	20	-	5	15	5/
14.	"	"	Miedermacherinnen	15. 2.41	15. 5.41	3 "	-	6	-	3	12	
15.	Schönmannschütz	1.440	Agronomie/Kibuz	20. 4.41	20.11.41	7 "	-	-	20	6	x	1/
16.	Sosnowitz	24.217	Agronomie	15. 4.41	15.11.41	7 "	-	-	60	6	60	
17.	"	"	Agronomie/Kibuz	25. 4.41	25.11.41	7 "	-	-	50	6	x	1/
18.	"	"	Angewandte Graphik	1. 5.41	1. 9.41	4 "	-	-	20	2	8	
19.	"	"	Damenschneiderinnen	18. 4.41	18. 7.41	3 "	-	-	20	3	18	
20.	"	"	Elektromonteure-									

Blatt-2-

Lfd. Nr.	GEMEINDE	Zahl der jüdischen Bevölkerung.	Kursus für	Eröffnungs-Datum	Prüfungs-termin	Dauer	Teilnehmerzahl: Abiturienten	Teilnehmerzahl: Unterricht-empfänger	Teilnehmerzahl: in Aussicht stehende	Wöchentlich: Tage	Wöchentlich: Stunden	Bemerkung Nr.
25.	Sosnowitz	24.217	Elektrotechnik-V	1. 3.41	1. 7.41	4 Monate	-	28	-	3	15	
26.	"	"	Feinbäckerei	25. 4.41	25. 8.41	4	-	-	30	3	15	
27.	"	"	Fussboden-u.Wand-plattensetzer	5. 5.41	5.10.41	5	-	-	80	3	15	
28.	"	"	Miedermacherei-I	1. 1.41	7. 4.41	3	-	11	-	3	15	5/
29.	"	"	Miedermacherei-II	1. 1.41	7. 4.41	3	-	12	-	3	15	5/
30.	"	"	Modistinnen-I	1.11.40	18. 4.41	3	10	-	-	3	15	6/
31.	"	"	Modistinnen-II	1.11.40	23. 4.41	3	11	-	-	3	15	6/
32.	"	"	Modistinnen-III	1.11.40	28. 4.41	3	14	-	-	3	15	6/
33.	"	"	Modistinnen-IV	1. 2.41	1. 5.41	3	-	16	-	3	15	8/
34.	"	"	Modistinnen-V	1. 3.41	1. 6.41	3	-	18	-	3	15	
35.	"	"	Modistinnen-VI	15. 4.41	15. 7.41	3 "	-	-	20	3	15	
36.	"	"	Ofensetzer	1. 5.41	1. 9.41	4 "	-	-	20	2	4	7/
37.	"	"	Strassenaufseher	1. 1.41	31. 7.41	5 "	-	28	-	3	15	2/
38.	"	"	Uhrmacher-I	1.11.40	1. 6.41	7 "	-	8	-	3	15	2/
39.	"	"	Uhrmacher-II	1.11.40	1. 6.41	7 "	-	9	-	3	15	
40.	"	"	Uhrmacher-III	20. 4.41	20.11.41	7 "	-	-	8	3	15	
41.	"	"	Uhrmacher-IV	15. 5.41	15.12.41	7 "	-	-	8	3	15	

Blatt-3-

Lfd. Nr.	GEMEINDE	Zahl der jüdischen Bevölkerung.	Kursus für	Eröffnungs-Datum	Prüfungs-termin	Dauer	Teilnehmerzahl: Abiturienten	Teilnehmerzahl: Unterricht-empfänger	Teilnehmerzahl: in Aussicht stehende	Wöchentlich: Tage	Wöchentlich: Stunden	Bemerkung Nr.
48.	Teschen	250	Damenschneiderei	10. 4.41	10. 7.41	3 Monate	-	-	15	3	12	
50.	"	"	Modistinnen	1.12.40	16. 4.41	4 1/2 Mon.	-	13	-	2	8	5/
51.	Trzebinia	1.174	Tischler	7. 4.41	7.10.41	6 Monate	-	-	20	6	30	
52.	Wadowitz	1.300	Damenschneiderei	1. 4.41	1. 7.41	3 "	-	8	-	4	20	
53.	"	"	Elektrotechnik	26. 3.41	1. 8.41	4 "	-	11	-	6	36	
54.	"	"	Holzschuhbearbeitung	11. 2.41	11. 5.41	3 "	-	9	-	6	48	2/
55.	"	"	Miedermacherei-I	14. 3.41	14. 6.41	3 "	-	15	-	6	24	
56.	"	"	Miedermacherei-II	14. 3.41	16. 6.41	3 "	-	15	-	6	24	
57.	"	"	Modistinnen	10. 2.41	20. 3.41	6 Wochen	14	-	-	4	20	4/
58.	"	"	Schlosser	15. 4.41	15. 9.41	5 Monate	-	-	27	6	30	
59.	Zawiercie	5.462	Damenschneiderei	1. 2.41	1. 8.41	6 "	-	23	-	5	15	
60.	"	"	Elektrotechnik	1. 1.41	15. 4.41	3 1/2 Mon.	-	28	-	4	12	5/
61.	"	"	Miedermacherei	1. 2.41	1. 5.41	3 Monate	-	23	-	6	18	2/
62.	"	"	Modistinnen	1. 2.41	1. 5.41	3 "	-	20	-	5	15	2/
63.	"	"	Agronomie/Kibuz	20. 4.41	20.11.41	7 "	-	-	50	6	x	1/
				vom Uebertrag:			104	418	545			
							118.	583	637			

1/ Die Arbeit in Kibuz ist dauernd.

2/ Die Teilnehmer des Kurses sind schon imstande leichtere Arbeiten selbstständig auszuführen.

3/ Der Kursus wird in Form von einer Werkstätte geführt.

4/ Die Prüfung zeugte von der Vorbereitung der Teilnehmer zur Ausübung des Berufes.

5/ Die Schulung auf dem Kurse ist bereits zu Ende und die Examen werden in der nächster Zeit stattfinden.

6/ Der Kursus wurde bereits beendet, die Prüfungen wurden verschoben.

7/ Der Kursus wurde am 6.2.d.J. unterbrochen und setzte am 9.3. seine Tätigkeit fort. Deshalb wurde auch der Prüfungstermin verschoben.-

Sosnowitz, den 6. April 1941.

The letter was addressed to Dr. Chaim Posner, Dr. Zilbersztajn, and Natan Szwalb. This letter was transferred from Turkey to Switzerland but was intercepted by the German spies and translated back into German with the secret messages left in Hebrew.

A copy of the letter which was preserved in the German Ministry of Foreign Affairs is shown on page 172.

Here I have to make a comment; as little as it was from certain organizations, to the inmates in the ghettos, it was a great help. The other comment is; that it would have meant much more to the Jews in the ghettos if most of the help, supplies or even the monies, were not stolen by the leaders in the ghettos. To this I am showing documents that will prove my allegations and suspicions of the ghetto leaders. I could say much more about the Moniek Merins in the ghettos, but…

With all the stealing and mismanagement in the ghetto, plenty of work was done in the "Public Welfare" section in Eastern Upper Silesia. (The public welfare system was active in all of the ghettos, but my interest lay in the Upper Silesia District.)

According to documents of Ost-Oberschlesien there were 32 communities with 27 soup kitchens in operation where 350,000 dinners were given out to 13,925 ghetto inmates monthly. Bendzin and a couple of other communities operated orphanages with 115 children in them. In five communities 460 children received once a day a meal. 270 ghetto inmates were taken care of in old age homes. In 13-17 communities, nourishment stations gave food to 555 children ages 4-8. Milk and other stuff was distributed to 970 infants.

Cash relief was given to 3,503 native families and 1,244 other people who came into the ghetto. About 4,096 of the entire ghetto population received winter relief and/or Passover relief.

Sosnowiec had a transit camp "Durchgangslager," where Jews were held over before being shipped to the slave labor camps. I remember when in 1941 my sister Laja was there, before she was transferred to a slave labor camp in Gabersdorf in Czechoslovakia, I did sneak in the "Durchgangslager" to a basement window to bring food to my sister.

One hundred people were freed in 1940 through bribes and many later wound up in other labor camps or Auschwitz Concentration camp. Most of them never came back. Perished.

The JDC did much to help the Jews in the ghettos and I am sure that they, the JDC, knew how much the leaders of those ghettos pocketed. But some of it did trickle down to the inmates in the ghettos. It is recorded of how much the JDC sent to those ghettos. The rivalry between the leaders of the ghettos, of who should run the show, is also known.

Rumkowski, the head of the Litzmannstadt (Lodz) ghetto, would have liked to run the show, including the Eastern Upper Silesia ghettos where Moniek Merin reigned supreme, and to receive all the money and to be the distributor, but there was not much trust in him — not by the Germans nor by the JDC.

The relationship between Moniek Merin, the head of the "Zentrale" in Sosnowiec, and the JDC were more friendly. Moniek Merin could connive his way in with the Germans and the JDC.

In 1941 the "Wohlfahrtsvereinigung" in Sosnowiec received all funds from the JDC for Eastern Upper Silesia and even Warteland.

In January of 1941, as shown by the documents pictured on page 181, Merin requested the Lisbon office of the JDC to get him a transit visa to visit Lisbon, Portugal. He never received that permission. The documents also show that more than once he had asked for that permit. (All the documents from "Ost-Oberschlesien" except a couple are from the private collection of the author.)

The 26th of January 1941 Upper Silesia was divided into two administrative parts. Upper and Lower Silesia.

Fritz Bracht, the Gauleiter of Upper Silesia, resided in Katowitze. He was appointed to his job on the 9th of February, 1941.

Bendzin, Sosnowiec and Dombrowa were part of the Upper Silesia region from the Kielce district, as well as parts of the Krakow region like Oswiecim (Auschwitz renamed by the Germans), Biala, Zywiec, Wadowitze, Trzebinia and Jaworzno. Over one million Jews lived in Upper Silesia alone.

Upper Silesia was an industrialized section of Poland and Germany, much dependent on the coal industry there as well as the zinc, textile and paper industry.

In May of 1941, Hitler himself stated in one of his orders to convert Upper Silesia into a German area.

Life in the ghetto went from bad to worse. We had no illusions that we could or would survive. The rationing became every year less and so became the ways of organizing some more food. But even this we could withstand if it was not for the "Resettlement" of more and more of the Jews from the ghetto. We could never be sure if we will not be the next ones. (Resettlement, was plain and simple the liquidation of the Jews, but in a finer language.)

The "Resettlement," too, was a sort of income for Moniek Merin. He always found ways to enrich the coffers of the Judenrat. I remember instances in the ghetto where Merin promised to release people from the "Sammelpunkt," the assembly place where the Jews gathered to be shipped to labor camps or liquidation. People who still had some money paid as much as the market would bear, only to find out later that this was a trick by Merin. These were the most despicable acts of the Judenrat with human emotions and to make them pay for their sufferings. I can testify to many of these acts. As if it was not enough that we were constantly blackmailed by the Germans. (I could write a whole volume just on the blackmail and suffering inside the ghetto caused by our leaders.)

Even the Judenrat faced every day the hardship of preparing the lists of the ghetto inmates. The lists had to be arranged by age, sex, occupation, how many in the family and so on. (List on page 194.)

New births had to be reported not just to the Bureau of Vital Statistics in the ghetto but to German authorities as well. Otherwise no ration cards will be issued.

Certificates were known to be issued in the Bendzin ghetto to sick people to exempt them from forced labor. Some people were brought home to Bendzin from slave labor camps to be treated in the Bendzin hospital or even sent to the hospital in Katowice. For all these favors people had to pay to the "Judenrat." The Jewish police, too, had special ID cards that exempted them from other work.

During the German occupation Jews were not allowed to conduct religious services, yet, in secret almost every ghetto had its prayer homes. Only a few people would assemble so not to draw attention of the Germans. One instance is known where in Sosnowiec there were communal prayer on Rosh Hashana in 1940 permitted by the German authorities.

How foolish those leaders of the Judenrats were, not wanting to realize that the Germans cannot and will not let them live, and yet how easy they, the "Judenrat," made it for the Germans to do their dirty work.

In Sosnowiec as well as Bendzin, for that matter all of Eastern Upper Silesia which was incorporated into the Reich, the Jews for the longest time were subordinate to the Polish commissar. No decision by the Jewish council could be taken without a commissar's permission and naturally this meant bribes so they would look the other way and not interfere with the council's matters. Moniek Merin did not like it and had enough influence with the Germans to abolish that office of the commissar. This did not stop the other Poles from causing trouble.

When the order of the "Final Solution" reached Bendzin, a German official from the economic branch of the administration in Bendzin, who did the audit of the German factories and businesses that used Jewish labor, sent a report on May 12, 1943 emphasizing the importance to the war effort of the Jewish "labor," concluding with the following statement as published in the book the *Judenrat*:

"It is in the interest of the state, the nation, and the entire military leadership to continue production at the highest capacity. Under no circumstances should it be allowed to be shattered or stopped, by removing the Jewish workers. The productive labor force, irrespective of its ethnic origin, is necessary for the management of all factories and for all people who are responsible for their output."

Nothing helped, no letter, no intervention, no reasoning. The Bendzin ghetto in Srodula was liquidated in August of 1943.

Benjamin Graubart, who was active in the leadership in the "Kehila" before the war, was elected chairman of the Jewish community of Bendzin just a few days after the German occupation of that city. He tried very much to resist some orders of the Gestapo to make it easier for the Jews. However, it did not last long. Moniek Merin, who became "Leiter" of the Jewish communities in Eastern Upper Silesia, when he started to please the Gestapo too much to the liking of Graubart, who was an honest man and could not hurt his people, the only way left to Graubart was hand in his resignation.

In summer of 1940 Merin sent in his brother Chaim to take over Graubart's place, who would just be a stooge for his brother. To the brother Merin it meant more to please the Gestapo and make himself be liked by them, than to please or help his people. When he was transferred to Sosnowiec as chairman of the council, Chaim Molczadzki was named to position of Council Chairman of Bendzin. Molczadzki was another one who would follow Merin without reservations.

Merin did a lot of despicable things, but the most outstanding one is the sending to Auschwitz to a certain death, Becalel Cukier, the chairman of the Council in Chrzanow, who was a respected leader before the war in his community. Merin set up in his place Dr. Boehm who was in the Sosnowiec "Zentrale" knowing that Dr. Boehm will be faithful to Merin.

Fanny Czarna, from the "Zentrale" in Sosnowiec, became Moniek Merin's right hand in the "Zentrale." She took part in all of the important meetings and even the ones that were not so important. Almost all documents from the Zentrale were signed by Fanny Czarina.

The Jewish Council considered themselves as privileged groups. Labor camps, deportations, resettlements and even forced labor did not include them. However, to the German authorities they were considered as slave labor. To us, the inmates of the ghetto, they were just considered despicable traitors who sold us out.

I remember many of those despicable acts by the Judenrat in Bendzin, by the Jewish police and especially by Moniek Merin.

I remember in June of 1942 when Merin called a meeting of all the young people in the Bendzin ghetto (I was then 20 years old), and delivered to us a passionate speech, telling us to report voluntarily to the "Arbeitseinsatz" for work in the slave labor camps, telling us that by going voluntarily we can save the rest of the ghetto inmates. Whom was he kidding?!! Just about two months before that my younger brother Bernard was taken away to a slave labor camp.

I don't think that he had any luck that time. But he got his 500 young men, with the help of the "Sonderbeauftragter fur Arbeitseinsatz," after he failed to convince the German shop managers to give him the people.

It did not help any of the ghetto inmates that he got the 500 slave laborers nor did it help my mother who just two months later went with a transport to Auschwitz where the whole transport was gassed and cremated.

The Judenrat only thought of saving their own skin. But it did not help them a bit. They, too, were Jews, and once the Germans had no use of them, they too were liquidated.

Paul Wiederman states in his book *Plowa Bestia,* The Blond Beast, about the Judenrat, of which he was a member, in a certain meeting about delivering Jews for "Resettlement," how Merin tries to justify his actions. The meeting was called with the representatives of the ghettos of Bendzin, Sosnowiec, Dombrowa and others. Merin insisted that they have to obey the orders and demands. Michal Laskier, a member of the Jewish Council, disagreed with Merin. He felt that the Council should not deliver the Jews even though they were considered by the Germans as the sick, maimed and old. They wondered about the morality if they listen to Merin.

The chairman of the Jewish Council in Bendzin Chaim Molczadski as usually a student and devotee of Moniek Merin agreed with him. Moniek Merin said that as a statesman he knows which is the best and the fate of the ghetto inmates was sealed.

There were other times before that when even the Rabbis thought that we have to obey orders. They agreed with Merin because, in their

ÄLTESTE DER JÜD. KULTUSGEMEINDEN
Ost Oberschlesien
llg.
/1732/40

SOSNOWITZ

An

Herrn Alfred Szwarcbaum
in Bendzin

Ich beauftrage Sie hiemit, im Namen der Zen-
le der Jüdischen Kultusgemeinden in Ost-Oberschlesien die
nötigen Vorarbeiten für Emigrationszwecke der hiesigen Juden
in der Schweiz zu treffen.

Gleichzeitig mache ich Sie aufmerksam, all-
Bemühungen zu machen, ausser Emigrationsmöglichkeiten auch
finanzielle Hilfe für die Juden in Ost-Oberschlesien zu br-
gen.

Nähere Anweisungen werden Sie von mir unm-
bar vor der Abreise in die Schweiz erhalten.-

Merin.

This is a photostatic copy of the first letter written by the Eldest of the Ghettos, M. Merin, to Mr. Szwcrzbaum, while he was still in Bendsburg authorizing him to get Jews out of the ghettos. This was March 12, 1940. By May of 1940 Mr. Szwcrzbaum was already in Switzerland helping Jews get into Interment Camps.

The leader
The Eldest of the Jewish Communities
in East Upper Silesia.

Sosnowitz 12 March 1940
Market st.12 III floor
Telephone 61.323
Herrn Alfred Szwarcbaum
in Bendzin

I empower you herewith in the name of the "Zentrale der Judischen Kultusgemeinden in Ost Oberschlesien the necessary preparations to make for emigrations of the Jews here to meet in Switzerland.

In the same time I am drawing your attention to make every afford except emigration to help the Jews in East Upper Silesia financially

More instructions you will receive from me before you leave for Switzerland.

Signed
M. Merin.

It bears the Official Seal of the Eld st of the Jews Of the Jewish Committee in East-Upper Silesia.

The Leader

The Eldest of the Jewish Communities

In East Upper Silesia

Sosnowitz, d. August 10, 1940

Marktstrasse 12, III Stock

Fernsprecher 61.323

Herrn Alfred Szwarcbaum (Delegate of the Joint Distribution Committee)
Luzerne, Switzerland

Pens. Jaques Av. Romine 64

Dear Sir:

To our great surprise we did not receive any news from you. The only news we received was through intermediaries, Herrn Laskier and Herrn Boehm. Your silence is not known to us. We do hope, however, to receive from you a letter in the near future.

We enclose herewith a copy of the letter from the "Joint" in Budapest, in which we asked for help. As it looks from that letter, the "Joint" is asking about our finances and the Aide Committee in which it stated in the letter of the 4th of this month.

We sent you a copy of all of these writings and are waiting impatiently your answer.

M. Merin

Bears official seal of The Eldest of the Jewish Communities in East Upper Silesia.

978

DER LEITER
DER AELTESTENRÄTE DER JÜDISCHEN KULTUSGEMEINDEN
in Ost Oberschlesien

SOSNOWITZ, den 10. August 1940
Marktstrasse 12, III Stock
Fernsprecher 61.323

Abt.: I
Nr. Z/S/9291/40
Betr. Unterstützung vom "Joint"

Herrn
Alfred Szwarcbaum
Lausanne
Pens.Jaques Av.Romine 64

Sehr geehrter Herr,

zu unserem grossen Verwundern haben wir von Ihnen keine unmittelbaren Nachrichten. Wir erhielten nur eine Nachricht durch Vermittlung des Herrn Laskier und Herrn Boehm. Die Ursache Ihres Schweigens ist uns unbekannt. Wir hoffen, in allernächster Zeit einen Brief von Ihnen zu erhalten.

Gleichzeitig übersenden wir Ihnen eine Abschrift des Briefes des "Joint" in Budapest, an welchen wir die Bitte um Unterstützung gerichtet haben. Wie aus diesem Briefe ersichtlich ist, wünschte der "Joint" einige Materialien über unsere Finanz- und Fürsorgetätigkeit, welche wir ihm samt Schreiben vom 4.d.M. übersandt haben.

Alle diesbezüglichen Schreiben und Materialien übersenden wir Ihnen in der Anlage zur gefl. Kenntnisnahme und erwarten mit grossem Interesse Ihre Nachrichten.-

Beilagen.-
Einschreiben.
Durch Eilboten.

In Ost Oberschlesien

M. MERIN

November 15. 1940

We hope that the matter with our writing to one another is solved and ask you to keep up our contact.

We are expecting your most honored writing with great interest

With kindest greetings
and
mutual respect
signed; M. Merin

P>S>Does the JOINT give you regularly your monthly fee? If that fee is too much for you please let us have that money direct through the JOINT.

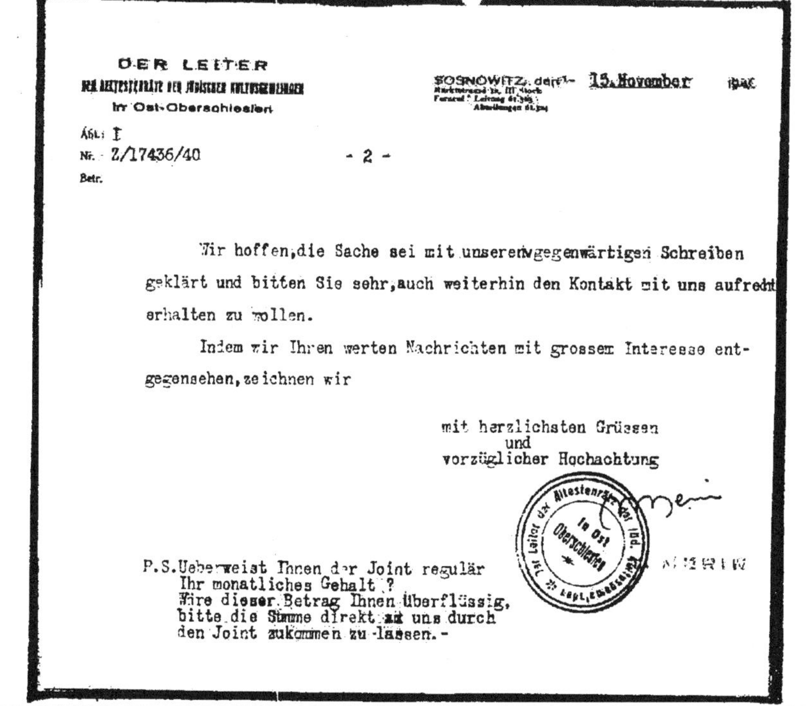

DER LEITER
DER ÄLTESTENRÄTE DER JÜDISCHEN KULTUSGEMEINDEN
in Ost-Oberschlesien

SOSNOWITZ, den 15. November 1940

Abt.: I
Nr. Z/17436/40

- 2 -

Betr.

Wir hoffen, die Sache sei mit unserem gegenwärtigen Schreiben geklärt und bitten Sie sehr, auch weiterhin den Kontakt mit uns aufrecht erhalten zu wollen.

Indem wir Ihren werten Nachrichten mit grossem Interesse entgegensehen, zeichnen wir

mit herzlichsten Grüssen
und
vorzüglicher Hochachtung

Merin

P.S. Ueberweist Ihnen der Joint regulär Ihr monatliches Gehalt ?
Wäre dieser Betrag Ihnen überflüssig, bitte die Summe direkt an uns durch den Joint zukommen zu lassen.-

Official letter from the Eldest of the Jews in Upper Silesia, Monik Merin. This is the second page from a long letter dated November 15, 1940. Later, Merin, together with the entire Jewish Council of Upper Silesia, was executed in Auschwitz.

Der Leiter der Aeltestenräte der jüdischen Kultusgemeinden in Ost-Oberschlesien
Fernsprecher 61-323, 61-324

An Herrn Alfred Szwarcbaum, Lausanne Blatt 2 vom 1.12.1940

Da es uns an der Zusammenkunft mit Herrn Tropper äusserst gelegen ist, bitten wir Sie innigst, uns bei der Erlangung einer Einreisegenehmigung nach Lissabon behilflich sein zu wollen.

Wie uns unser Pressburger Mitarbeiter mitteilt, wird vielleicht die Jointkonferenz in Budapest stattfinden.

Wir bitten Sie jedoch alle Schritte zu unternehmen um uns die Reise nach Lissabon zu erledigen.

Wir werden Sie noch über diese Angelegenheit in Kenntnis setzen.

Für Ihre Bemühungen waren wir Ihnen zu grossem Dank verpflichtet und begrüssen Sie

mit Schalom

Personalien des Herrn Merin

Merin Moszek, geb. am 22.2.1904 zu Sosnowitz
wohnhaft in Sosnowitz, Oderstrasse 39.-

EILSCHREIBEN
Durch Eilboten

THE LEADER.
THE ELDESTEN OF THE JEWISH COMMUNITIES
IN EAST UPPER SILESIA.

Sosnowitz 1,December 1940
Market str. 12 III floor
telephone 61.323

Herrn
Alfred Szwarcbaum
Lausanne
Ave. du Leman 31
Villa Mirabelle

With thanks we confirm the receipt of your honored writing of the 23rd of t.m. and send you with wishes the actual rapport of the . Land preservation works

Reg; Food shipments.

from your list of produce, almost all of it we can use, all the products mentioned. The most important however are; CHOCOLATE IN BARS
CHEESES IN BOXES
SMOCKED SALAMIES
BISQUITS

We are asking of you when possible the shipments of food items as soon as possible to send.

Reg. JOJNT MATTERS.

We did receive from the JOINT a support in the amount of $5000.- for the month of October $5000.- for the month of November t.y. Even though this help is far from satisfactory, all affords have to be made to get a more substantial amount.

In connection with MR Tropper's presence in Europe we did get in touch with the JOINT in Lisbon, to get for Mr. Merin and Mr. Dir.Borenstein / JOINT WARSAW a travel permit to Lisbon to produce

SECOND PAGE.

BECAUSE IT IS VERY IMPORTANT TO US TO MEET WITH MR. TROPPER . we beg of you to help us to get a permit to get to Lisbon.

We beg of you to make every effort to make for us the trip to Lisbon a fact.

We will get to you again in this matter. For your efforts we are obliged to you and greet you.

With Shalom
I.A. CZARNA.

It bears the Official Seal of the Eldesten of of the Jewish Committee in East Upper Silesia.

Personal of Mr. Merin
MERIN MOSZEK, born on 22.2.1904. in Sosnowitz
living in Sosnowitz, Oderstrasse 39.

REGISTERED
by EXPRESS.

DER LEITER
DER AELTESTENRÄTE DER JÜDISCHEN KULTUSGEMEINDEN
in Ost-Oberschlesien

Abt.: Zentrale Hauptbüro
Nr. I- 138/41
Betr. Z/H

SOSNOWITZ, den 13 Januar 1940
Marktstrasse 12, III Stock
Fernruf: Leitung 61.323
Abteilungen 61.324

Herrn

Alfred Szwarcbaum

Lausanne

Ave du Leman 31
Villa Mirabelle

Wir bestätigen den Empfang Ihres Briefes vom 8 ds. Mts. und es ist uns unverständlich, wieso Sie unseren Brief vom 18. Dezember v.J. so spät erhalten haben.

Die Einschreibbriefe werden nicht prompter als die gewöhnlichen befördert und das könnte auf den Erhalt des Schreibens keinen Einfluss haben.

Nicht desto weniger bedauern wir lebhaft, dass die Verzögerung die Liebesgabenaktion unmöglich gemacht hat. Wir sind jedoch daran nicht schuldig.

Wir haben inzwischen auch aus Wien erfahren, dass Herr Tropper bereits nach New-York zurückgekehrt ist. Wir wären Ihnen sehr verbunden, wenn Sie uns mitteilen könnten, ob und wann Herr Tropper in Lissabon weilen wird. Wir bitten Sie, uns auch weiterhin auf dem Laufenden halten zu wollen.

Ihren weiteren Nachrichten mit grossem Interesse entgegensehend, zeichnen wir

mit vorzüglicher Hochachtung

/Fanny Czarna/

The Leader
The Eldest of the Jewish Communities
In East Upper Silesia

Sosnowitz, d. January 13, 1940
Marktstrasse 12, III Stock
Fernruf: Leitung 61.323
Abteilungen 61.324

Herrn Alfred Szwarcbaum

Luzerne

Ave du Leman 31
Villa Mirabelle

We confirm the receipt of your letter of the 8th of this month and cannot understand why you did not receive the letter of December 18th of last year.

The registered letters are not really checked and cannot have any bearing on those letters.

Nonetheless, we are aware of the delay in the delivery of goodwill packages of food for which we are not at fault.

Meantime we have received notice that Herr Tropper left for New York already. We would greatly appreciate it if you let us know if and when he is in Lisbon. We ask you to keep us informed of the first developments.

Your future news is awaited with great interest.

Fanny Czarna

Bears official seal of The Eldest of the Jewish Communities in East Upper Silesia.

The Leader
The Eldest of the Jewish Communities
in East Upper Silesia.

Sosnowitz January 27. 1941
Market st. 12 III floor

Herrn
Alfred Szwarcbaum
Lausanne
Ave du Leman 31
Villa Mirabelle

I have your writing of the 12th t.m. and rush to express our thanks for you willingness to help.

We are begging you for Mr. Merin a Visa so Lisbon to procure. For the Pass we will ourselves try after we have received the Emigration Visa.

For your affords we thank you in advance.

Signed
M.Merin.

It bears the Official Seal of the Eldest of the Jewish Communities in Upper Silesia.

DER LEITER
DER AELTESTENRÄTE DER JÜDISCHEN KULTUSGEMEINDEN
in Ost-Oberschlesien

Abt.: Zentr-Hauptbüro
Nr. I/310/2241
Betr. Einreisevisum.-
Z/Lo

SOSNOWITZ, den 27. Januar 194
Marktstrasse 12, III Stock
Fernruf: Leitung 61.323
Abteilungen 61.324

Herrn
Alfred Szwarcbaum
Lausanne
Ave du Leman 31
Villa Mirabelle

Im Besitze Ihres Schreibens vom 20.d.Mt. eilen wir, Ihnen für Ihre Hilfsbereitschaft unseren Dank auszudrücken.

Wir bitten Sie für Herrn Merin ein Einreisevisum nach Lissabon gefl. beschaffen zu wollen. Um die Durchreisevisas werden wir uns nach Erhalt des Endvisums selbst bemühen, und auch die Ausreise besorgen.

Für Ihre Bemühungen danken wir im Vorhinein und zeichnen

mit vorzüglicher Hochachtung

A LETTER FROM THE GHETTO

Religious services, although severely restricted, were continued in many ghettos as long as possible. This is brought out by the letter shown below. This letter is from The Eldest Council of the Jewish Community in Upper Silesia. It is signed by the Council's secretary and it was dated on August 28, 1941. It states as follows:

Re: The Feast of Tabernacles

In view of the forthcoming Feast of Tabernacles, we humbly ask if you could obtain tomatoes and myrtle branches for our district.

We would ask you, in such a case, to let us know what, if any, preparations we should meet here to receive the complete Esrogim set on time.

For a possibly quick answer we are indebted to you.

With best regards
(signed) F.S. Czarna
Fanny Sarah Czarna

DER LEITER
DER ÄLTESTENRÄTE DER JÜDISCHEN KULTUSGEMEINDEN
in Ost-Oberschlesien.

SOSNOWITZ, den 28. August 1941
Marktstrasse 12, III Stock
Fernruf: Leitung 61-323
Abteilungen 61-324
Postfach 295

579

Abt.: Zentr.Hauptbüro
Nr. I 2484/41
Betr. Laubhüttenfeiertage.-
Cz. Z/Lo

Herrn
Alfred Schwarzbaum

Lausanne
Vilamont 23

In Hinsicht auf die herannahenden Laubhüttenfeiertage fragen wir Sie höflichst an, ob Sie für unser Gebiet Paradäpfel und Mirtenzweige besorgen könnten.

Wir bitten Sie, uns gegebenenfalls mitzuteilen, ob und welche Vorbereitungen wir unsererseits zu treffen haben, um rechtzeitig in den Besitz der Esrogim-Komplette zu gelangen.

Für eine baldmögliche Antwort wären wir Ihnen sehr verbunden

Mit besten Grüssen

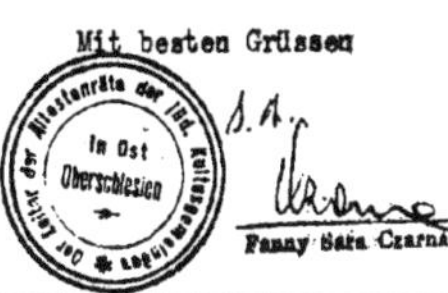

THE LEADER
THE ELDESTEN OF THE JEWISH COMMUNITIES
IN EAST UPPER SILESIA.
Centr. Main office.
Re; The Feast of Tabernacles.

SOSNOWITZ 28. August 1941
Market st.12 III floor
annex 61-324
P.O.Box 295

Herrn
Alfred Szwarcbaum

Laussanne
Villamont 23

In view of the forthcoming Feast of Tabernacles we humble ask if you could obtain tomatoes and myrtle branches for our district.

We would ask you, in such a case, to let us know what, if any, preparations we should meet here to receive the complete Esrogim set on time.

For a possibly quick answer we are indebted to you.

With best regards
signed; F>S>Czarna.
Fanny Sara Czarna

The Seal of The Aeltestenrat

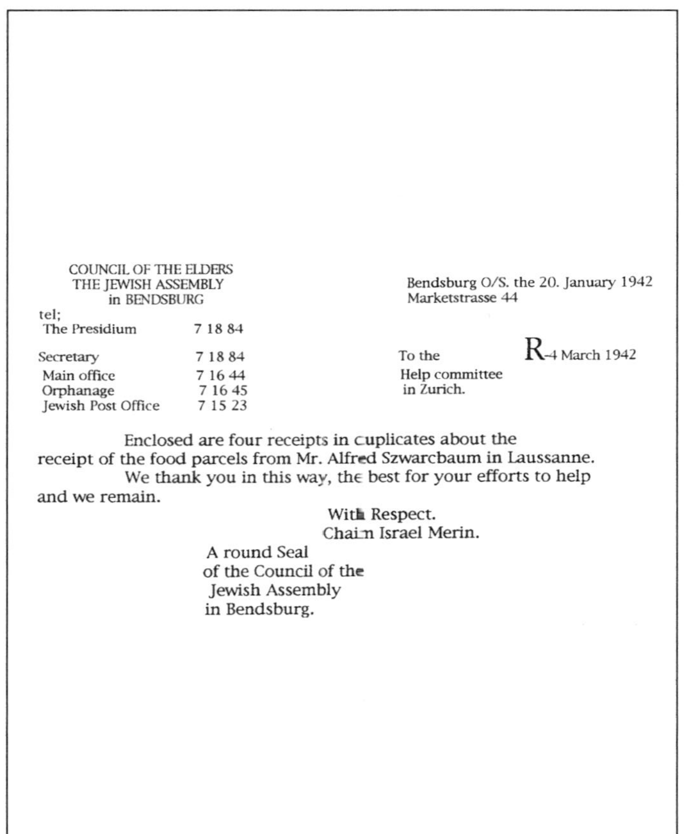

COUNCIL OF THE ELDERS
THE JEWISH ASSEMBLY
in BENDSBURG

Bendsburg O/S. the 20. January 1942
Marketstrasse 44

tel;

The Presidium	7 18 84
Secretary	7 18 84
Main office	7 16 44
Orphanage	7 16 45
Jewish Post Office	7 15 23

To the
Help committee
in Zurich.

R-4 March 1942

Enclosed are four receipts in cuplicates about the receipt of the food parcels from Mr. Alfred Szwarcbaum in Laussanne. We thank you in this way, the best for your efforts to help and we remain.

With Respect.
Chaim Israel Merin.

A round Seal
of the Council of the
Jewish Assembly
in Bendsburg.

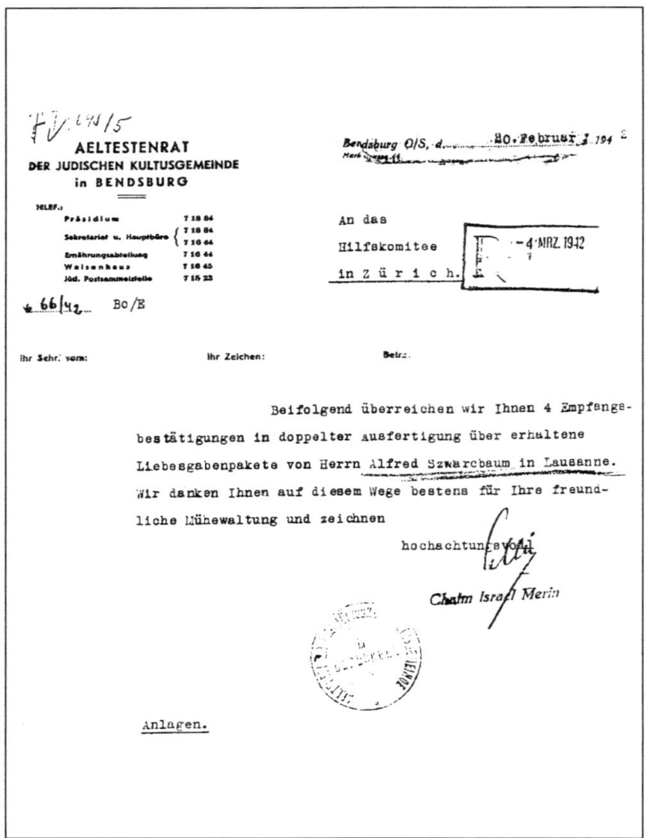

AELTESTENRAT
DER JUDISCHEN KULTUSGEMEINDE
in BENDSBURG

Telef.:

Präsidium	7 18 84
Sekretariat u. Hauptbüro	7 18 84 / 7 16 44
Ernährungsabteilung	7 16 44
Waisenhaus	7 16 45
Jüd. Postsammelstelle	7 15 23

66/42 Bo/E

Bendsburg O/S, d. 20. Februar 1942

An das
Hilfskomitee
in Zürich.

-4 MRZ 1942

Ihr Schr. vom: Ihr Zeichen: Betr.:

Beifolgend überreichen wir Ihnen 4 Empfangsbestätigungen in doppelter ausfertigung über erhaltene Liebesgabenpakete von Herrn Alfred Szwarcbaum in Lausanne. Wir danken Ihnen auf diesem Wege bestens für Ihre freundliche Mühewaltung und zeichnen

hochachtungsvoll
Chaim Israel Merin

Anlagen.

VORSTAND
DER JUDISCHEN INTERESSENVERTRETUNG
in BENDSBURG

Bendsburg, d. 29.Januar 1942

TELEF.:
Präsidium } Sekretariat } 71-884
Ernährungsabteilung 71-644
Waisenhaus 71-645

Herrn
Alfred S c h w a r z b a u m,
L a u s a n n e / Schweiz/
Villamont 23.

Nr. 41/42.
Bo/B.

Ihr Schr. vom: Ihr Zeichen: Betrifft:

Wir erhielten an unsere Adresse weitere 12 Päckchen enthaltend a je 2 Doden Oelsardinen, die wir an unsere charitativen Institutionen verteilten.

Wir danken Ihnen bestens für Ihre Aufmerksamkeit und empfehlen uns Ihnen auch weiterhin.

Der Vorsitzende,
Chaim Israel Merin

The Executive
The Jewish Community
in Bendsburg

Bendsburg, d. January 29, 1942
Marktstrasse 44.

Telephone:

Herrn Alfred Schwarzbaum (Delegate of the Joint Distribution Committee)
Luzerne, Switzerland
Villamont 23.

We received delivery at my address of 12 packages each of 2 dozen sardines which we handed out to our charity organization.

We do thank you for thinking of us and hope you will do so again.

Chairman Chaim Israel Merin

Bears official seal of The Eldest of the Jewish Communities in Bendsburg.

DER LEITER 2/II/7. 302
DER AELTESTENRÄTE DER JÜDISCHEN KULTUSGEMEINDEN
in Ost-Oberschlesien

SOSNOWITZ, den 6.lutego 1942
Marktstrasse 12, III Stock
Fernruf: Leitung 61.323
Abteilungen 61.324
Postfach 295
12,

Abt. Zentr.Hauptbüro
Nr. Z/332/42
Betr. Liebesgaben

Herrn
Alfred Szwarcbaum
Lausanne
Villamont 23

Anbei überreichen wir Ihnen eine Aufstellung der erhaltenen Liebesgabenpakete, die bis heute eingegangen sind, in zweifacher Ausfertigung.

Wir eilen, Ihnen unseren verbindlichsten Dank für Ihre Mühewaltung und Hilfsbereitschaft auszudrücken und sehen mit grossem Interesse Ihren weiteren Nachrichten entgegen.-

Mit vorzüglicher Hochachtung

Fanny Sara Czarna

The Leader
THE ELDESTEN OF THE JEWISH COMMUNITIES
in EAST UPPER SILESIA.
ZENTRAL MAIN OFFICE
Z/332/42
RE; LOVEGIFTS.

SOSNOWITZ. the 6. February 1942
marketstrasse 12 III floor
tel; main 61-323
annex 61 324
P.O.box 295

Herrn
Alfred Szwarcbaum
Lussanne
Villamont 23

Enclosed we send you a list of the received packages that up till today reached us in duplicates.

We hurry to you our thanks for your help efforts and await with great anticipation for your farther correspondence.

Seal of the Judenrat

With respect.
I.A. Czarna
Fanny Sara Czarna.

Council of the Elders
THE JEWISH ASSEMBLY
in BENDSBURG.

Bendsburg O/S. the 28. February 1942
Market street 44

tel;

The Presidium	7 18 44
Secretary	7 18 44
Main Office	7 16 44
Food Supply	7 16 44
Orphanage	7 16 45
Jewish Post Office	7 15 23

To the

Help Committee

Zurich

Enclosed we are sending to you 4 receipts in duplicates about the food parcels we received from Mr. Alfred Szwarcbaum in Laussanne.

We thank you in this way for your friendly help and affords.

Respectfully

Michal Israel Laskier

A round Seal
of the
Jewish Assembly
in Bendsburg.

AELTESTENRAT
DER JUDISCHEN KULTUSGEMEINDE
in BENDSBURG

Bendsburg O/S, d. 28. Februar 1942
Marktstrasse 44

TELEF.:

Präsidium	7 18 84
Sekretariat u. Hauptbüro	7 18 84 / 7 16 44
Ernährungsabteilung	7 16 44
Waisenhaus	7 16 45
Jüd. Postsammelstelle	7 15 23

Nr. 30/E

An das

Hilfkomitee

Zürich.

Ihr Schr. vom: Ihr Zeichen: Betr.:

Beifolgend überreichen wir Ihnen 4 Empfangsbestätigungen in doppelter Ausfertigung über erhaltene Liebesgabenpakete von Herrn Alfred Szwarcbaum Lausanne. Wir danken Ihnen auf diesem Wege für Ihre frdl. Mühewaltung und zeichnen

hochachtungsvoll

Michal Israel Laski

Anlagen.

2021/1D

DER LEITER
der Aeltestenräte der Jüdischen Kultusgemeinden
in Ost-Oberschlesien

SOSNOWITZ den 25. März 1942
Marktstrasse 12, III Stock
Fernruf: Leitung 61.323
Abteilungen 61.324
Postfach 295

Abt. Zentr. Hauptbüro
Nr. Z/ I 816/42
Betr. Liebesgaben

Herrn
Alfred Szwarcbaum
Lausanne

Wie wir von der Frau Zynger erfahren haben, beklagen Sie sic dass Sie bin nun keine Bestätigung über die übersandten Liebesgabe pakete erhalten haben. Dies wundert uns sehr, da wir Ihnen mit unser Schreiben vom 6. Februar d.J. Nr. Z/332/363/42 eine genaue bestätigte Aufstellung der erhaltenen Pakete in zweifacher Ausführung übersan haben. Seit dieser Zeit sind keine Pakete mehr eingegangen.

Ordnungshalber übersenden wir Ihnen nochmals die in Rede stehende Aufstellung und hoffen, Ihrem Wunsche entsprochen zu haben.

2 Anlagen.-

Aeltestenräte der Jüd. Kultusgemeinden in Ost Oberschlesien

Fanny Sara Czarna

THE LEADER
THE COUNCIL OF THE ELDEST OF THE JEWISH COMITTEE
IN EAST UPPER SILESIA.

Sosnowitz the 25. March 1942
Market street 12, III floor
tel,; leaders 61,323
branches;61,324
Post office box 295

Zentr. Main Office
Z/ I 816/42
reg' love gifts.

Herrn
Alfred Szwarcbaum
Laussanne

As we found out through Mrs. Singer you complained that you did not get receipts for sending the food parcels that we received. we are very much surprised, since we confirmed the receipts of February of this year, # Z/332/363/42 and have sent to you this receipt in duplicates. Since then we did not receive any more packages.

We are sending to you again the receipts of the before mentioned packages and hope to have satisfied your wishes.

OFFICIAL SEAL

Signed and stamped

Fanny Sara Czarna

Council of the Elders
THE JEWISH ASSEMBLY
in BENDSBURG O/S

TO THE
HELP COMITTE
ZURICH

No. 480/Bo/E

Bendsburg O/S the 3, July 1942
Marketstrasse 44

Enclosed we are sending to you 2 receipts in duplicates for food packages from Mr. Alfred Szwarcbaum in Laussanne

We thank you this way best for your friendly efforts and remain.

With respect
The President.

Seal

Signed and typed
Chaim Israel Molczadzki.

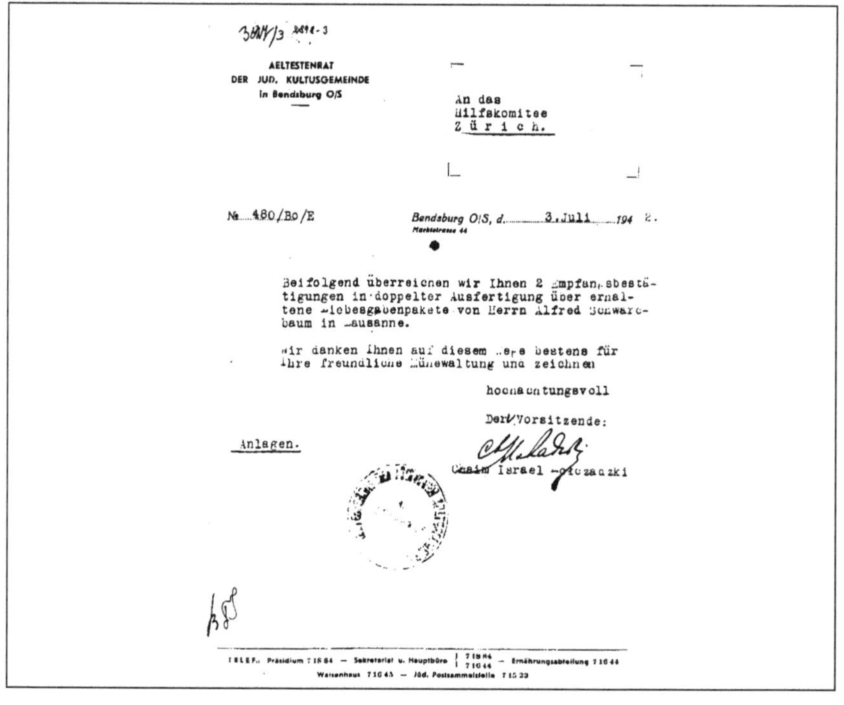

AELTESTENRAT
DER JUD. KULTUSGEMEINDE
in Bendsburg O/S

An das
Hilfskomitee
Z ü r i c h.

№ 480/Bo/E

Bendsburg O/S, d. 3.Juli 1942.
Marktstrasse 44

Beifolgend überreichen wir Ihnen 2 Empfangsbestätigungen in doppelter Ausfertigung über erhaltene Liebesgabenpakete von Herrn Alfred Schwarcbaum in Lausanne.

Wir danken Ihnen auf diesem Wege bestens für Ihre freundliche Mühewaltung und zeichnen

hochachtungsvoll

Der Vorsitzende:

Anlagen.

Chaim Israel Molczadzki

TELEF.: Präsidium 7 18 84 — Sekretariat u. Hauptbüro 7 18 84 / 7 16 44 — Ernährungsabteilung 7 16 44
Waisenhaus 7 16 43 — Jüd. Postsammelstelle 7 15 23

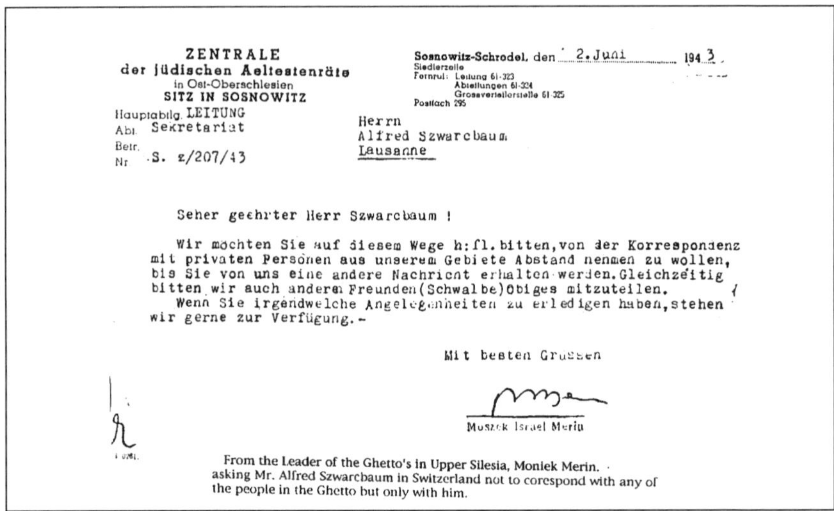

ZENTRALE
der jüdischen Aeltestenräte
in Ost-Oberschlesien
SITZ IN SOSNOWITZ

Sosnowitz-Schrodel, den 2. Juni 1943.
Siedlerzeile
Fernruf: Leitung 61-323
Abteilungen 61-324
Grossverteilerstelle 61-325
Postfach 295

Hauptabtlg. LEITUNG
Abt. Sekretariat
Betr.
Nr. S. z/207/43

Herrn
Alfred Szwarcbaum
Lausanne

Seher geehrter Herr Szwarcbaum !

Wir möchten Sie auf diesem Wege h:fl. bitten, von der Korrespondenz mit privaten Personen aus unserem Gebiete Abstand nehmen zu wollen, bis Sie von uns eine andere Nachricht erhalten werden. Gleichzeitig bitten wir auch anderen Freunden (Schwalbe) Obiges mitzuteilen.
Wenn Sie irgendwelche Angelegenheiten zu erledigen haben, stehen wir gerne zur Verfügung.-

Mit besten Grüssen

Muszek Israel Merin

From the Leader of the Ghetto's in Upper Silesia, Moniek Merin. asking Mr. Alfred Szwarcbaum in Switzerland not to corespond with any of the people in the Ghetto but only with him.

From the Leader of the Ghettos in Upper Silesia, Moniek Merin, asking Mr. Alfred Szwarcbaum in Switzerland not to correspond with any of the people in the Ghetto but only with him.

VERZEICHNIS der best atten judeschen Leichen, die wahrend der Aussiedlung in der zeit v.22-26 Juni1943auf der Flucht erschosen wurden

L.Nr.	Zu-u.Vorname	Alter	Anschrift	
1.	Broder Juda Lajb Iz rael	31	R. Kochstr.	37
2.	Zejdman Moschek chaim "	26	Marktstr:	19
3.	Schwarcberg Icek Izrael	Steinstr.	Steinstr.	4p.
4.	Lederman Nusyn Dawid "			
5.	Radoszycki Beryś izrael	40	Fr iedrichstr.	17
6.	Rubinlicht Lajzer Izrael	62	Fr iedrichstr	57
7.	Lipszyc Dan Izrael		Friedhichstr.	23
8.	Grundman Josek Izrael			
9.	Najfeld Srul Dawid Izrael	21		
10.	Goldberg Mendel Izrael	50	Friedrichstr.	50
11.	Żabner Szmul Majer Izrael	20	Kasernenstr.	62
12.	Ertenberg Josef Izrael	22	Kl.Schrodel	
13.	Staszewski Szulim Izrael			
14.	Lipszyc Abram Hersz Izrael	18	Steinstr.	
15.	Lewin Pe res Lajb Izrael	17	St einstr:	
16.	Guzy Lajzer Icek I srael	20	R.Kochstr.	78 5
17.	Wis ner Hersz Izrael	70	Kasernenstr:	37
18.	Gitler Ajzyk I srael	63	Wolfbergstr.	5
19.	Skocylasz Motel Izrael	29		
20.	Landau Nuta Izrael	27		
21.	Lipszyc Dawid I srael	55		
22.	Lau don Beniamin Izrael	67	Kl.Schrodel	23
23.	Lindenbaum Majer Izrael	69	A.Weg	4
24.	Niegoslawski Mo rdka Izrael	52	Steinstr.	49
25.	Joskowicz Dawid -Izrael	24		
26.	Sch midt Julius Dr. Izrael		Bergmanstr.	78
27.	Zelmanowicz Chil Izrael	28		
28.	Szenherc Hirsch Izrael	50	Kl. Schrodel	
29.	Rozen Chaim Icek I srael		Steinstr:	33
30.	Ferleger Chaim Josek Izrael	25	Steinstr:	
31.	Men delbaum Simon Izrael	65	Marktstr.	37
32.	Ajzenhendler Wo lf Izrael	52		
33.	Roberye Salek Izrael	22	Kasernenstr.	102
34.	Landau Dobra Sara	21	Kasenenstr.	37
35.	Landau Hena Ruchla Sara	57		
36.	Landau Chawa Sara	29		
37.	Lipszyc Chawa Sara		Friedrichstr.	
38.	Frenkiel Fajgla sara			
39.	Brauner Sara Sara		Kasernenstr:	. 37
40.	Posenica Szejndla sara		Bergmahstr.	
41.	Wega Marjem Rywka sara			
42.	Źmigr od Helen a Sara	39	Bergmanstr.	
43.	Abramowicz Per la Sara			
44.	Lokaj Szajndla Sara	24		
45.	Jakubowi cz Tauba Hinda Sara			
46.	Frydler Ita Sara	77	R. Kochstr.	36
47.	Frochzwajg Rajl a Sara	29		
48.	Lederman Sala Sara			
49.	Aro nowicz Liwcia Sara			
50.	Jochimowicz Sura Fajgla Sar a		Steinstr.	
51.	Flach Anna Sara			
52.	Plesner Hinda Fajgla Sara			
53.	Brajtman Masza Sara	60	Kl.Schrodel	
54.	Cymbler Ruchla		1.weg	40
55.	Durchschlaufer Chana Sara		Kl.Schrodel	27 6
56.	Guzy Fajgla		R. Kochstr.	73
57.	Aleksandrowicz Wigder Izrael		Wolfberg	26
58.	Wasserman Icek Izrael			

Unbekante weibliche Personen 11
Unbekante manliche Personen [illegible]

A list of names, addresses and ages of Jewish dead that were killed during the "Evacuation" of the Ghetto on June 22-26, 1943 (according to the Germans, while trying to escape).

opinion, it was God's will. RUBBISH, RUBBISH. God did not help them either.

It did not help them in May 1943 when Merin in cahoots with the Gestapo, promised us to ward off another "resettlement action" after the two that had taken place before, that if we deliver our valuables to the Gestapo, we will be safe. The Jews had no other choice but to deliver it, and delivered they were: loads of crates and boxes full of our most valuable item. Mostly the religious items that the people held off to the last minute.

This was May 1943, and in August 1943 our ghetto in Bendzin was liquidated, made "Judenrein" clean of Jews.

Oh, yes. I have to mention here that on June 26, 1943, just two months before the liquidation of the ghetto, the leaders of the ghetto with Moniek Merin were shot at the famous "Black Wall" in Auschwitz.

The whole story is given in an article published by this author in 1964 in the *Clinical Pediatrics* printed by Lippincott in Philadelphia (see page 199).

Merin, the wise man of the Eastern Upper Silesia ghettos, like Rumkowski of Lodz, thought that they were chosen by God to lead the Jews out of the German bondage. Merin had big plans for the Jewish people who will survive the war. These people were sick for power and were ready to send to their death million of Jews as long as they can have a future.

There were some that would not deliver Jews for resettlement. Such a case was in one of the Upper Silesia ghettos of Dombrowa. The chairman of that Jewish Council, Adolf Weinberg, refused to deliver a list of Jews for resettlement. Some members of the Council were executed for such an act.

Chapter Ten

We cannot shoot these…Jews
We cannot poison them. We shall
however take measures that shall lead
to their eventual annihilation

Hermann Göering

Mail in the ghetto

The following article by Arnold Shay appeared for the first time in the *Clinical Pediatrics,* March, 1964, Vol. 3, #3, published by J.B. Lippincott Company, Philadelphia, Pennsylvania under PHILATELY. Titled: GHETTO MAIL. It was later published in different magazines (with the author's permission), in the United States and Poland.

So much has been written about the ghettos of World War II that many people think they know all there is to know about them. No inexperienced outsider, however, can possibly know what it meant to live in a ghetto. Nor do people want to know or even discuss the matter. As little information as there is about ghettos in general, there is even less information about those on the German-Polish border.

Not long ago, I was approached by friends who are avid stamp collectors. They asked how I, a former inmate of ghettos and concentration camps, could interest myself in collecting mail from ghettos, prisoners of war, internment and concentration camps. Having personally experienced the horrors of both the ghetto and concentration camp, the collecting of items relating to these unforgettable experiences for the express purpose of documentation for posterity represented a worthwhile challenge to me. Actually, I am a general collector with a special interest in Germanic philately.

Several years ago, I spotted a few items from concentration camps and ghettos at a philatelic exhibition. These gems struck a respondent chord in me and I decided then and there to build up a collection of just such material as a sideline to what I had brought with me from Germany. Since then I have had the good fortune of acquiring a number of important items of which I am extremely proud. At best, desirable items are rare and difficult to obtain. When found, such material commands a high price. Not many philatelists are interested in this specialty and this is to the good, for significant collectable material is scarce and hard to find.

Very little has been written about the philatelic aspects of the smaller ghettos. A few articles have been written about the larger Warsaw, Litzmannstadt and the Theresienstadt ghettos, but the smaller ones where people vanished by the thousands have not been described. It is my intention to describe briefly a few ghettos that I knew well (and) because so few people have any knowledge of them.

I was confined to the Bendsburg ghetto in Upper Silesia. This region changed hands several times; first from Austria-Hungary to Poland; from Poland to Germany and finally from Germany back to Poland, its present possessor. This was the territory that Hitler wanted as a corridor to the Baltic Sea. Bendsburg (as it was renamed by the Germans from Bendzin) was occupied on September 4, 1939. The fourth day after the beginning of the war, immediately after occupying this area, the Germans began to show their complete disregard for the defeated public in general and the Jews in particular, with many acts of utter barbarism.

For the Jews, there followed a rapid succession of events, leading finally to their extermination. (As described in the book with my biography, *Hell Was My Home*, and now in my new book on the history of the city of Bendzin and its people, its life and its martyrdom of the Jews of the Zaglembia Region.)

First, they (the Jews) were required to wear an armband bearing the Star of David (emblazed in blue). This was replaced by the infamous "Yellow Star," secondly by the open ghetto, thirdly by the closed ghetto and fourth and finally by "Judenrein" or liquidation (of the Jews). I personally experienced all of these events with the exception of extermination. (I don't know how.) During the short period of time when Bendsburg was an open ghetto, the Germans designated an extremely limited number of streets where non-Aryans could live.

They were permitted to use only one side of the street while the other side was reserved for unrestricted use by the Aryans. We were permitted to use the mail box to mail letters and the letter carrier could still bring letters addressed to us. When the closed ghetto was established, however, sending a letter became a most difficult and almost impossible task.

It was required that all mail sent by inmates of the closed ghetto be delivered unsealed to the Jewish Council. The Council then censored the letters and sealed the envelopes. Over the rear flap they affixed the following (rubber stamp);

"Einlieferer;
Aeltestenrat der Judischen Kultusgemeinden

in Bendsburg O,S,
Sammelstelle fur Postsendungen!"

Translated this reads as follows:

"Sender,
Eldest of the Council of the Jewish Community
in Bendsburg Upper Silesia,
Mail Collection Center"

There were several other varieties of cancellations in addition to the one mentioned above. Even though the wordings varied somewhat, the implications for these notations were identical since all of them indicated that the council accepted full responsibility for contents of the letter. After being censored by the council, mail was brought by a special messenger to the German Post Office where it was usually held back until such time as the authorities saw fit to censor it further. This procedure usually took days and frequently even months. The Germans placed considerable responsibility on the Jewish officers in the ghettos.

As might be expected, the Jewish censor was much more severe than was his German counterpart because the penalty for even a minor infraction by an inmate of the ghetto was death. Under such circumstances, it remains only to the imagination to realize how thoroughly mail was read and censored. There were regulations governing not only the mail but also regulations governing all phases of life. These laws were uniform in all of the ghettos.

In my collection are a number of items of exceptional interest in that they illustrate so well the modus operandi of the ghetto. Among these are the following: An official letter from Moniek Merin, Eldest of the Council of the Jewish Community in the Bendsburg Ghetto; another from Chaim Moldczadski, President of the Jewish Community in the Bendsburg Ghetto, as well as a letter from Fanny Czarna, who was the private secretary of Moniek Merin and, as such, perhaps the most prominent figure in all of the ghettos in Upper Silesia.

With the exception of a few individuals who were in league with the Germans, the people mentioned above were the only Jews authorized to communicate with the German authorities. In their hands rested the life or death of the inhabitants of the ghettos. Ironically, these dignitaries were sent to Auschwitz where they were exterminated even before the ghettos they controlled were liquidated.

Although there were a number of ghettos in Upper Silesia, those in Sosnowitz, Bendsburg and Dombrowa were the most important. Early in 1943, only two remained; Schrodel in Sosnowitz and Kamionki in Bendsburg. So few Jews remained at this time that there was no need for barriers of any sort between these two areas. The Eldest of the Ghetto, Moniek Merin, came to power almost immediately after the Germans occupied Upper Silesia. He established the ghettos, he ruled them with an iron hand and everywhere his word was absolute law.

His aides and cohorts were his brother Chaim, Fannie Czarna, a Dr. Lowenstein and a man by the name of Borenstein (first name unknown). On June 19, 1943, the Gestapo called this quintet to Kattowitz for trial. From there they were sent to Auschwitz and on July 6, 1943, this entire group of five dignitaries from the ghettos in Upper Silesia were shot at the "Black Wall." The liquidation of the remaining Jews began on August 1, 1943, and was completed in one week, bringing to a close the final chapter on the infamous ghettos in Upper Silesia.

Some Jews remained in the former ghetto officially for a month to clean and collect the Jewish properties.

Figure 1. Cover from ghetto in Bendsburg showing censorship stamp of the Council as well as that of the German authorities.

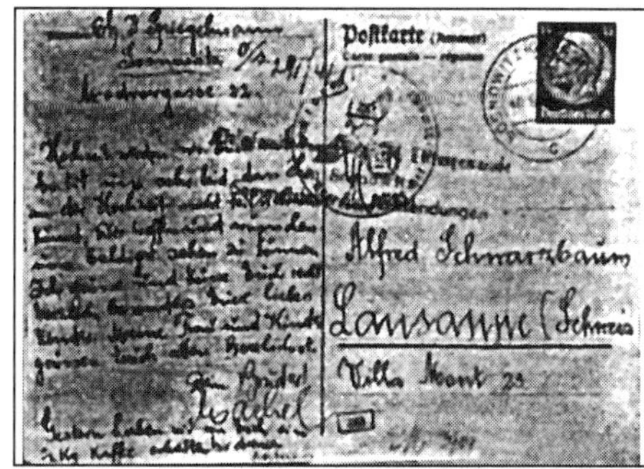

Figure 2. Cover from the ghetto in Sosnowitz showing censorship stamp of the Council as well as that of the German authorities.

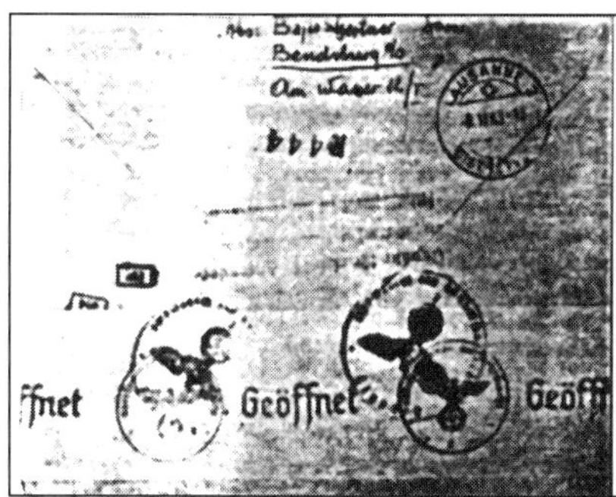

Figure 3. This interesting modification of the censorship stamp of the Council reads "Gewahr fur richtiger absenderangabe wird ubernommen. Postsammelstelle der Jud. Kultusgemeinde." Translated this reads as follows: "Verification for the right identity of the sender is the responsibility accepted by the Mail Collection Center of the Jewish Community."

Figure 4. Front of the cover shown in Figure 3. This cover is from the ghetto in Dombrowa in the District of Bendsburg.

Kundenschein I Odcinek Kontrolny	Kundenschein II Odcinek Kontrolny	Kundenschein III Odcinek Kontrolny	Kundenschein IV Odcinek Kontrolny
№ 402063	№ 402063	№ 402063	№ 402063
August 1944 — Sierpień 1944	August 1944 — Sierpień 1944	August 1944 — Sierpień 1944	August 1944 — Sierpień 1944

Faksymile

B 1 Chleb 1000 g Sierpień 44	B 5 Chleb 1000 g Sierpień 44
B 2 Chleb 1000 g Sierpień 44	B 6 Chleb 1000 g Sierpień 44
B 3 Chleb 1000 g Sierpień 44	B 7 Chleb 1000 g Sierpień 44
B 4 Chleb 1000 g Sierpień 44	B 8 Chleb 1000 g Sierpień 44

LEBENSMITTELKARTE
KARTA ŻYWNOŚCIOWA
für nichtdeutsche Erwachsene und Jugendliche über 14 Jahre
dla nieniemców dorosłych i młodzieży ponad 14 lat
Gültig für den Monat August 1944
Ważna na miesiąc sierpień 1944
№ 402063

Name u. Vorname: / Nazwisko i imię
Adresse: / Adres
Nicht übertragbar — Bez prawa odstąpienia
Bei Verlust kein Ersatz
W razie zagubienia duplikat wydany nie będzie
KUNDENLISTENNUMMER — NUMERY LIST KONSUMENTÓW
I Nr. III Nr.
II Nr. IV Nr.

N 2 Produkty zbożowe 100 g Sierpień 44	N 1 Produkty zbożowe 100 g Sierpień 44
M 2 Marmolada 250 g Sierpień 44	M 1 Marmolada 250 g Sierpień 44
F Mięso 3 Sierpień 44	F Mięso 1 Sierpień 44
F Mięso 4 Sierpień 44	F Mięso 2 Sierpień 44

B/M Chleb 1000 g albo Mąka 750 g Sierpień 44	A Różne 8 Sierpień 44	A Różne 7 Sierpień 44	A Różne 6 Sierpień 44	A Różne 5 Sierpień 44	A Różne 4 Sierpień 44	A Różne 3 Sierpień 44	A Różne 2 Sierpień 44	A Różne 1 Sierpień 44	K Kawa 125 g Sierpień 44	Z Cukier 300 g Sierpień 44

Ration Card for non-Jews for the month of August 1944. This card has much more food than the card for Jews.

M Mąka 24 Paźdz. 41	M Mąka 26 Paźdz. 41	N Różne 47 Paźdz. 41	N Różne 48 Paźdz. 41
M Mąka 25 Paźdz. 41	M Mąka 27 Paźdz. 41	N Różne 46 Paźdz. 41	N Różne 49 Paźdz. 41
N Różne 43 Paźdz. 41	N Różne 44 Paźdz. 41	N Różne 45 Paźdz. 41	N Różne 50 Paźdz. 41
B Chleb 4 Paźdz. 41	B Chleb 8 Paźdz. 41	B Chleb 12 Paźdz. 41	
B Chleb 3 Paźdz. 41	B Chleb 7 Paźdz. 41	B Chleb 11 Paźdz. 41	B Chleb 15 Paźdz. 41
B Chleb 2 Paźdz. 41	B Chleb 6 Paźdz. 41	B Chleb 10 Paźdz. 41	B Chleb 14 Paźdz. 41
B Chleb 1 Paźdz. 41	B Chleb 5 Paźdz. 41	B Chleb 9 Paźdz. 41	B Chleb 13 Paźdz. 41

№ 037081

LEBENSMITTELKARTE
KARTA ŻYWNOŚCIOWA
Gültig für den Monat Oktober 1941 — Ważna na miesiąc październik 1941
in
Kreis / miejscowość
Name / nazwisko
Wohnort / miejsce zamieszkania
Strasse / ulica
Nicht übertragbar — Bez prawa odstąpienia
Bei Verlust kein Ersatz
W razie zagubienia duplikat wydany nie będzie
KUNDENLISTENNUMMERN — NUMERY LIST KONSUMENTÓW
I Nr II Nr
III Nr IV Nr

Z Cukier 18 Paźdz. 41	Z Cukier 19 Paźdz. 41	N Różne 52 Paźdz. 41	N Różne 54 Paźdz. 41
Z Cukier 16 Paźdz. 41	Z Cukier 17 Paźdz. 41	N Różne 51 Paźdz. 41	N Różne 53 Paźdz. 41

N Różne 42 Paźdz. 41	A Marmolada 30 Paźdz. 41	A Marmolada 28 Paźdz. 41
N Różne 41 Paźdz. 41	A Marmolada 31 Paźdz. 41	A Marmolada 29 Paźdz. 41
N Różne 40 Paźdz. 41	N Różne 37 Paźdz. 41	N Różne 32 Paźdz. 41
N Różne 39 Paźdz. 41	N Różne 36 Paźdz. 41	N Różne 33 Paźdz. 41
N Różne 38 Paźdz. 41	N Różne 35 Paźdz. 41	N Różne 34 Paźdz. 41
N Różne 56 Paźdz. 41	F Mięso 23 Paźdz. 41	F Mięso 22 Paźdz. 41
N Różne 55 Paźdz. 41	F Mięso 21 Paźdz. 41	F Mięso 20 Paźdz. 41

Ration Card for Jews in the Ghettos in Poland. This one is for the month of October 1941. It is printed in Polish and German. You had to write in your name and address. Every member of the family received one card a month. This one has coupons for flour, all kinds of bread, sugar, marmalade and at the bottom two coupons for meat. Jews received much less rationing than the Poles.

Chapter Eleven

If horses were being slaughtered as are Jews of Poland, there would now be a loud demand for organized action against such cruelty to animals.

Rabbi Meyer Berlin, to U.S. Senator P. Wagner

The Underground in Bendzin

The Jewish underground movement did not receive financial help from abroad, while the non-Jewish underground received arms, training and money.

There is no written order of the Germans as for the establishment of the Jewish Police in the ghetto as with the Jewish Council; however, the ghetto police, "Ordnungsdienst-Order Service," was established on the German say so. The Germans tried many times to show that the ghetto police was initiated by the Jewish Council.

The ghetto police served also as the judges of the courts until an official court was set up later and there are many instances where the ghetto police acted on their own, exceeding the laws far and beyond their duties. There are known facts where the ghetto police in Bendzin arrested and sealed off homes for non-payment of taxes.

I witnessed one fact where the apartment of Josko Gutman, on Plebanska 8 in Bendzin, had his apartment sealed off in the building that he with his family owned, by one member of the Judenrat because this member of the Judenrat liked his apartment and later moved in. I still remember who this man was but I cannot say his name now for many reasons. The main reason is that his son, who is prominent in the Jewish community, would suffer for it. He is dead...

There were other cases where Jews were handed over to the Gestapo by the ghetto police for unpaid taxes in Bendzin. The Gestapo made weekly visits to the Judenrat in Bendzin. Parents of youngsters who did not report for forced labor in Bendzin and Sosnowiec were arrested by the ghetto police.

On April 26, 1940, in a public announcement, the Jewish Council warned that daily lists of people who did not report for forced labor will be handed over to the authorities for punishment. This was no idle threat, it happened. Ration cards were withheld for the whole family for not reporting to slave labor.

In Bendzin, Sosnowiec and the entire Eastern Upper Silesian area, Fanny Czarna, Moniek Merin's right hand, chief of the "Zentrale," was the administrative supervisor of the ghetto police.

The ghetto police had no special uniforms. However, they wore special hats with a badge and armbands with their ranks inscribed, and wooden or rubber clubs of which they made use at every occasion. In Bendzin and Sosnowiec the badges were of metal with the blue Star of David in the center and engraved above the star. Either O.D. Ben. or O.D. Sosn. around the star was in German and Polish (Jewish Order Service). The hat itself was white with a blue band at the bottom (in our ghettos, there were different ones in Warsaw and so, too, in Litzmannstadt) and a black visor and black strap above the visor with the exemption of an officer where the strap above the visor would be silver or gold color. In the center in front of the hat, on the white part, there was the number the police was issued.

Besides all this the police had to wear the common issued Yellow Star on the left hand breast or before that the white armband with the Blue Star of David. Is there any wonder that they were hated by the ghetto inmates?

August 12, 1942, when I was with my mother at "Punkt" (like the "Umsclagplatz," the gathering place for the ghetto Jews where they were selected and sent to Auschwitz) where we sat in mud and heavy rain all night and the next morning when the "Selection" started and my mother was sent to the lines to be shipped to Auschwitz, I tried to help mother and a Jewish police hit me over the head with his club so hard that I blacked out and when I came to my mother was already taken away. I still do not know why they did not take me too.

The Jewish police from Bendzin and Sosnowiec were sent to the smaller ghettos in Upper Silesia to help with their "Resettlement." Is it not nice how these policemen were helpful to one another? I do hope that none of them survived. If they did, as some did, I hope that they don't have a peaceful night.

Some of the police were planted by the underground and served as liaison between the underground and the Judenrat. That kind were very few. Moniek Merin gave specific orders not to help the underground, as he was violently opposed to the underground. There is a recorded case where a young woman from the underground was captured by the Sosnowiec police and the commandant of the Sosnowiec police, Goldminc, beat and tortured that young woman.

We all opposed the councils and the Jewish police from the start. They showed right away their cooperation with the German authorities and they wanted to prove to us, the ghetto inmates, that they are our superiors. Numerous beatings, arrests and extortions are sited by the council and the ghetto police.

A lot of these functionaries in the ghettos and camps, like the ghetto police and members of the Judenrat, were judged after the war by Courts of Honor as well as by the courts of the State of Israel, when the war had stopped and we were placed in the Displaced Persons Camps (D.P.) and the remnants of those who survived were not ready to forgive and forget what those people did to us as fellow Jews.

Naturally the trials began. In the American Zone, the Central Committee of Liberated Jews with offices in Munich started the trials.

In the British Zone Bergen-Belsen was the place since it was the largest D.P. Camp there.

And so it was in Italy "The Court of Honor at the Central Organization of Survivors in Italy."

And there were also local courts that took up the issue. One was in Landsberg where there, too, was a large concentration of holocaust survivors.

And so many, Jewish former "elite" in the ghettos and camps were judged. Some were found guilty, some innocent. It is true that in some cases when a Jew was forced to carry out criminal acts against other Jews, his own life was at stake. Acts like this had to be considered. And in most cases they were.

As I mentioned before, a lot of these were judged, but my story is about Bendzin, Sosnowiec and in general Eastern Upper Silesia, then I will dwell only on persons of that region.

I will start with a former member of the Council in Bendzin, Julius Zigel, chief of the Department of Labor, who was judged in Italy by the Court of Honor for harming Jewish workers and other lawless acts. There were four witnesses and he was sentenced on July 19, 1946. He confessed that he acted improperly but not criminally. But the court saw his actions as criminal and harmful to the Jewish community he served for five and a half years. He was forbidden to hold any position in the Jewish public life.

Roman Merin, a former member of the Council in Sosnowiec who was the chief of a department in the Zentrale of the Councils of Elders of

Israel Szyjowicz and Cesia Danciger

Danciger

Jewish Police Badge

Elazar Rubenlicht

Herman Szer Felczer

Eigenhändige Unterschrift — Podpis własnoręczny

M. Szeps

Hiermit wird bescheinigt, dass—Niniejszym zaświadcza się, że

Szeps Majer

geboren am — urodzony dnia 24. XII. 1892

Wohnhaft in Bendzin—zamieszkały w Będzinie

Marktstrasse 7.

beim Vorstand der Jüd. Interessenvertretung in Bendzin als zatrudniony jest w Zarz. Przedst. Ludn. Żyd. w charakterze

Ordner Nr. 26.

beschäftigt ist.

Der Vorsitzende
Przewodniczący

Bendzin, d. 24. III. 1941

Gültig bis zum
Leg. ważna do dn. 30. VI. 1941

Chaim Israel Merin

(siehe nächste Seite) — (patrz stronę nast.)

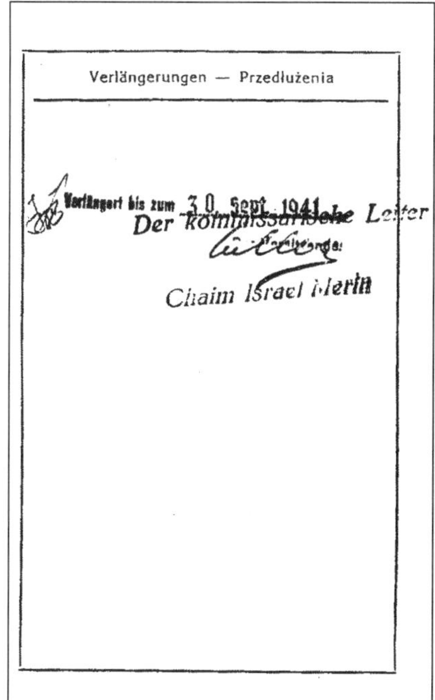

Verlängerungen — Przedłużenia

Verlängert bis zum 30. Sept. 1941

Der kommissarische Leiter

Chaim Israel Merin

Inhaber dieses Ausweises, der Ordner Szeps Majer, ist seitens der Jüdischen Interessenvertretung in Bendzin zur Erfüllung von Ordnungspflichten beauftragt. Wir bitten alle Dienstbehörden, ihm bei Ausübung seiner Pflichten Unterstützung zu gewähren.

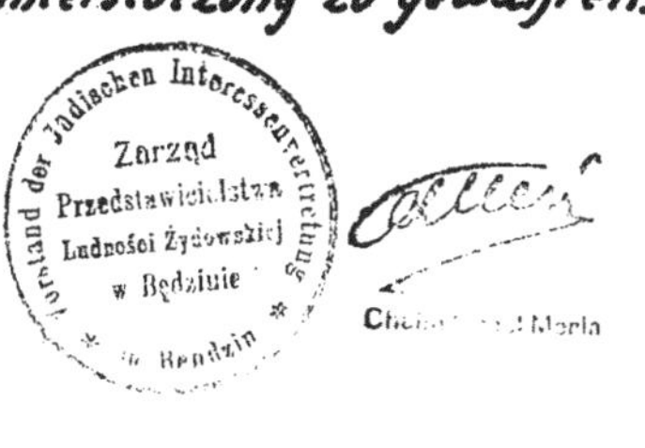

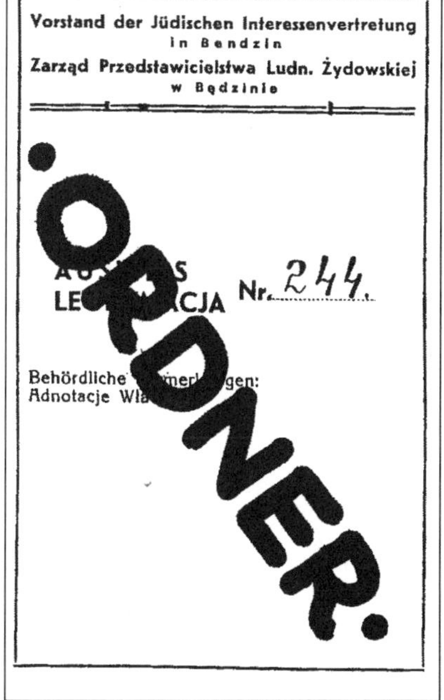

Vorstand der Jüdischen Interessenvertretung
in Bendzin
Zarząd Przedstawicielstwa Ludn. Żydowskiej
w Będzinie

ORDNER

Nr. 244

Behördliche
Adnotacje Wła

the Jewish Religious Community in Eastern Upper Silesia, was found guilty after a number of witnesses testified. The verdict was announced on May 26, 1949 by the Central Committee of Liberated Jews in the American Zone. He was charged among others of watching that no Jew escaped from the assembly square during a round up in the ghetto. (I personally could not judge Ziegel even though I knew of his actions in the Ghetto.)

To me he acted fine when my father was killed by the Germans in his own bed. When my father had all his ribs crushed by the Germans with a rifle butt, and he was spitting blood, I needed medication for my father. Ziegel helped me obtain the medication even though I knew him only from the Zionist movement. Later on he helped me with a permit to get my father buried. I don't sing praises for him but I needed him then and he helped me.

Mair Kiwkowicz, a Jewish policemen in the Olkush Ghetto (in Eastern Upper Silesia), was found guilty by the Court of Honor in Munich for harming Jews in the ghetto, for requisitioning furniture from Jews as well as other "harmful acts" against Jews in the Olkusz Ghetto.

Zajnvel Zelinger, an official of the "Durchgangslager" in Sosnowiec who was later the Jewish Elder in Sachenheim Labor Camp and after that Forman in the Blechhammer Camp, was rehabilitated after a public trial even though he was accused of betraying a group of underground activists to the Gestapo. But survivors also testified that he treated Jewish camp inmates well and helped organize religious services for Orthodox Jews.

Hersz Bernblat, chief of the Bendzin Ghetto Police, was sentenced on February 5, 1954 in Tel-Aviv-Jaffa court in Israel to a jail term of five years, but the sentence was quashed by the Supreme Court. Bernblat was sentenced on two counts; a) for carrying children from the orphanage and handing them over to the Germans during the "action" of August 1942, and b) for not allowing people destined for deportation, or whose fate was yet undecided, to join the group of people who were to be left in the ghetto or sent to a labor camp.

I have to add a personal note to this. I witnessed both accounts. I was there when the children from the orphanage were put on trucks to be shipped to Auschwitz, and b) I mentioned before where I was hit over the head for trying to help my mother at the "Umschlagplatz." And yet when I was requested to appear in court as a witness against Bernblat, by Alfred Szwarcbaum who, too, was from Bendzin and who knew that I was mistreated by Bernblat, I did not go to the trial because I did not like the accusers of Bernblat, where some of them were not reliable enough in my judgment to judge Bernblat. It was more a matter of who the accusers were, and some of the accusers were not even in the Bendzin ghetto when all this happened. There were others that were not better and maybe worse than Bernblat and live a nice life here in the states or Israel and even Germany or Poland.

Judge Landau said about the judging of the Judenrat and the police; "Everyone cares for himself and his family, and the prohibition of criminal law, including the Nazis and Nazi Collaborators (Punishment) Law, were not written for heroes, extraordinary individuals, but for simple mortals with their simple weaknesses."

Collaboration of the non-Jews was on a voluntary basis, not so with the Jewish collaborators where their lives and the lives of their families were always threatened.

In the official German pronouncements it was stated that the councils represented the Jewish interests. Like in the Bendzin Council where its title said it all; Interessenvertetung der Judischen Kultusgemeinde in Bendsburg. The councils were led to believe that they truly will be able to protect and defend Jewish interests. But the end was that by carrying out the persecution of their brethren they brought on self-destruction where the council members and the Jewish police were the final victims, with the exception of a small percentage (only 12% survived). To me even this is too many. They died together with the ghetto inmates and some even before.

At the end here I want to quote a passage in the "Appendix I" in the "Judenrat by Isaiah Trunk" on page 582:

"We shall now examine some of the purely negative evaluations. We shall take as a sample the second chairman of the Bendzin Council of Elders, M. (Moldczadski Chaim)... He carried out the German orders with the greatest severity... Obediently and devotedly carried out the orders of the Gestapo and M. Merin regarding Jews deported to Auschwitz. But at the same time he cared for the children in the orphanage, secured food for them with no profit to himself, and also provided food for the Borochov-kibbutz."

One who knew Moldczadski personally stated "from my own personal experiences and contacts during the war," he tried to find some positive features in his behavior. He even mentions as a "virtue" the fact that he did not extort money for personal gain. The evaluation of another party, a comrade of Moldczadski, an official of the Bendzin Jewish Council and a member of the Zionist underground movement, takes up four large pages. We shall make here only a few quotations; "…Right from the first day he (Moldczadski) became Merin's right hand, his and the Gestapo's devout servant… He shared with Merin responsibility for all the bad deeds of the Bendzin Jewish Council. Always before a deportation Merin tried in various ways to convince the Jews that nothing wrong was going to happen to them. Thus, for instance, on August 11, 1942 (on the eve of the 'selection' for deportation), he addressed them in the following words; 'Jews, put on your holiday clothing and joyfully proceed to the indicated assembly places. Nobody stay home.' He who would not report would not be allowed to remain in Zaglembie there after. He ruled in the Jewish Council with a strong arm…"

As he was a recent newcomer in Bendzin (born in Baranowicze, he had been sent to work for the Jewish National Fund in Bendzin before the war), he had no sympathy for the Bendzin Jews and acted disgracefully during the large scale deportation of 5,000 in June 1942. He used to say; "I do not debate with the Germans." He proved himself a mean scoundrel, trampling on the heads of people.

The witness was in delegation of Zionist Labor groups asking to free two council officials from the duty to serve in the ghetto police; one a member of the Hitachtud and another from the Poalei Zion Left group.

The delegation pointed out that these two men and the underground movement in general were against serving in the police. The chairman's answer was:

"I am not a Jewish representative and am acting here on behalf of the Gestapo. I am the boss here and things will happen as I wish." Still, because the men had the support of the party underground, he had to release them as unfit for police duty…

He fought everyone who opposed Merin. He used to scream: "Whatever Merin does is good — he is a God-blessed leader." He was also responsible for the misdeeds of the police in the course of carrying out his orders. He behaved as a beast much as the police did in the time of expulsions and actions.

The witness also related that the well known underground activist Frumka Plotnicka once criticized the chairman for behavior unbecoming a former party member. When he gave her a rude answer, she slapped him in his face, saying that he could now go and report to the Gestapo that she had hit him in the face. The witness concluded that "out of fear of revenge by the underground he kept quiet about the incident."

The conclusion of the three evaluations are clear enough. We have here a representative of a council who was a follower of the policy in which some other council members also believed, that by offering the "Nazi Moloch" hundreds they would be able to save thousands, and that no moral canons were admissible in applying this policy. One witness clearly states that Moldczadski considered Merin a "God-blessed leader," and he fell under his spell without reservations. Carrying out drastic measures inadmissible from the point of view of moral standards, he evoked a deep negative reaction on the part of those who revolted against them, which in turn influenced the witnesses in their evaluation of the ethical standards of the men responsible for the measures.

A selection taking place: those capable of work being led off; older ones facing immediate death (an S.S. photograph).

Separated into columns of men and women, they wait for the selection to begin. The SS man on the right smoking a cigarette is believed to be Josef Mengele, the most notorious camp doctor. His white gloves can be seen.

Sleeping banks in the women's barracks.

Women prisoners after being undressed, shaved, and given prison dress.

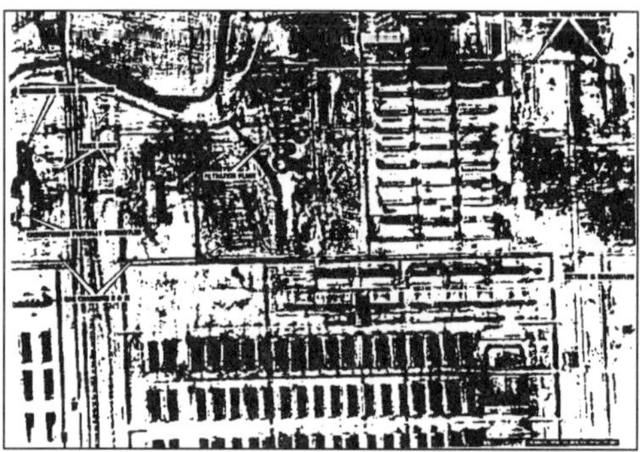

Auschwitz and Birkenau were photographed by Allied planes. This photograph was taken in December 1944. Oswiecin is the Polish name, which the Germans changed to Auschwitz.

One of the gas chambers. Resistance in daily life. It is worth repeating: Nazi regulations were designed to make life impossible, both in the camps and in the ghettos. To obey them meant to die sooner or later. To disobey them meant to die immediately. So they were obeyed as much as necessary. And they were disobeyed as much as possible.

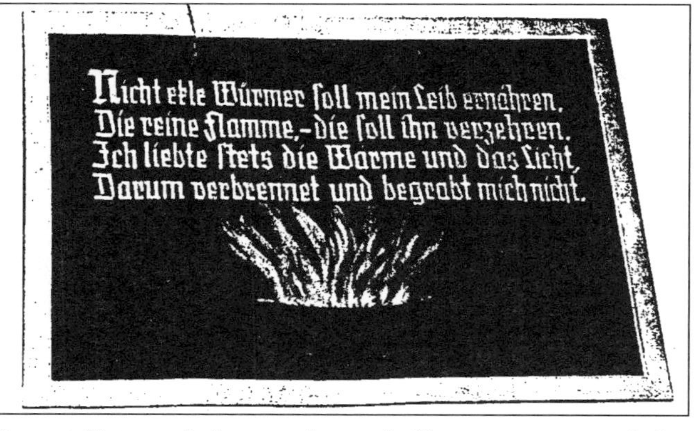

Bronze tablet on wall of crematorium reads: "Let not worms eat my body. Let it be consumed by fire flame. I love always warmth and light. Therefore burn, do not bury me."

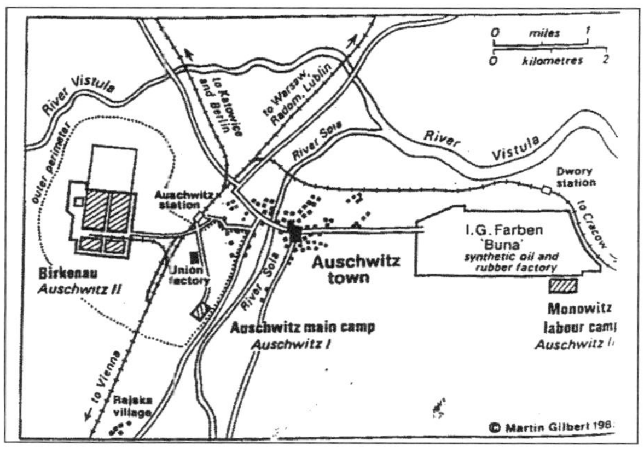

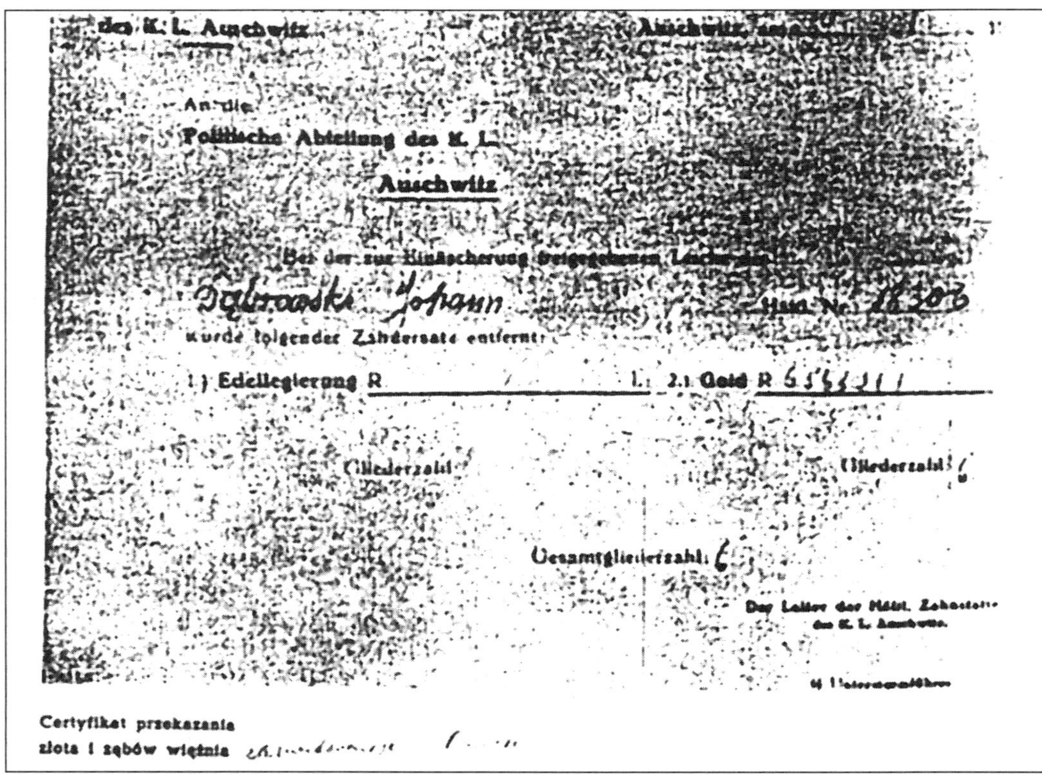

des K. L. Auschwitz Auschwitz,

An die

Politische Abteilung des K. L.

Auschwitz

Bei der zur Einäscherung freigegebenen Leiche

Dąbrowski Johann Häftl. Nr. 18203

wurde folgender Zahnersatz entfernt:

1.) Edellegierung R 2.) Gold R 5 5 5 3 1 1

Gliederzahl Gliederzahl 6

Gesamtgliederzahl: 6

Der Leiter der Häftl. Zahnstelle
des K. L. Auschwitz.

Certyfikat przekazania
złota i zębów więźnia

Auschwitz, a certificate of delivery of gold and teeth of a prisoner.

Chapter Twelve

Poland; the law of existance requires uninterrupted killing so that the better may live.

Adolf Hitler

The Establishment

Most contemporaries of the Jewish catastrophe were neither perpetrators nor victims. Many people, however, saw or heard something of the event.

The process of destruction of the Jews was based on three premises. First, no segment of Jewry will be exempt from the anti-Jewish laws. Second, relationship between Jew and non-Jew must be severed with least harm to the German economy. Third, the killing had to be conducted in a manner that would limit psychological repercussion to the perpetrators, avoid unrest among victims and to prevent unrest among non-Jews.

All these preparations required the participation of functionaries in a wide variety of offices.

Below is a list of special organizations and their special roles in the destruction process.

Reich Chancellery	Coordination of laws and decrees
Interior Ministry	Definition of term Jew
	Prohibition of mixed marriages
	Decrees for compulsory names
	Dismissals from civil service
	Deprivation of property
Churches	Supply of proof of non-Jewish descent
Justice Ministry	Elimination of Jewish lawyers
	Inheritance questions
	Divorce questions
	Regulation of names of enterprises
Party Boycott Committee	Boycott of Jewish enterprises
Party Chancellery	Participation in decisions involving the status of Jews

Reich Chamber of Culture	Dismissals of musicians, artists, and journalists and barring of writers
Education Ministry	Elimination of Jewish students, professors and researchers
Propaganda Ministry	Suggestions to the press
Economy Ministry	Regulations for the acquisition of Jewish firms
Dresdner Bank and other banking concerns	Intermediaries in takeover of Jewish firms
Various firms in retailing, wholesaling, manufacturing, and construction	Acquisitions of Jewish firms Dismissals of Jewish employees Utilization of Jewish forced labor in cities, ghettos and camps Contracting for measures of destruction such as supply of poison gas
Finance Ministry	Discriminatory taxes Blocked funds Confiscation of personal belongings Special budgetary allocations, such as clearing Warsaw ghetto ruins
Foreign Office	Negotiations for deportations of Jews in foreign countries and of foreign Jews in the Reich
Transport Ministry	Transports to ghettos and camps Utilization of forced Jewish labor Acquisitions of Jewish personal property
Armed Forces	Logistic support of killing operations in the occupied USSR Direct killing in Serbia and the occupied USSR Ghettoization in the occupied USSR Discriminatory measures and deportations from France, Belgium, and Greece Regulation of forced Jewish labor in armament plants

	Employment of forced Jewish labor by army offices
	Transport questions
Municipal authorities in the Greater German Reich	Movement and housing restrictions
Protectorate administration in Bohemia and Moravia	Anti-Jewish measures patterned on those of the Reich
Generalgouvernment in occupied central Poland	Confiscation, Ghettoization, Forced labor, Starvation measures, Preparations for deportation
Ministry for Eastern occupied Territories	Anti-Jewish measures patterned on those of the Reich
Reichskommissariat of the Netherlands	Anti-Jewish measures patterned on those of the Reich
Führer Chancellery	Staffing of the Belzec, Sobibor and Treblinka death camps
SS and Police	
Reich Security Main Office	Marking of Jews in the Reich Supervision of the Jewish communities in the Reich and Protektorat Einsatzgruppen killings in the occupied USSR Preparations of European-wide deportations
Main Office Order Police	Guarding of ghettos, trains and camps Participation in roundups and shooting
Economic-Administration	Administration of Auschwitz and Majdanek (Lublin)
Higher SS and Police Leaders in occupied Poland	Deportations to death camps Administration of the Chelmno (Kulmhof), Belzec, Sobibor and Treblinka death camps
Higher SS and Police Leaders in the occupied USSR	Shootings

Each organization was responsible for a specific segment in the destruction process. Thus several agencies employed "Specialists in Jewish Affairs" like the Interior Ministry, Economy Ministry, Finance Ministry,

Foreign Office, Transport Ministry, the Ministry for Eastern Occupied Territories and the Reich Security Office. Only Eichmann, who sat in the Reich Security Main Office, became known as a symbol of all perpetrators. Most of them survived the war and some were even retained in office by the Allies and some in their own businesses. It was not talked about all that much in public.

Many survivors like I, say "I am one of the few who survived, the strange thing however is not that I lived through it but that I was not destroyed."

There is an unmistakable rank order among the Jews who lived through those years. The decisive criteria are, exposure to risk and depth of suffering writes Raul Hilberg, who in my opinion is one if not the greatest historian of the Holocaust. The greatest respect from the survivors, however, commend the survivors who came from the woods and the ones who came out from the "Extermination" camps.

Compiled by Arnold Shay
With excerpts from the book
Perpetrators, Victims, Bystanders
By Raul Hilberg

Headquarter of the Camp Buchberg
Buchberg – Bavaria

Buchberg July 14th 1945.

To whom it may be concerned.
1 st/ Sgt. SMITH

I [illegible] [illegible] the leader of the camp Buchberg from May 10th 45. up to date have the pleasure to constate, that the American soldiers from the guard of the camp Buchberg have done all they could for the inhabitans of the camp.
They treated all the people alike and the people filled with them as friends.
In my name and in the name of all inhabitans of the camp we thank for their friendship to us.

With our best compliments and
best wishes

Lagerführung Buchberg
[illegible]

The last camp (for this writer) where I was liberated in May of 1945 by the American troops.

Celebration Session of the Presidium of the City of Bendzin to commemorate the 600th anniversary of the city.

Bendzin. The ruins of the Castle as a motif on one of the first stamps minted in Poland after the war in 1946.

Chapter Thirteen

"I know from my own experience that prisoners, especially those in concentration camps, are oppressed and tormented and brought to the verge of despair far more by psychological than by the physical effect and impressions of the camp's regime and life. One must mention here the uncertainty and the lack of hope to regain freedom — the majority of prisoners were sent to camp for an indefinite period of time — together with the terror and uncertainty of tomorrow, which were always oppressing them."

Rudolph Hoess,
Commandant of Auschwitz
in his biography

D.P. Camps

I have in my collection a newspaper *AJR Information* issued by the Association of Jewish Refugees in Great Britain, October 1946, issue #10, which still shows the misery we survivors had to go through after the liberation from the concentration camps.

"Brave New World"

A film script written at the end of the war and never translated to the screen was, not long ago, read by the author to his friends. It had the visionary ending of the victorious Allied armies parading at Brandenburg Tor before the survivors of the concentration camps and ghettos, partisan groups and extermination centers. The script was written before those camps and ghettos were liberated.

The storm of protest which swept through the press and other instruments of public opinion in the summer of 1945 seemed to suggest that the vision of that writer might come true; the "living dead" of Bergen-Belsen and other places of horror were the martyrs for whom the world bowed in deference. The obituary devoted to them was on the most lavish scale modern publicity could conceive.

Of course, everyone labored on the assumption that the "living dead," however, made remarkable recoveries and gradually more Jews came to the open from their hiding places, from labor camps, from partisan groups and from Soviet Russia, amounting to something like a million. And little was left from the generosity which was so lavishly bestowed upon the dead martyrs when it appeared that quite a number of them were still alive.

We are so entangled in technical terminology speaking of "Displaced Persons," and so on, that we have departed from measuring events in Europe and elsewhere by normal human standards. The expected reaction towards the survivors of the Nazi massacres would have been a welcome wherever they return, a helping hand in restoring their property, hailing them as warriors coming home from a victorious battle. Instead, they have met with hostility, refusal of restitution, discrimination and pogroms. The other expected world reaction would have demanded the restoration of the human right to choose their own residences; i. e., to leave it at their discretion to go and settle wherever they like; according to their wishes, they ought to have been allowed to go to Palestine, the U.S.A., the British Commonwealth and South America. Instead, only a trickle of them succeeded in joining their families and starting life anew. As a whole, they were denied that basic right of selecting their domiciles. The gates of the world have remained shut.

Reluctantly and, no doubt, slightly embarrassed, the Allies have placed thousand of them in camps. Since when have been concentration camps, even if the inmates are treated humanely, the reward for martyrs whose fate the world had loudly mourned when they deemed them dead? The vanquished aggressors are permitted to live in individual freedom, and their victims are herded together in camps. In Germany and Cyprus, Greece and Italy — barbed wire has become the approved method of dealing with resurrected corpses.

There is a strong movement in this country for releasing the German prisoners of war although no formal peace has been concluded with Germany and the majority of those prisoners are proven Nazis. One way or the other — we agree that it is inhuman to keep men behind barbed wire indefinitely. Is there in the "brave new world" for which we were said to be fighting no alternative but to penalize the victims and to commute the aggressors?

No doubt it would have been a fine gesture, as suggested in that film script, if the Allied troops had paraded at the Brandenburg Tor before the survivors of the concentration camps. But from this idealistic vision to the victimization of the victims is a long way indeed.

That is exactly how we the survivors felt then. Not that the feeling has changed, but we realize now that we were and are still the victims. The world has not learned a thing even after World War II.

But, we are here, we accomplished a lot without anybody's help, we brought up beautiful families in spite of all the hardships we had to go through. And our future generations will still contribute to the world as before, with poets, philosophers, men in medicine, Nobel prize winners, and after all the atrocities committed against us, we will remain human.

CCG Form 55

CONTROL COMMISSION COURT
GERICHT DER KONTROLL-KOMMISSION

FORM OF RECOGNIZANCE—WITNESS
FORMULAR DER VERPFLICHTUNGSERKLÄRUNG EINES ZEUGEN

I Arnold Schijowitz of Goslar
Ich (Name of Witness) *aus*
(*Name des Zeugen*)

Mauernstr. 33
(Address of Witness)
(*Anschrift des Zeugen*)

hereby acknowledge myself to be bound over in the sum of Rm 200.–
erkenne hiermit an, gegen eine Summe von

to appear and give evidence at the trial of Otto Locke
verpflichtet zu sein, vor dem *Gericht*

at ... on date and time to be notified.
in *am*

or at such other place as I may be notified on such date as I may be informed and to remain at such place of trial until the termination thereof or until I am released.
oder an einem solchen Ort zu solcher Zeit zu erscheinen und als Zeuge auszusagen, wie mir bekanntgemacht wird, und am Ort der Verhandlung bis zu deren Beendigung zu bleiben oder bis ich entlassen werde.
I understand that should I not appear a warrant will be issued for my arrest.
Es ist mir bekannt, dass im Falle des Nichterscheinens Haftbefehl gegen mich erlassen wird.

Witness E. Schyplens
Zeuge

Celle, 15/6/48.

[illegible]

CONTROL COMMISSION COURT
GERICHT DER KONTROLL-KOMMISSION

WITNESS SUMMONS
ZEUGEN-VORLADUNG

To Arnold ... SCHIJOWITZ, tailor
An

Address Goslar, Mauerstr. 33
Anschrift

1. You are ordered to attend the Control Commission High Court
Sie werden hiermit geladen, vor dem Kontroll Komm. Obere *Gericht*

at Brunswick, Burgplatz 2
in

on 26th August 48 at 0930 hrs to
am *um* (time) (*Uhr*) *persönlich*

give evidence in the trial of LOCKE, Otto
zu erscheinen, um als Zeuge in der Strafsache aufzutreten gegen (Name of accused) (*Name des Angeklagten*)

on a charge of — *der wegen der folgenden strafbaren Handlung angeklagt wird:*

Crime against humanity — Verbrechen gegen die Menschlichkeit

2. You are ordered to bring with you the following documents/articles:
Sie haben die folgenden genannten Dokumente und Gegenstände zur Verhandlung mitzubringen:

3. You will be liable to punishment if you fail to comply with this order.
Unentschuldigtes Fernbleiben wird bestraft werden.

By Order
Im Auftrage von

Prosecutor
(Signature of person authorised)
(*Autorisierte Unterschrift*)

Zugestellt am 13/8.48, 9.30 Uhr
Seifert, Pol.-Wm.

Published Every Friday Since 1887 (ISSN 0021-6437)

JEWISH EXPONENT

Berlin Releases Two War Criminals

BONN (JTA)—The West Berlin Senate has pardoned and released two Nazi criminals serving life sentences on 30 charges of murder. Each had served 21 years.

THEY ARE Otto Locke, 62, convicted of the murder of seven Jewish inmates of the Birkenau concentration camp, and Gottfried Matthes, a 72-year-old doctor, who was convicted of murdering 23 mentally defective Germans in the Polish town of Grottkau.

Matthes was medical director of the State Health Authority at the time.

In Brussels, Maurice Pioro, president of the Belgian Union of Deportees and Families, urged Nazi victims to help bring war criminals to justice by pressing charges against former SS men and other Nazi officers responsible for crimes committed during World War II.

According to Pioro, West Germany has started civil actions against four Nazi war criminals, but it is taking an inordinately long time to bring them to court because there is no outside pressure.

SUCH PRESSURE can be exerted by public opinion, by the deportees themselves or members of their families, Pioro said.

The four criminals in question are Constantin Canaris, Kurt Asche, Ernst Ehlers and Karl Fielitz. The Belgian government transferred more than 6,000 documents to the West German authorities earlier this year to facilitate the prosecution.

See the attached "Form of Recognizance-Witness" issued by The Control Commission Court at the trial of Nazi criminal Otto Locke. June 5, 1948
Arnold Shay...Witness

NAZIS PARDONED

BONN (JTA)—The Berlin Senate has pardoned two Nazi criminals serving life sentences. They are 62-year-old Otto Locke, who was responsible for the deaths of seven Jewish inmates of Birkenau concentration camp, and Gottfried Matthes, who, as medical officer in charge of the health office in the Polish town of Grottkau, killed Germans suffering from mental illness.

Locke and Matthes have served 20 and 21 years of their sentences respectively and are no longer fit to be held in custody, for, in the view of leading criminologists, prison inmates undergo a personality decline between the 15th and 20th year of imprisonment. For this reason, the Berlin Senate is applying the unwritten law of not continuing sentences beyond the 20th year.

Chapter Fourteen

We love Adolf Hitler,
because we believe,
with a faith that is deep
and unshakable,
that he was sent us
by God to save Germany

Field Marshal Hermann Goering

Instructions How To Treat Employed In Germany Foreign Labor Force

Statehood:
"Ostarbeiter"

As such to be treated all non-Germans who as of 22.6.1941 live on the former Russian soil and registered by the German Working Commission for work in the Reich on transportations. Citizenship for instance, Ukrainian, Russian, Polish, Greek, Rumanian, and others do not count. The "OST" Arbeiter are not considered Volksdeutsche, and Russian Immigrants that are on German territory before 22.VI.1941.

Marking: Square patch "OST" on the right side of your chest attached to the upper part of your clothing. Responsible for the orders to the local and city police stations.

Identification: Working Card with a detailed personal, picture, finger print, place of work. Responsible for fulfilling the order are the local and city police stations.

Place: A camp with wiring to make escapes impossible. Leaving with a German Guard, the Guard has to have a proper I.D. as a work supplier, special permit for the "Ostarbeiter." Leaving without supervision in groups of 10-15 people. Entrance to movies, theaters, restaurants, sport fields is forbidden.

Escapes: Give personal details, the camp address of the last working place, the address in your own country of birth, register at the city police station immediately, /STAPO/ to the run-aways, shoot without warning.

The Caught: (Escapees) After the first time, return to the same working place. If it is unknown, turn over to the place of work. After the second and following times, report without fail to the police in

Sochum, turn over the case to the GESTAPO in Sochum. In the same time give a report about the case to the STAPO in Dortmund.

Aversion to work: In lighter cases punishment by the place of work. In harder cases; arrest, report to the STAPO or even in special cases notify by telephone.

1) Sexual Contacts. 2) No morals. 1) Allowed among themselves, to interfere if pregnancy is interrupted. In case of homosexuals, arrest without fail, telephone, notify STAPO. Sexual contact with Germans or other foreign workers is forbidden. Notify STAPO. 2) Immediate arrest, notify STAPO as in point 1.

Political crimes: Immediate notifying by phone to STAPO, wait for orders from STAPO.

Criminal cases: Arrest, notify STAPO, without fail notify the Courts.

Religion: With help of a priest, also in case of Christianity, marriage and death is (strictly) forbidden. Not to go to church.

Legal cases: Directive of the STAPO of the 13,6,1942, 4D3, instructions 30.7,1942, IV FD3, following instructions of 29,6,1942.-1916/42 of 30.9. 1942-1537/42. of 31.8. 942.1537/42 of 3.11.1942-5/10/42.

POLES

Poles as such are considered: a) all people with Polish citizenship living as of 1.9.1939, inside the territory of the General Government including Lvov as well as the Region of Bialostock or near the East terrain/ Wartegau, Danzig/ East Prussia. b) People with Polish citizenship from Western Europe. c) People with no Polish citizenship, Ukraine, and others as the punk a). d) Polish citizens living on German territory before 1.9.1939.

Marking: a/ Gray ID card, work permit with picture, finger print. b) Passport or similar. c) Same as in a).d) Passport or alike.

Place: (Living Quarters) Collecting Camp, Exclusions: Field workers, smaller working places, tailors, shoemakers and alike. Leaving the place of work and taking advantage of public transportation only with the permission of the local police.

Escapes: Notify immediately the STAPO giving all details, address of the last working place, address of stay in his own country.

Escapees: (When caught) Sending by force to the last working place, inform the Division of Labor for the return to work.

Aversion to work: (Faulencer) In lighter cases try to make the conflict easy with the help of reporting to the STAPO. In more difficult instances; arrest, hearing and submitting a report in two copies immediately to the STAPO, do not give the case to the Prosecutor of the Courts.

1) Sexual contacts; 2) No morals. Permitted among themselves, marriage between themselves. With German or other nationals is forbidden. Non-interference with self-motivated abortions or private paying for abortions. Homosexuals arrest, report to STAPO. 2) Arrest, hand the case over to the STAPO. If possible without a hearing, otherwise attach three copies. Handing the case over to the Prosecution or the courts is forbidden.

Political crimes: No hurry for arrest, handling the situation in the right manner. Without fail hand the case over to the STAPO, eventually by telcphone submit information. Do not turn the case over to Prosecutor or the courts.

Criminal cases: Look into the case and hand over to the STAPO with two copies of the case. Listen to and report. Wait for advice. In case of arrest do not bring attention. Do not hand the case over to the Prosecutor or the courts.

Religion: Only special ceremonies and only one Sunday a month as well as the main holidays, between the hours of 10-12 A.M. Partakers only who live in a 5 km radius. To and from the ceremonies only under guard. The use of the Polish language is forbidden even in songs or Confession. Taking part in German ceremonies is forbidden.

Legal: The Order by the Police in case of the markings of the workers in the Reich. For Poles 8.3.1940. Regional Order for Poles of 27.3.1940, 19.5.1940, 3.15.1942. General Order of the STAPO in Dortmund of 17.6.1940. in case of chase and arrest of 11,132.1941. For the Ukrainian Laborers, civilians, the ones coming from Galicia, the Order of 20.3.1942. "Instructions How To Treat The Civilian Work Force" of 25.6.1942-3635/42, IV d3, of 7.6.1942.-3704/42 IV d3.

CZECHS LIVING IN THE PROTECTORATE

Markings: Identification without markings.

Identification: ID card for permission to get citizenship, and a substitute ID card and workers book.

Place: Same as Poles.

Escapes: Report to the office of labor.

Escapees: (If caught) Same as Poles.

Aversion to work: Same as Poles.
Sexual contacts and Morality: 1) Among themselves allowed. In other cases report to STAPO. 2) Same as Poles.
Political crimes: Same as Poles.
Criminal cases: Handling by the local police.
Religion: No limitations.
Rights: General Order of the STAPO of Dortmund of 11.7.1939. provincial arrest (Chechs).

ITALIANS

Markings: Without identifying markings.
Identification: Passport or alike.
Place: Same as Poles.
Escapes: Report to STAPO and state what made them do it.
Escapees: (Caught) Include the STAPO arrest in minor cases.
Aversion to work: Report to STAPO, wait for orders, arrest only in special case. If possible wait for decision from the STAPO by telephone.
Sexual contact and Morality: Crimes and especially contacts with Germans. Report immediately to the STAPO, wait for decision. Do not involve the Prosecutor or the courts.
Political crimes: Same as Poles.
Criminal cases: Same as Poles from Protectorate.
Religion: No limitation.

FRENCH, BELGIANS, FLEMISH, DUTCH, CHORVACS, SLOVACS HUNGARIANS, RUMANIANS AND BULGARIENS

Markings: No identification markings.
Identification: Passport or alike.
Place: Report to STAPO.
Escapees: (If caught) Same as Poles.
Aversion to work: Same as Poles.
Sexual contacts and Morality: Same as Italians.
Political crimes: Same as Poles.
Criminal cases: Same as Protectorate.
Religion: No limits.

Chapter Fifteen

Hatred, burning hatred — that is what
we want to pour into the souls
of our millions of fellow Germans
until the flames of rage ignites
our Germany and avenges
the corrupters of our nation.

Adolf Hitler

Third Reich History

Adolf Hitler. Born in Austria and settled in Munich in 1913. He enlisted in the German army in World War One. He became a corporal and received the Iron Cross First Class for bravery.(?)

After the war he came back to Munich and joined the German Workers Party. In 1920 he became the leader of that party and the party was renamed the "National Socialist German Workers Party" (NSDAP).

November 1923. The "Bear Hall Putsch" in Munich, which was supposed to bring Germany under nationalist control. The putsch failed. Hitler was arrested after fleeing and was sentenced to five years in the Landsberg Fortress. He served only nine months.

In prison he dictated to Rudolf Hess the now infamous "Mein Kampf" (My Struggle).

January 30, 1933. Hitler takes office in the Reichstag and on March 5, 1933 he won the Reichstag election with a bare majority.

1934. The Presidency and Chancellorship are united in the person of the Führer. All parties are outlawed and opposition brutally suppressed.

1935. In the fall the "Nuremberg Laws" are promulgated for the "Protection of German Blood and Honor."

Prohibitions are to intermarriage or extramarital intercourse between "Jew and persons of German blood," the use of the "Reichs Flag," German employment in Jewish household, and a few other laws against the Jews.

November of the same year, a second law is enacted called: "The Reich Citizenship Law," stating that only persons of the "German or Related Blood" can be a citizen of Germany.

1938. Austria which was Hitler's dream is annexed, then the Sudetenland.

1939. September 1. Poland is invaded and World War II begins.

1941. France is defeated, Belgium and Holland invaded, Denmark and

Norway occupied. In June of that year Germany invades Russia.

1945. Germany lost the war. Hitler insists that the Germans fight to the end. He, however, remained in his bunker in Berlin where on April 29 he married Eva Braun. Next day April 30th he commits suicide.

Reinhard Heydrich was the chief of the Reich Security Main Office. On September 20, 1939, he issued a directive called "The Jewish Question in Occupied Territories." It ordered the movement of all Jews into ghettos.

Heydrich's car was bombed in Prague by members of the Czech resistance on May 27, 1942, and he died shortly thereafter. In honor of Heydrich, the extermination of the Jews of Poland was given a code name "Operation Reynhard."

Globocnik, Odilo. S.S. Lieutenant General in charge of operation "Reynhard," the plan for the extermination of the Polish Jews.

The early killings of the Jews, Heydrich called "Interim" or "Temporary Measures."

Daluege, Kurt. Commander in Chief of the "Reich Police" and later "Deputy Protector of Bohemia and Moravia." Responsible for the destruction of the town of Lidice in revenge for Heydrich's assassination.

The "Extermination Camps," Belzec, Sobibor and Treblinka, were especially built for "Operation Reynhard In the General Government."
The amounts of food each Jew was allowed:

Bread	14.0 oz.
Meat products	4.5 oz.
Sugar	1.75 oz.
Fat	.9 oz.

At its best the Jewish ration was about 350 calories a day.

Krupp, Alfred. In sole control of "Krupp Industries," the largest producer of guns, tanks and ammunition in the Third Reich, used over 100,000 slave laborers, including Jews from Auschwitz and elsewhere, of which 70,000 to 80,000 died. Krupp family members were early supporters of Hitler and gave ten million Reichsmark a year to the Nazis. Sentenced to twelve years and loss of all money and property in 1948. Freed in 1951. All property and personal fortune estimated at close to $100 million returned to him.

Schirar, Baldur von. In charge of "Labor Mobilization" for the Third Reich. Responsible for the extermination of tens of thousands of Jewish workers in Poland, and for deporting five million people from their homes in occupied territories to work as slave labor in Germany.

Pohl, Oswald. Chief of the "S.S. Economic and Administrative Department" in charge of the economic side of the "Final Solution," in which all valuables seized from the gassed Jews, including clothing, human hair, tooth fillings, gold spectacles, were sent back to Berlin.

Speer, Albert. Reich Minister for armament and war production. Admitted responsibility to the using of slave labor in factories under his control and for using S.S. supplied concentration camp prisoners for his production lines.

Streicher, Julius. Fanatic anti-Semite and favorite of Hitler. Owner and publisher of the extremely popular newspaper *Der Sturmer*, which used as its banner "THE JEWS ARE OUR MISFORTUNE," and printed stories of Jewish ritual murders, sex crimes and other lies. Streicher constantly called for extermination of the Jews, both in his newspaper and in his frequent speeches, which attracted very large audiences.

Liebenschel, Arthur. Commander of Auschwitz.

Eichmann, Adolf. Obersturmbannfuhrer Lieutenant Colonel, in charge of the "Department of Jewish Affairs, Bureau IV-B-4," the section of the "Reich Central Security Office" in Berlin, responsible for deporting Jews. He was hanged in Israel May 31, 1962.

Wirth, Christian. Administrative head of "Operation T4," the "Mercy Killing" program in Germany. Assigned to begin extermination of Jews in Chelmno death camp. In charge of extermination squads at Belzec, Sobibor and Treblinka Death Camp.

The basic plans for the "Final Solution" were drawn up at the Wannsee Conference in January of 1942. With the expert advice of the two men in charge of the "Euthanasia Program," Christian Wirth and Victor Brack, six of the camps became the killing centers. All of them used carbon monoxide gas. Auschwitz and later Chelmno used "Zyklon B." The six camps that classified as "Extermination Camps," were in Poland (NOT BY CHANCE):

Operation started in the following order.

Chelmno	December	1941
Auschwitz	February	1942
Belzec	March	1942
Sobibor	April	1942
Treblinka	July	1942
Majdanek	September	1942

We will never know the exact numbers of the people killed at each camp, because there are no records of the people that went straight from the trains to the gas chambers. However, there are approximate numbers of the victims and the survivors of each camp.

CAMPS	VICTIMS	SURVIVORS
Chelmno	360,000	3
Belzec	600,000	2
Sobibor	250,000	64
Treblinka	800,000	less than 40
Majdanek	500,000	less than 600
Auschwitz	2,000,000 to 4,000,000	

It is generally believed by historians of that period, that the number of Jews killed is higher than six million. These are the figures in the Encyclopedia Judaica:

Polish and Soviet area	4,565,000
Germany	125,000
Austria	65,000
Czechoslovakia	277,000
Hungary	402,000
France	83,000
Belgium	24,000
Luxemburg	700
Italy	7,500
Holland	106,000
Norway	760
Rumania	40,000
Yugoslavia	60,000
Greece	65,000
	5,820,960

On recommendation of doctors from the Leipzig clinic, that a "baby born blind, an idiot — at least it seems to be an idiot, with a leg and an arm missing" — should be killed. That finally persuaded Hitler to sign a decree legalizing Euthanasia, on September 1, 1939.

Brent, Karl. Hitler's personal physician and one of the main doctors involved in "Operation T4," the Euthanasia program.

Rauff, Walter. S.S. Colonel who organized the development and production of the "Mobile Gas Vans" estimated to have killed 97,000 Jews and Russians. He had failed at first his S.S. heredity test because his fiancee had been married to a Jewish lawyer. Eventually Himmler's office accepted her submission, that her marriage had been "an oversight" due to the fact that she had "not studied racial biology…and was unaware of the consequences of this marriage." Rauff died of lung cancer in Santiago, Chile, in May 1983 after several attempts to secure his extradition had failed.

Himmler had made the right choice, it was said in the hierarchy of the German killers, in appointing Rudolf Hoess as Camp Commandant of the Auschwitz Concentration Camp. He obeyed orders when Himmler, on a visit to Auschwitz in March 1943, told him "The construction work must be pushed on, regardless of all present or future difficulties," with the vast expansion of his program of genocide.

Hoess, Rudolf. Commander of Auschwitz 1940 to 1943, noted in his memoirs that, "Auschwitz became the greatest human extermination centers of all time." He stated, "I never personally hated Jews, but Himmler had ordered it and had even explained the necessity and I never gave much thought to whether it was wrong."

Although, as Hoess said, Himmler ordered records to be burned "after every large action." The total number of Jews gassed at Auschwitz is known to be about 2.5 million or more. According to Hoess, this was the figure supplied by Eichman, before Berlin was surrounded.

Auschwitz was originally military barracks for the Polish army. Himmler built another camp nearby at Birkenau in 1941. This was known as Auschwitz-Birkenau.

The Allied planes were involved in reconnaissance and limited bombing missions against some of the industrial installations outside Auschwitz-Birkenau. The Allies have never satisfactorily answered why they failed to bomb the camp, even though by late 1944 they had conclusive proof of what was going on there and they could easily have used the bright flames from the crematoria as their target sites. Not only could hundreds of thousands of lives have been saved during the final month of the war, but casualties to inmates, who were housed far away from the crematoria, would have been negligible. The Allies never even attempted to bomb the railway lines leading to the camp, which would have cut off the means of bringing inmates of the murdering machine.

Those are the names of some of the murderers of Auschwitz: Lagerfuhrer Schwarzhuber, Dr. Mengele, Dr. Thilo, S.S. Unterfuhrers-Boger, Buntrock, Baretzki, Hustek, Steinberg, Kurschus, Schultz, Gorges, Unterfuhrer Voss, Wachtmeister Kurbanik.

Kramer, Josef. Commander of Birkenau and Bergen Belsen concentration camps. Known as "The Beast of Belsen" for his sadistic cruelty towards prisoners.

Hoessler, Franz. Auschwitz Administrator.

Klein, Fritz. Auschwitz Camp Doctor.

Mengele, Dr. Josef. Chief Medical Officer at Auschwitz. In charge of selections of Jews to the gas chambers and horrifying medical experiments, particularly on twins and Gypsies.

Mengele was at the ramp when new transports arrived at Auschwitz, he selected who shall live and who shall die. Those considered too old, too weak to work, were sent straight to the gas chambers. All their possessions were taken away and sent later to Germany.

Dr. Mengele had been transferred to Gross Rosen together with several other doctors from Auschwitz, including Dr. Munch. Even during the final hours of the war, the S.S. hierarchy attempted to keep its killing machines operating and fully staffed.

Dr. Victor Cpesius, the chief pharmacist of Auschwitz, was charged with complicity in joint murder on at least four separate occasions of 2,000 deaths each. He was sentenced to nine years of hard labor.

Berger, Gottlob. S.S. Main Office. One of Himmler's foremost experts on racial selection.

Bear, Richard. Commandant of Auschwitz I.

Brack, Victor. S.S. Colonel and top official in the "Reich Main Office." Active in the construction of the Polish death camps. In charge of "Operation T4" the "Mercy Killing" of at least 100,000 Germans judged "unfit for life." He set up "Mobile Gassing Vans" in Riga and Minsk to exterminate Jews judged "unsuitable for work."

Eicke, Theodor. S.S. General and inspector of all concentration camps and S.S. concentration camps guard formations. Used Dachau and its prisoners as a training school for concentration camp guards, laying down exact instructions on punishment, beating, solitary confinement and shooting of prisoners.

Heyde Werner, head of the "Reich Association for Hospitals and Sanatoria." Ensured their cooperation in "Operation T4," the "Mercy Killing" of 100,000 Germans judged "unfit for life."

Frick Friedrich, wealthy industrialist, supporter of the Nazi movement and one of three most prominent employers of slave labor in the Third Reich. Bought and used 48,000 slave laborers, of whom 80% died.

Frich, Wilhelm. Reich Minister of the Interior from 1933 to 1943. Responsible for setting up the laws that eliminated Jews from German life. Climaxed in the Nuremberg laws.

Thierack, Otto. Reich Minister of Justice, S.S. Major General. Drafted the “Extermination Through Work” decree, put into effect against Jewish concentration camp prisoners.

Wiesliceny, Dieter. S.S. Deportation Expert in Slovakia, Greece and Hungary.

Muller, Heinrich. Head of the Gestapo as Adolf Eichmann’s direct superior, signed orders for immediate delivery to Auschwitz of 45,000 Jews for extermination and countless other orders of the same kind.

N.S.D.A.P. “National Socialistische Deutsche Arbeits Partei,” National Socialist Workers Party. Otherwise known as the Nazi Party.

S.S. In abbreviation for “Schutzstaffel” (Protective Units). Written with the two lightning symbols. They were called “The Black shirts” or “Storm Troopers.”

“Waffen S.S.” Were the fighting units, the police and the concentration camp guards.

In the following two chapters the author is
bringing out his "Kadish" to remember the
six million Jews that perished in the Holocaust.
They were written for the 'Yom Hashoa' every year.
May their souls be held in everlasting memory.
Arnold L. Shay

Chapter Sixteen

We were forced to come to a grim decision that this people must be made to disappear from the face of the earth... We have tackled (the assignment) and carried it through without our man and our leader suffering any damage in their minds and souls.

Heinrich Himmler

Kadish

In Memory of the Six Million

We say Kadish for the dead
Yet there is no mention
Of the dead in the Kadish
    So the Kadish is for the living
    The ones who will remember
    The loved ones we lost
We will remember the dead
Never forget the murderers
The ones who took their lives.
    We say Kadish for each dead
    We must say Kadish Six Million times
    For the Six Million Kedoshim.
Kadish we say, with
Eyes full of tears, pain
And anger in our hearts.
    Anger against the world
    That was so silent
    And G-d that was just looking on.
    How can we forget Six Million Jews
Over One Million innocent children?
No! We will not forget
We can never forget them
Ours is their debt.
    In the Vilna ghetto
    In a basement on the wall
    "ZACHOR"was written in blood.
    From the ghetto in Bendzin
On the wall at the train station
The plea was about the same.
"Bracia pomscicie nasza smierc"

Brothers take vengeance
For our death.
The Nazi murderers did their best
To erase and deny
Their beastly deeds
We must do our utmost
To remember the victims
Our silence will kill them again.

Compiled by:
Arnold L. Shay

Yiskor

In memory of the six million.

Thirty-seven years have past
Since we were assigned a new
Life.

But the memories are still ague
With our inner fight and
Strife.

We have to recall those years
No matter how much pain they
Bring

Of life filled with fears
A time, when even birds forgot to
Sing.

With reverence we still remember
Six million lives that
Perished.

Of our people with pain in our hearts
Their memory forever we will
Cherish.

Arnold L. Shay
1981

Meditation in Holy Memory to the Six Million

With reverence we bow our heads as we kindle the lights in holy memory of the six million innocent Jews who perished at the hands of the Nazis in the cruelest way, while the world was looking on.

It still is impossible to comprehend even for us survivors, that all this was allowed to happen.

Let us promise now, that we shall never forget, nor can we forgive the murder of those innocent souls, who died just for being born a Jew.

We, the survivors, may be able to forgive for the pain inflicted upon us, but, do we have the right to forgive for the six million who are no more with us??

Let their memory be a shining light for us. Let us, if only in their memory, strengthen, and support, with all our hearts and being, the only thing that can keep us alive, our beloved state of Israel.

Am Israel Chaiby Arnold L. Shay
Lakewood, New Jersey
Memorial 1983

To This I Beare Witness

The 1939 German Blitzkrieg became a pretext for the extermination of Jews.

The German soldier became transformed into an instrument of genocide.

Cruel decrees, wrecking, looting and burning, wholesale arrests of Jews, terror, oppression, death became the order of the day.

Collective punishment was administered indiscriminately against young and old, infants were stabbed at their mother's breast.

Prominent Jewish citizens were tortured, traditional Jewish community leaders were shot before the eyes of their wives and children.

The brutal sadism left the victims and witnesses emotionally paralyzed and semi-conscious.

Those were the graphic pictures of the first days of the German occupation.

The systematic process of fear, oppression and degradation, led to the total destruction of European Jewry.

Through scientific and barbaric means, starvation of the children, the writhing of the aged.

The anguish of the dying mothers and the agony of the gassed fathers, all vibrating, pounding and waking the conscience of every human being. This was the civilized world.

God!! Why?? Why were you silent?? Could you not hear our cries, our agony, our calling to you in desperation?

Could you not see the flames and smoke of the crematories engulfing your children??

You and the whole world were silent. Nobody would hear our cries.

This passiveness strengthened the Nazis and their lust for Jewish blood grew.

The world is now trying to forget and mitigate its own share of the guilt, by placing the entire blame on one madman with the abstract racist system.

We, the victims, we the survivors of the Holocaust, will continue to testify that this is a blatant lie.

The Holocaust came with the agreement and cooperation of the German majority,

We testify that the entire Christian world had laid the groundwork for the Holocaust long, long before it started.

The gas chambers of Auschwitz were only completed in 1942, but they were 1,500 years in the process of building, through hatred, discrimination, degradation, false accusations, inquisitions and pogroms.

To this I testify, to this I bear witness.

We also bear witness to the small groups of righteous Christians who endangered their own lives to help the Jews sometimes from death.

We honor the people of Denmark and their King Christian X, the only country in the world that was not silent and resisted the Nazi murderers, and rescued their Jewish neighbors from destruction.

History will record them as the only righteous people in their generation. We, the survivors, speak of them with reverence.

The physical forces of darkness and evil were at last shattered and destroyed.

The Holocaust left six million Jewish men, women and children dead. And entire communities annihilated. Orphans and nameless mass graves remain.

During the darkest days of the Holocaust, intense resistance was everywhere.

Young and old, men and women — all resisted, the mothers giving food to the child.

The teachers continuing to instruct the young ones, Zionists studying Hebrew, historians recording ghetto history for posterity.

Rabbis studying Torah — all concealed under the threat of death, in many of the ghettos.

Jews, the few weapons, battered a ruthless sophisticated, German army.

And death camps revolted, some even blowing up the crematoriums. From Warsaw to Bendzin, from Treblinka to Auschwitz.

Jewish resistance fought the enemy alone. Without any outside help. This I witnessed, to this I testify.

The spirit of martyrdom, in all of its aspects, must not overshadow the spirit of heroism.

Heroism is enveloped in martyrdom — survival is struggle — struggle is resistance. We did it all. Let us not forget it.

Every Jew who survived the Holocaust, be it in the concentration camps, ghettos, in the woods, in hiding or on forged papers, defied the enemy. However, the enemy's hatred and poison did not contaminate us. This is resistance in the best tradition of our people, in the spirit of our ethics.

The history of the Holocaust asks very crucial questions, not only about the past but also about the future, directed not only to the Jews but to all people with a conscience.

To understand the future one must remember that past, for without the past, there is no future.

Today's younger generation, which was not in th e time of Auschwitz, is now critical, incensed and angry at their older generations apathy and indifference. This is their heritage from the chapter Auschwitz.

But we must learn and teach from the past and make it relevant to our contemporary times. We must apply what has been learned from the past in order to protect the future.

The tragedy of Auschwitz must never happen again. Not in Europe, not in Russia, not in Israel and not here in the Cradle of Liberty.

This is our "ani maamin" to our Kedoshim. This is the testament of the six million Jewish martyrs.

Ym Eshkach Germania
Tishkach Yemini.
If I forget you Germany
May my right hand forget its cunning.

Compiled and read by
Arnold L. Shay
in the Kibutz in New Jersey, 1969
on Yom-Hashoa in Temple Beth Shalom
Coconut Creek, 1988

Lest We Forget

Forty years are now past
Since the birth of our nation
Forty-five years, we put to rest
Since the liberation.
        Our hearts are still with tears
        And dreams of past are here to stay
        Our lives are still with fears
        And dreams of past will not go away
How long can one live in that shadow
Of crematorias that give no way
Visions of atrocities that will not fade,
How long do we survivors have to pay?
        The second and third generation of ours
        Live with a past that know family few
        There are no graves to bring some flowers
        For that generation that they never knew.
For us, the few that are still around
Time cannot heal our open wounds
Thoughts and visions are too abound
The years could not silence the sound.
        Of our parents that have no graves
        That marched to death with prayers on their lips
        With their ashes and bones, streets are paved
        The heavens cried and the sun went eclipse
Will there ever be rest
For our morbid dreams
We have tried our best
at night...To muffle our screams.
        We can still hear the voices
        Of cry for help, in their need
        The world too, heard their screams
        But no one, no one, gave any heed.
So it is only us survivors to carry the burden
To live with dreams of years past
Very few care, how much we are hurtin'
Or that we the survivors, can find no rest.

But remember the dead, do not forget
That our parents too had a past
Pray that the world will be peaceful yet
And maybe, just maybe, we too can rest.
They have written on walls, with their blood "Zachor"
For the whole world, not to forget
So only to us, it is left to settle the score
So far our job is not done yet.
So remember dear friends
We must tell the story
To you survivors, I stretch my hand
With you my "family" I am in my glory.

I dedicate this poem as a Kadish to our parents, who like us were victims of Nazism but are not here to tell their story.

To the 45th anniversary of the Warsaw Ghetto Uprising.

To the 40th anniversary of the rebirth of the state of Israel.

Arnold L. Shay
1988

"Kristalnacht"

On this night of November 9-10, we remember the horror and tragedy of "Kristalnacht," the night of the broken glass.

That night of arson, property destruction and murder, formalized what was to become known as the Holocaust.

For the first time a demonic political and social order had nothing to fear from citizens, from Jews, from the church or from the world.

"Kristalnacht" calls us to respond with a sense of sorrow over the capacity of human beings to inflict suffering and death upon his fellow human beings.

The Nazi anti-Jewish outrage committed on November 9-10, 1938, was officially sanctioned by the regime as a provocation by the assassination of a member of the German Embassy in Paris, by the son of a Polish Jew living in Germany until their deportation the month before, to Poland.

The Germans had created an atmosphere of tension, and on the night of the 9-10 of November of 1938, there were widespread attacks on the Jews, Jewish owned property and synagogues.

No complete tally of the destruction exists, but at least 30,000 Jews were arrested, 815 Jewish owned stores were destroyed, 29 warehouses and 171 Jewish dwellings were set on fire or otherwise destroyed, 191 synagogues and schools were set on fire, and a further 76 completely demolished.

Thirty-six Jews were killed and 36 severely injured.

After the damages were tallied, the insurance companies were ordered not to pay to the Jews. The Jews had to bear all the expenses, even those of the non-Jewish owned businesses that were damaged by accident, the Jews had to pay for the damages.

Arnold L. Shay
November 9-10, 1979
Richland, Washington

Chapter Seventeen

I am of the opinion that bronze tablet should be laid, recording that we had the courage to carry out this great and so necessary a task.

Odilo Globocnik, S.S. Chief of Lublin
Police Director of Operation Reynhard

Six Extermination Camps

HITLER'S "FINAL SOLUTION OF THE JEWISH QUESTION" WAS TO ESTABLISH DEATH CAMPS WHERE ALL OF THE JEWS IN EUROPE WOULD BE EXTERMINATED. SIX DEATH CAMPS SAW NEARLY SIX MILLION JEWS ENTER, AND VERY FEW LEAVE ALIVE.

THIS TEMPLE OF BETH-ZION-BETH-ISRAEL IN PHILADELPHIA, HAS INVITED SIX MEMBERS OR GUESTS WHO ARE EITHER HOLOCAUST SURVIVORS OR CHILDREN OF SURVIVORS TO LIGHT SIX CANDLES, ONE FOR EACH MILLION JEWS, AND FOR EACH DEATH CAMP WHERE THEY PERISHED.

MR. ARNOLD SHAY, WHO HAS SET UP AN EXHIBIT IN THIS TEMPLE TO COMMEMORATE YOM-HASHOA, HAS A SHORT HISTORY OF THOSE SIX CAMPS. HE WILL READ IT TO US AS A KADISH TO THE SIX MILLION KEDOSHIM.

Yiskor; SIX MILLION JEWS...SIX DEATH CAMPS

1) CHELMNO

CHELMNO HAD THE HONOR OF BEING THE FIRST DEATH CAMP TO BE COMPLETED, IN DECEMBER OF 1941. CHELMNO WAS LOCATED 60 KILOMETERS FROM LODZ, AND THEREFORE CHOSEN TO REDUCE THE LODZ GHETTO OF ITS JEWS. ITS KILLING METHOD WAS CRUDE.

JEWS WERE PACKED INTO MOBILE GASSING VANS AND EXHAUST FUMES WERE PUMPED INSIDE THE VAN. BUT THIS METHOD WAS FOUND TO BE TOO SLOW AND NOT EFFICIENT ENOUGH FOR THE NAZIS. THE NAZIS DID NOT LIKE THAT THE GAS PRESSURE WAS IRREGULAR AND DID NOT KILL ITS VICTIMS FAST ENOUGH. SOME OF THE VICTIMS DIED IN LINGERING AGONY. BETWEEN 250,000 AND 300,000 JEWS WERE

KILLED IN CHELMNO.

2) BELZEC

BELZEC, NEAR LUBLIN, WAS THE SECOND DEATH CAMP TO BE COMPLETED. THIS WAS A DEMONSTRATION OF GERMAN EFFICIENCY.

AT THE BEGINNING, JEWS WERE HERDED INTO PERMANENT CHAMBERS, HUNDREDS AT A TIME, WHERE THEY CROUCHED NAKED IN THE COLD WITHOUT FOOD OR WATER.

THEN A TRUCK ENGINE PUMPED ITS EXHAUST INTO THE CHAMBER. THE ENGINE USED TO BREAK DOWN FROM OVERWORK AND THE VICTIMS REMAINED IN THE GAS CHAMBERS FOR HOURS UNTIL THE ENGINE WOULD BE FIXED TO WORK AGAIN.

BELZEC WAS HONORED TO BE THE FIRST CAMP SELECTED TO USE THE NEW ZYKLON-B PRUSSIC ACID FUMES, TO KILL MORE JEWS QUICKER, MORE EFFICIENTLY.

WITH THIS IMPROVEMENT, BELZEC COULD AND DID KILL OVER A HALF-MILLION JEWS IN ONLY NINE MONTHS OF OPERATION. THERE WAS ONLY ONE KNOWN SURVIVOR OF BELZEC.

3) SOBIBOR

SOBIBOR, TOO, WAS LOCATED NEAR LUBLIN AND RESERVED EXCLUSIVELY FOR JEWS, AND EXCLUSIVELY AS A KILLING CAMP. JEWS WHO WERE SENT TO SOBIBOR WERE DOOMED TO IMMEDIATE EXTERMINATION.

WOMEN AND YOUNG GIRLS WERE UNDRESSED AND HAD THEIR HAIR CUT, THEN MARCHED IN ROWS TO A ROOM MARKED "SHOWER ROOM." THEY WERE PUSHED IN WITH ONE PERSON TO A SQUARE FOOT.

THE GASSING LASTED FROM 10 TO 30 MINUTES. SOBIBOR NEVER ACHIEVED THE GREAT KILLING POWER OF OTHER DEATH CAMPS. "ONLY" A QUARTER OF A MILLION JEWS WERE KILLED IN SOBIBOR.

4) TREBLINKA

TREBLINKA WAS ORIGINALLY BUILT FOR THE PLANNED LIQUIDATION OF THE WARSAW GHETTO JEWS. BUT FOR

SOME UNKNOWN REASON IT WAS NOT READY IN TIME. NEVERTHELESS, IN ONLY TWO SHORT MONTHS, 300,000 JEWS WERE DEPORTED TO TREBLINKA.

THERE WERE DAYS WHEN AS MANY AS 10,000 JEWS LEFT THE "UMSCHLAGPLATZ" IN WARSAW AND SHIPPED TO TREBLINKA. TREBLINKA DID NOT DEPEND ON ORDINARY DIESEL ENGINES TO PUMP THEIR EXHAUST GAS INTO THE DEATH CHAMBERS.

TREBLINKA USED THE ENGINES OF CAPTURED RUSSIAN TANKS AND TRUCKS. 800,000 JEWS WERE KILLED AT TREBLINKA.

5) MAJDANEK

MAJDANEK, NEAR LUBLIN, WAS ORIGINALLY A LABOR CONCENTRATION CAMP. ALONG WITH TREBLINKA, IT WAS TRANSFORMED INTO A DEATH CAMP IN THE EARLY PART OF 1942. MAJDANEK HAD AIRTIGHT CHAMBERS DISGUISED AS ORDINARY POLISH FARMERS HUTS. THEY WERE HERMETICALLY SEALED AND THE EXHAUST GAS FROM A RUSSIAN CAPTURED U-BOAT MOTOR WAS PUMPED IN.

LATER, MAJDANEK WAS A BIT MODERNIZED, AND USED MORE EFFICIENT PRUSSIC ACID FUMES TO KILL ITS VICTIMS. MAJDANEK AND TREBLINKA HAD THE HONOR TO RECEIVE THE 31,000 JEWS FROM THE BIALYSTOK GHETTO. BUT THIS WAS ONLY A SMALL PORTION OF THE 1,380,000 JEWS THAT WERE KILLED AT MAJDANEK.

6) AUSCHWITZ

AUSCHWITZ WAS CHOSEN BY HEINRICH HIMMLER, CHIEF OF THE GESTAPO AND THE S.S., IN JUNE OF 1940 AS AN IMPORTANT DEATH CAMP, BECAUSE IT WAS EASY TO REACH BY RAIL.

IT WAS NEAR A LARGE AND DENSE JEWISH POPULATION AND BECAUSE IT WAS IN POLAND, WHERE MILLIONS OF JEWS COULD BE KILLED AND BURIED WITHOUT CONTAMINATING SOIL.

JEWS WERE SENT TO AUSCHWITZ FROM ALL OVER THE NAZI CONQUERED TERRITORIES: ITALY, FRANCE, BELGIUM, BULGARIA, NORWAY, GREECE, YUGOSLAVIA, RUMANIA,

TURKEY, HUNGARY, AND EVEN NORTH AFRICA.

AUSCHWITZ BECAME THE LARGEST DEATH CAMP THE WORLD HAS EVER KNOWN. HERE THE NAZIS PERFECTED EXTERMINATION BY ZYKLON-B GAS WHICH REDUCED ASPHYXIATION FROM 32 MINUTES (BY CARBON MONOXIDE) TO 15 MINUTES, IN NOVEMBER OF 1944.

AS THE AMERICAN ARMED FORCES CLOSED IN FROM THE WEST, AND THE SOVIET ARMY APPROACHED FROM THE EAST, HIMMLER ORDERED THE GASSING TO BE STOPPED. THOUSANDS OF JEWS WERE THEN SENT OUT OF AUSCHWITZ TO OTHER CONCENTRATION CAMPS OR LABOR CAMPS INSIDE GERMANY.

ON JANUARY 27TH, 1945, AS THE SOVIET TROOPS ENTERED AUSCHWITZ-BIRKENAU, THEY FOUND 648 DEAD INMATES, 7,000 SICK INMATES OF WHICH 180 WERE CHILDREN, AND 4,800 INMATES NEEDED IMMEDIATE ATTENTION.

THE TASK BEING MORE DIFFICULT FOR THE INMATES CAME FROM MANY PARTS OF EUROPE, USING 22 DIFFERENT LANGUAGES.

RESEARCHED AND COMPILED BY:
ARNOLD L. SHAY
YISKOR, APRIL 1986

In Memory of Six Million

Over twelve million people disappeared in the camps in Germany under the Nazi regime. I, as a Jew and an inmate of those camps, am totaling my writings IN MEMORY OF SIX MILLION.

In my studies of the period of 1933-1945 of history and documentation, of which I do have an extensive collection, I come across different documents. The one that I am submitting now is of great importance to me since it comes from the American troops that were among the ones to liberate those camps and saw the atrocities first hand.

It is a copy of a document marked "Secret" and submitted by a member of the American team to investigate the concentration camps. (I do not know the rank as a military man or otherwise of the signer of this report.)

I have made and written many studies on different concentration camps and ghettos, but almost all the information comes from German documents. This time, however, it is from the Allies.

I know that even this will be disputed by some who deny that there was a Holocaust, but this is proof beyond a shadow of a doubt of what happened in the concentration camps.

This document was written on three legal size pages marked 'SECRET' top and bottom of each page, except the last page, where the word 'SECRET' appears only on the top of the page.

I tried to keep everything the way it was originally written, with capital letters where capital letters appear and dates, names and numbers with the original spelling. Nothing was changed, altered or misinterpreted.

I do not remember where I got this document, I do get so many that it is hard to keep track. I am collecting these documents since 1945, since I was liberated by the AMERICAN TROOPS at Buchberg after we were driven there the last minute from Kaufering "Lager 11" a sub-camp of Dachau.

THESE documents are of great importance, as far as preservation of history goes. I have a lot of them and some just 'bug' your mind.

I do hope that with this and maybe other documents like this I WILL be able to make some contribution to the study of that period and shed some light as to what happened in those camps to millions of innocent people.

I know that there is not enough paper nor ink to describe the horrors and atrocities committed by the Nazis in those camps. However, I do feel that the story must be told, especially by us the survivors.

Some of the articles I have written are personal accounts, but most of them are part of the history of the Third Reich, that will leave a black silence mark of shame for the German people and the whole world that kept, for generations to come.

War-Doc
Arnold L. Shay

P.S. The whole document mentioned here is chapter nineteen.

SHLOSHIM

ACCORDING TO JEWISH TRADITION, WE MOURN AFTER THE DEAD FOR THIRTY DAYS. IT IS NOW THIRTY YEARS, AND WE STILL MOURN. WE WILL MOURN UNTIL THE LAST OF THE SURVIVORS OF THIS HORRIBLE INHUMANITY TO MAN'S FELLOW MAN, WILL PART THIS EARTH. AND THEN I BELIEVE, AND TRULY HOPE, OUR CHILDREN AND CHILDREN'S CHILDREN WILL REMEMBER AND TELL THEIR CHILDREN WHAT HAS BEFALLEN THE JEWISH PEOPLE.

MY WISH FOR OUR CHILDREN TO KNOW OUR PAST IS NOT A "LUGE," THE AUSCHWITZ LIE, OR REASONS OF HATE, BUT FOR AVOIDING A REPETITION OF THE PAST.

IT IS ONLY THIRTY YEARS, WHICH IN HISTORY IS A VERY SHORT TIME, BUT GERMANY IS CRACKING HER WHIP AGAIN. GERMAN STUDENTS WERE RIOTING THIS PAST JANUARY ON HITLER'S BIRTHDAY. A YOUNG LAWYER, MANFRED ROEDER, APPOINTED HIMSELF SPOKESMAN FOR THE RIGHT-WINGERS, AND HIS SLOGAN IS "RETURN TO THE GERMAN REICH, DOWN WITH DEMOCRACY."

WHEN INTERVIEWED, HE STATED THAT EVERY TRIAL AGAINST A GERMAN, EVEN IF HE BE GUILTY, IS A CRIME AGAINST GERMANY. WITH THE SAME SLOGANS, ROEDER AND HIS CLIQUE DEMONSTRATED IN FRANKFURT, IN FRONT OF DR. ROBERT KEMPTNER'S OFFICE. KEMPTNER HAS BEEN ASSISTANT PROSECUTOR AT THE NUREMBERG TRIALS. AT THE HIGHER SCHOOL OF LEARNING IN SALZBURG, THE STUDENTS ACCEPTED AS THEIR BIBLE A BOOKLET CALLED "DIE AUSCHWITZ LUGE," THE AUSCHWITZ LIE.

ROEDER WROTE A LETTER TO OTTO ROSEN, THE AUSTRIAN MINISTER OF THE INTERIOR, AFTER HE WAS EVICTED FROM AUSTRIA FOR ANTISEMITIC PROPAGANDA… "YOU ARE A COLONIAL SPOKESMEN FOR THE ZIONISTS INTERESTS, AND ONE DAY YOU WILL STAND TRIAL BEFORE OUR TRIBUNALS AS A COLLABORATOR WITH OUR ENEMIES."

FOR THE COMMEMORATION OF HITLER'S TAKEOVER OF POWER, THE "BUND NATIONALDEMOKRATISCHER STUDENTEN" DISPENSED ANTISEMITIC LEAFLETS STATING THAT THE

JEWS BETTER REALIZE THAT THERE ARE GERMANS AGAIN.

THE TRIALS NOW GOING ON IN GERMANY AND AUSTRIA AGAINST WAR CRIMINALS, ARE A MOCKERY OF JUSTICE, WITH THE DEFENDANTS TELLING BLATANT LIES. ONE EXAMPLE IS, THE TRIAL OF DR. LUDWIG HAHN, THE CHIEF OF THE SD IN WARSAW DURING THE LIQUIDATION OF THE GHETTO, THE ONE WHO TOOK CARE OF THE TRANSPORTATION OF THE JEWS TO TREBLINKA. HE HAD THE AUDACITY TO TELL THE PROSECUTOR THAT HE NEVER KNEW THE JEWS WERE BEING EXTERMINATED.

WHEN HE WAS TOLD BY THE PROSECUTOR THAT IT IS KNOWN THAT HIMMLER WAS THERE TO GET THE REPORT, HE TOLD THE PROSECUTOR THAT HE WAS THERE TO PLAY PING-PONG WITH HIM. WITH ALL THESE TRIALS, THE COURTS ARE SO LENIENT THAT IT IS ONLY A SHOW.

CAN WE FORGIVE OR FORGET??

NEVER!!

WRITTEN AND READ BY:
ARNOLD L. SHAY
1975

June 11, 1984

AN ODE TO ANN FRANK

'HAPPY BIRTHDAY' DEAR ANN, I WISH I COULD SAY
TO YOU, DEAR FRIEND, ON THIS MEMORABLE DAY.
THROUGHOUT THE WORLD YOU ARE REVERED NOW,
TO YOUR COURAGE AND STRENGTH, OUR HEADS
WE DO BOW.
YOU SHOWED US HOW TO LIVE, HOPE AND HAVE FAITH,
NEVER TO SURRENDER TO MAN'S BRUTAL WAYS.
WHEN ELDERS GAVE UP HOPE, YOU LAUGHED AND JOKED,
FOR YOU KNEW YOU WERE OUR ONLY HOPE.
ALTHOUGH YOU NO LONGER CAN HEAR OUR PRAYERS,
WE WILL NEVER FORGET YOU AND THE CHILDREN
WHO CARED.
TO US YOU ARE THE CHILDREN LOST,
YOU ARE MORE THAN A SYMBOL, YOU ARE A CAUSE.
SO HAPPY BIRTHDAY, DEAR ANN, WHERE EVER YOU ARE,
YOU WILL ALWAYS BE OUR SHINING STAR.

ARNOLD SHAY
SURVIVOR 135584

In May of 1984, Arnold Shay was commissioned to write an "Ode to Ann Frank," to commemorate her birthday.

That birthday was observed in the Chambers of Mayor Goode on June 11, 1984 by special proclamation of the Mayor of the City of Philadelphia. The reading of the "Ode" by Arnold Shay was attended by representatives of all major organizations and religions as well as students from different schools.

YIM ESHKACH

WHENEVER WE FIND OURSELVES IN A SITUATION OF MORAL CONFLICT MUST CHOOSE A COURSE OF ACTION. AS A BYSTANDER, EITHER WE LOOK AWAY OR WE GET INVOLVED.

EVERYONE WHO WAS TOUCHED BY THE NAZIS IN A PARTICULAR WAY HAD TO MAKE A CHOICE.

COOPERATE, LOOK AWAY OR RESIST. I CHOSE TO RESIST. HOWEVER, IF WE SHOULD FORGET OR LET ANYONE ELSE FORGET ABOUT THE SIX MILLION JEWS MURDERED IN COLD BLOOD FOR ONE AND ONLY REASON THAT THEY WERE BORN JEWISH.

THEN WE THE SURVIVORS, COMMITTED A BIGGER CRIME THAN THE ONES THAT PERPETRATED IT.

I CANNOT HELP BUT QUOTE THE BIBLE AND THE GREATEST ZIONIST LEADER THEODORE HERZL WHEN HE SAID "YIM ESHKACH YERUSHALAIM, TISHKACH YEMINI"…IF I FORGET THE O YERUSALEM, MAY MY RIGHT HAND FORGET ITS CUNNING.

I HOWEVER WANT TO CHANGE SOME WORDS IN THAT PROMISE, I SAY, YIM ESHKACH HAGERMANIM, TISHKACH YEMINI, IF I FORGET THE GERMAN CRIMES, MAY MY RIGHT HAND FORGET ITS CUNNING.

IT IS NOT EASY FOR ME AS A SURVIVOR OF FOUR OF THE MOST NOTORIOUS CONCENTRATION CAMPS TO SPEAK ON THIS SUBJECT, BUT I MADE MYSELF A PROMISE, NEVER TO FORGET MY BRETHREN THAT WERE SLAUGHTERED FOR THE SANCTIFICATION OF OUR NAME.

AT THE SAME TIME I CANNOT FORGET AND WILL NOT FORGET THE SIX MILLION OTHER NATIONALS THAT WERE MURDERED BY THE NAZIS.

IT DOES NOT MATTER IF I AM RELIGIOUS OR NOT, BUT I DO BELIEVE THAT ONE DAY I WILL MEET THOSE PEOPLE WHO DIED IN THE CAMPS AND I DO BELIEVE IN "DIN VECHESHBON" ACCOUNTABILITY, AND WHEN THEY WILL ASK ME WHAT I DID TO REMEMBER THEIR NAMES, WHILE I SURVIVED, I WANT TO HAVE THE ANSWER. I NEVER FORGOT THEM.

I WAS 17 YEARS OLD WHEN THE GERMANS MARCHED INTO

MY NATIVE TOWN OF BENDZIN IN POLAND. WHAT FOLLOWED FOR ME PERSONALLY IS TOO MUCH AND TOO PAINFUL TO RECOLLECT.

I WAS LOCKED INTO THE GHETTO, ESCAPED TO THE ARYAN SIDE WITH FALSE PAPERS, WAS CAUGHT A FEW TIMES AND FINALLY SENT TO AUSCHWITZ, THEN ORANIENBURG, SACHSENHAUSEN AND DACHAU, SURVIVED ALL THESE INHUMANE YEARS.

IN AUSCHWITZ I WORKED CLOSELY WITH THE UNDERGROUND, CONTINUING THE WORK I HAVE DONE BEFORE I WAS BROUGHT TO THE CAMP. I, TOO, WAS A VICTIM OF THE EXPERIMENTS IN AUSCHWITZ, AND YET I HAVE NEVER LOST HOPE.

I ALWAYS TRIED TO KEEP MY DIGNITY AS A HUMAN BEING AND THAT IS WHY I AM HERE TO TELL YOU IN SHORT OF WHAT HAPPENED IN THOSE YEARS.

JUST AS OTHERS HELPED ME TO SURVIVE, I, TOO, TRIED TO HELP MEN AND WOMEN SURVIVE THE WORST ATROCITIES OF THE NAZIS.

I HAVE READ ABOUT EVERYTHING THAT HAS BEEN WRITTEN ON THE HOLOCAUST, BUT I HAVE YET TO DISCOVER A BOOK WHICH DISCUSSES THIS ASPECT OF HUMAN DIGNITY THAT EXISTED EVEN IN THE CAMPS.

YOU CANNOT IMAGINE HOW VERY CRITICAL THIS DIGNITY WAS TO OUR SURVIVAL.

PROGRAMS LIKE THIS ONE ON THE HOLOCAUST SHOULD TAKE PLACE EVERYWHERE IN THE FREE WORLD. WE MUST INFLUENCE THE GERMAN GOVERNMENT TO EXTEND THE STATUTE OF LIMITATION, BECAUSE WE KNOW THAT THERE ARE THOUSANDS OF NAZI MURDERERS WHO HAVE NOT YET BEEN BROUGHT TO JUSTICE.

EVEN IF THEY CANNOT BE FOUND, LET THEM LIVE IN ALWAYS WITH THE FEAR THAT THEY MIGHT BE BROUGHT TO JUSTICE. I, TOO, STILL HAVE SLEEPLESS NIGHTS RELIVING THE TERROR OF THESE YEARS.

COMPILED AND READ BY:
ARNOLD L. SHAY

1987 YISKOR IN TEMPLE BETH SHALOM OF
COCONUT CREEK, FLORIDA.

CONCENTRATION CAMP AND GHETTO MAIL 1933-1945

CONCENTRATION CAMPS CAME INTO BEING DURING HITLER'S FIRST YEAR IN POWER 1933. BY THE END OF THAT YEAR THERE WERE SOME FIFTY OF THE CAMPS. MAINLY SET UP FOR THE STORM TROOPERS TO GIVE THEIR VICTIMS A GOOD BEATING AND THEN RANSOM THEM TO THEIR RELATIVES OR FRIENDS FOR AS MUCH AS THE TRAFFIC WOULD BEAR. IT WAS LARGELY A CRUDE FORM OF BLACKMAIL. SOMETIMES, HOWEVER, AND VERY OFTEN, THE PRISONERS WERE MURDERED, USUALLY OUT OF PURE SADISM AND BRUTALITY.

SHORTLY AFTER 1933, HITLER TURNED THE CONCENTRATION CAMPS OVER TO THE CONTROL OF THE S.S., WHICH PROCEEDED TO ORGANIZE THEM WITH THE EFFICIENCY AND RUTHLESSNESS EXPECTED OF THE ELITE CORPS. GUARD DUTY WAS GIVEN EXCLUSIVELY TO THE DEATH-HEAD UNITS, WHOSE MEMBERS WERE RECRUITED FROM THE TOUGHEST NAZI-ELEMENT, WHO HAD TO SERVE AN ENLISTMENT OF TWELVE YEARS (IT'S ODD BECAUSE THAT'S HOW LONG THE THIRD REICH LASTED), AND WORE THE SO VERY FAMILIAR TO US THE SCULL- AND- BONE INSIGNIA ON THEIR BLACK TUNICS AND HATS.

THE COMMANDER OF THE FIRST DEATH-HEAD DETACHMENT AND THE FIRST COMMANDER OF THE DACHAU CONCENTRATION CAMP WAS THEODORE EIKE WHOM HITLER HAD RELEASED FROM JAIL JUST FOR THAT PURPOSE. LATER ON EICKE WAS PUT IN CHARGE OF ALL THE CONCENTRATION CAMPS IN GERMANY.

THE SMALLER CONCENTRATION CAMPS WERE LATER CLOSED DOWN, AND THE LARGER ONES WERE EXPENDED, THE MAIN ONES. THE MAIN ONES THEN WERE DACHAU NEAR MUNICH, BUCHENWALD IN WEIMAR, SACHSENHAUSEN WHICH BECAME THE MAIN CAMP TO ORANIENBURG OF INITIAL FAME, NEAR BERLIN, RAVENSBRUCK IN MECLENBURG FOR WOMAN AND AFTER THE OCCUPATION OF AUSTRIA IN 1938 MAUTHAUSEN NEAR LINZ.

WITH THE OCCUPATION OF POLAND IN 1939, NAMES LIKE AUSCHWITZ, BELZEC, TREBLINKA, MAJDANEK, SOBIBOR AND CHELMNO, RUN CHILLS DOWN YOUR SPINE. AND WHO CAN FORGET THE GHETTOS OF WARSAW, LODZ (WHICH WAS RENAMED BY THE GERMANS LITZMANNSTADT) LUBLIN, BENDZIN (RENAMED BY THE GERMANS BENDSBURG) KRAKOW AND SO MANY, MANY OTHER GHETTOS IN POLAND. AND THE ENTIRE TOWN OF THERESIENSTADT IN CZECHOSLOVAKIA WERE TO BECOME ALL TOO FAMILIAR TO MOST OF THE WORLD.

THE CRIMES COMMITTED IN THESE CAMPS AND GHETTOS NEED NOT BE RECOUNTED IN THIS SHORT HISTORY, THEY WERE RETOLD IN THE CELEBRATED EICHMANN TRIALS OF 1961 IN ALL TOO VIVID DETAILS.

BUT, "LEST WE FORGET," SOME NUMISMATIC AND PHILATELIC ITEMS AS WELL AS NAZI MEMORABILIA FOLLOWS TO BE SHOWN BY THIS COLLECTOR (ARNOLD SHAY OF WYNNEWOOD, PA) AS A REMINDER OF THE ATROCITIES COMMITTED BY THE NAZIS.

WE SHALL NEVER FORGET, NOR CAN WE FORGIVE.

THIS WAS READ BY ARNOLD SHAY AS A KADISH TO THE SIX MILLION JEWS WHO PERISHED BY THE HANDS OF THE NAZIS IN WORLD WAR II. AT THE OPENING OF THE STAMP EXHIBITION OF THE "SOCIETY OF ISRAEL PHILATELISTS" IN 1963 IN PHILADELPHIA.

THE NEW HAVEN JEWISH FEDERATION AND THE JEWISH COMMUNITY CENTER ARE GRATEFUL TO MR. ARNOLD SHAY FOR MAKING THIS EXHIBIT AVAILABLE TO US.

MR. ARNOLD SHAY OF PHILADELPHIA HAS DEVOTED THE LAST THIRTY YEARS TOWARDS COLLECTING HOLOCAUST MEMORABILIA.

HE HAS MADE HIS EXHIBIT AVAILABLE AS A PUBLIC SERVICE IN DOZENS OF COMMUNITIES AS A TEACHING AID ABOUT THE HOLOCAUST.

HE, HIMSELF, IS A SURVIVOR OF THE WORST CONCENTRATION CAMPS, LIKE AUSCHWITZ, ORANIENBURG, SACHSENHAUSEN AND DACHAU.

THE FOLLOWING IS A FACT SHEET COMPILED BY MR. ARNOLD SHAY IN 1979 FOR THIS EXHIBIT.

HITLER OFTEN SAID THAT THE GERMAN REICH WHICH HE FOUNDED WOULD LAST FOR A THOUSAND YEARS. IT IS ASTONISHING THAT IT SHOULD HAVE LASTED FOR AS MANY AS TWELVE YEARS.

BUT, ITS INFAMY WILL LIVE AS LONG AS HISTORY ITSELF, FOR IN THE TERRIBLE RECORD OF HUMAN CRIMES, THE DEEDS OF HITLER AND HIS ACCOMPLICES SURELY SURPASSES ALL OTHERS IN THEIR ENORMITY.

NO STATISTIC CAN MEASURE THE PHYSICAL SUFFERING AND MENTAL ANGUISH THAT THE NAZIS CAUSED IN JUST TWELVE YEARS.

THE BRUNT OF THE HITLER CRIMES FELL CHIEFLY ON EUROPEAN JEWRY.

OVER SIX MILLION JEWS DIED DURING THIS BRIEF PERIOD; THEIR ONLY CRIMES WAS THEIR JEWISHNESS.

THIS WAS A WAR AGAINST THE JEWS. AND THE GERMANS USED THE MOST MODERN, SCIENTIFIC METHODS TO DO THEIR DARK DEEDS. OVER ONE MILLION JEWISH CHILDREN UNDER THE AGE OF TWELVE WERE SLAUGHTERED.

FROM THE VERY MOMENT THAT THE NAZIS TOOK POWER IN 1933, THEY CREATED A NETWORK OF CONCENTRATION CAMPS. THE FIRST WAS DACHAU AND WAS FOLLOWED BY MANY, MANY OTHERS.

THE FIRST INMATES OF THESE CONCENTRATION WERE NOT JEWS, BUT ANTI-NAZIS, MASONS AND POLITICAL OPPONENTS OF THE NAZI REGIME. THESE WERE FOLLOWED BY A NETWORK OF LABOR CAMPS, WHICH USED FORCED LABOR. THESE FORCED LABOR CAMPS WERE CREATED WITH THE OCCUPATION OF POLAND RIGHT AFTER THE OUTBREAK OF THE WAR. (1939 UP).

WHEN NAZI GERMANY INVADED AND CONQUERED MOST OF EUROPE, THE FINAL STAGES WERE DEATH CAMPS, A KIND OF CONCENTRATION CAMPS CREATED SOLELY FOR THE PURPOSE OF DESTROYING THE JEWS.

IN EASTERN EUROPE, WHERE THE LARGEST NUMBER OF

JEWS LIVED, THEY WERE FORCED TO LIVE IN GHETTOS, UNDER THE MOST HORRIBLE, INHUMANE CONDITIONS, WHICH WAS THE FIRST STEP TOWARDS THEIR SUBSEQUENT DEPORTATION TO THE DEATH CAMPS.

THE LARGEST AND MOST INFAMOUS DEATH CAMP WAS AUSCHWITZ, WHICH TOGETHER WITH OTHER EXTERMINATION CAMPS, WAS ESTABLISHED IN POLAND.

IN AUSCHWITZ, THE GERMANS USED GAS CHAMBERS AND CREMATORIUMS TO DESTROY THOUSANDS OF JEWS DAILY.

ALONG WITH THE JEWS, GYPSIES WERE ALSO MURDERED AS WELL NUMEROUS OTHER NATIONALITIES.

OTHER DEATH CAMPS, WERE TREBLINKA, SOBIBOR, CHELMNO, MAJDANEIC AND BELZEC.

AFTER OCCUPYING SOME OF THE SOVIET TERRITORY, THE NAZIS USED S.S. COMMANDOS TO SLAUGHTER JEWS IN MASS GRAVES.

MANY JEWS DIED IN LABOR CAMPS FROM STARVATION, OVERWORK AND PRIVATION.

OTHER ETHNIC GROUPS WERE ALSO PERSECUTED, NOT TO THE EXTENT OF THE JEWS BUT PERSECUTED. THOUSANDS OF POLES DIED DUE TO THE TERRIBLE WORKING CONDITIONS.

THE NAZIS ALSO MURDERED THOUSANDS OF SOVIET PRISONERS OF WAR.

THE NAZIS DID NOT FEEL A RESPONSIBILITY TO THE SOVIET PRISONERS OF WAR BECAUSE THE SOVIET UNION WAS NOT A PART OF "THE INTERNATIONAL GENEVA CONVENTION FOR THE RIGHTS OF PRISONERS OF WAR." (NOT THAT IT BOTHERED THEM TOO MUCH TO KILL AMERICAN OR ENGLISH P.O.W'S).

IT IS ESTIMATED THAT CLOSE TO SIX MILLIONS OF NON-JEWS WERE ALSO MURDERED IN THE DEATH CAMPS, CONCENTRATION CAMPS AND SLAVE LABOR CAMPS.

THESE INCLUDED: POLES, RUSSIANS, GREEKS AND SO MANY OTHERS. IT IS RECORDED THAT AUSCHWITZ ALONE HAD MORE THAN 27 DIFFERENT NATIONALITIES AS PRISONERS.

THE GERMAN NAZI GOVERNMENT SUCCEEDED IN ESTABLISHING A NETWORK OF CAMPS, OF WHICH THE PURPOSE WAS TO TERRORIZE THEIR OPPONENTS AND SUBSEQUENTLY TO DESTROY THE JEWS.

THEY STOPPED AT NOTHING TO ACHIEVE THEIR PURPOSE. SIX MILLION JEWS AND CLOSE TO SIX MILLION OTHER NATIONALITIES DIED IN THESE CAMPS.

AFTER THE LIBERATION OF THE CAMPS, MANY THOUSANDS OF PRISONERS CONTINUED TO DIE BECAUSE OF DISEASE AND THEIR WEAKENED CONDITION.

THE AMERICAN, BRITISH AND RUSSIAN MILITARY AUTHORITIES SENT IN TO GERMANY TEAMS OF PHYSICIANS AND NURSES TO HELP THESE UNFORTUNATE FORMER PRISONERS.

DESPITE THEIR EFFORTS, IT IS ESTIMATED THAT SOME 100,000 VICTIMS WHO LIVED TO SEE THEIR LIBERATION DIED BECAUSE OF THEIR WEAKENED CONDITION.

NOTE:

THIS SHEET OF INFORMATION WAS HANDED OUT TO ALL VISITORS TO THE ARNOLD SHAY EXHIBIT.

NEW HAVEN 1979.

Chapter Eighteen

When Jewish blood spurts
From the knife. Then things go twice as well

From the Horst Wessel Song.
A Nazi Anthem

To the city of my youth, Bendzin

Compiled by Abram Blat, Israel

Translated into English by Arnold L. Shay, U.S.A

GOD REMEMBER THE LIGHT SOULS
THAT WONDER DISTRAUGHT
LIKE IN DESERT ROADS.
THAT WERE LEAD IN DISMAY
TO POLISH CAMPS AND LATVIAN TRAPS.
 GOD REMEMBER THE NIGHTS FILLED WITH NIGHTMARES
 EYES LIKE TUNNELS AND HEARTS LIKE RAVINES
 SOULS LIKE VERBS AND BUNDLES OF BONES
 LEFT IS NO ONE, LEFT IS NO ONE.
GOD DO REMEMBER THE CRIES OF THE CHILDREN
AND THEIR PRESSED ARMS SEEKING THE BREASTS
LIKE WONDERS IN THE DESERT, THE LOGGED, THE LOGGED
IN THE DARKNESS OF THE WOODS ON SLAVIC COASTS.
 ISKOR! THE SON IS SHOWING IN THE EARLY MORNING
 ON THE GRASS ON THE STONES ON THE DESTRUCTION OF HOMES.
 (AND IT IS STILL BLOSSOMING THE FRONTS IN OUR HOMES.)
 ON THE WALL THE CRADLED SHADOW AND MOSS HUGS THE STONES.
ISKOR! MAY MY PRAYER REACH THE HAVENS
MY PRAYER FOR EVERYONE MY PLEA FOR ALL
IN MEMORY OF MY GRANDFATHER, THAT WAS PUT TO SHAME
WITH JOY ON THEIR LIPS CARRIED THEM THEIR PAIN.
 ISKOR! DRIED ARE THE SOCKETS OF TEARS
 OUR HEARTS ARE FLEECING, LIKE CUTS FROM THE WIND
 (THEY WENT IN ROWS JUST LIKE SHEEP
 TOGETHER THE FATHER, THE MOTHER, THE CHILD.)
GOD. PLEASE REMEMBER THE LIGHTHEARTED SOULS
THAT ARE SEEKING THEIR PEACE IN YOUR BRIGHT KINGDOM

THAT HOLLOWED YOUR NAME EVEN TO THEIR LAST
ON THE WALL OF SACRIFICE, IN THE CHAMBERS OF GAS.
THE BELLS OF AUTUMN HAVE ALREADY RUNG
THE TORCHES ARE LIT SO FREE AND COLORFUL
IN OUR HOMES WITH US ARE STILL THE MEMORIES
WHERE HAVE YOU DISAPPEARED ? OH GOD MY LORD.

THE SONG OF BENDZIN

BY: A.W. WERTHEIM, ISRAEL
TRANSLATED INTO ENGLISH BY: ARNOLD L. SHAY, U.S.A.

OH BENDZIN! THE CITY OF MY YOUTH,
THE CRADLE OF MY DREAMS.
HOW FAR ARE YOU AWAY FROM US,
LIKE INTO A FOG HAVE YOU DISAPPEARED
EVERY CORNER WITHIN YOU — IS A NEST OF MEMORIES
THAT TORTURES AND CARESSES SO DEEP,
LIKE A LOVING WIND.

I SAW YOU IN YOUR ADORING FULLNESS,
YOU SHONE ALL AROUND
A CITY FULL OF SCHOOLS AND SO RICH WITH LIBRARIES
YOUR OLD, SO WELL KNOWN WHITE CASTLE
AND THE PRZEMSZA RIVER
CAPTURED SILENTLY HAVE THEY MY HEART,
I CAN SEE THEM EVEN NOW.

WHERE ARE YOU TREASURED CHILDREN,
FROM SCHOOLS AND FROM CHEDER
IN HER LOVE OF LIFE,
BOYS FROM THE ROOMS OF WORK?
HOW MUCH PAIN HAVE YOU ENDURED, IN HUNGER OF MARTYRDOM?
DID NOT YOUR MOTHERS EYES SHED TEARS OVER YOU
THAT FELL ON YOUR GRAVE

MY FIRST BREATH OF AIR, HAD I IN YOUR STREETS, SO LOVELY
IN RAB MOISHE THE BATLEN' CHEDER AT THE BELLY OF THE GREENS
SUMMER, WINTER, AT THE NIGHTFALL LIGHT AND DREARE
THE FIRST LEAFS OF MY LIFE I HAVE WEAVED THERE AND SPINNED.

PAINFUL MEMORIES OF THE OLD MARKET NUMB,
DESERTED ARE THE STREETS
NOT EVEN A MARK OF A JEWISH CHILD IS THERE LEFT
STREETS, DIRT ROADS FROM MY CITY,
LISTEN TO MY QUESTION THAT I ASK YOU MY LITTLE SHEEP,
TO WHERE HAVE THEY BEEN BANISHED?

DID NOT THE "ASHMEDAI" WILDLY CHASE THEM FOR THE SACRIFICE
IN AUSCHWITZ CITY OF PAIN,
IN MAJDANEK ON THE SACRIFICIAL ALTER.
WHERE THE AIR IS FULL HUMAN-BURNING-STAIL STENCH —
IN THE DRY HOLES,
AND SPRINGS FROM THE GRAND CHILDREN AND GRANDFATHERS.

WHAT CADDLES IN THE DARKNESS THE SYNAGOGUE STREET NOW AT NIGHT?
IN THE OLD "BETH HAMEDROSH" WHERE THE VOICES ARE NOW STILL?
IN HOW MANY DESERTED PILES ARE THE HOLY ASHES OF YOU PEOPLE BURNING?
THE SHADOW HAS WITH AN ANGRY JOY ALL OF THEM DESTROYED.

OH BENDZIN THE CITY OF MY CHILDHOOD,
THE CRADLE OF MY DREAMS
HOW FAR HAVE YOU GONE FROM US,
LIKE IN A FOG SO DEEP DISAPPEARED
EVERY CORNER WITHIN YOU, A NEST FULL OF MEMORIES
THAT TORTURE AND CORRESS SO DEEP LIKE A LOVING WIND

"OHN A HEIM"

THIS POEM IN YIDSH, WHICH LATER BECAME THE SONG OF THE BENDZIN GHETTO, WAS WRITTEN BY AN UNKNOWN IN THE BENDZIN GHETTO ON AUGUST 12, 1942, WHEN THE "MAIN RESETTLEMENT" TOOK PLACE, AND WHEN MOST OF THE JEWS OF BENDZIN WERE SENT TO AUSCHWITZ, WHERE THE WHOLE "TRANSPORT" WENT STRAIGHT TO THE GAS CHAMBERS. "MY MOTHER WAS IN THAT TRANSPORT."

THIS POEM WAS TRANSLATED FROM
YIDDISH INTO ENGLISH BY: ARNOLD L. SHAY.

WITHOUT A HOME, AND WITHOUT A ROOF —
WANDERING WERE WE ALL THROUGH THE NIGHT
NOT KNOWING WHERE
NOR WHAT WILL BE OUR ZEEL.
AT THE "PUNKT" WE WERE ALL CHASED
AND SURROUNDED WITH A CHAIN OF POLICE AND S.S.
HOW MUCH LONGER WILL OUR PAIN LAST?
THIS HELL. WORST IT CANNOT BE.
REFRAIN; WITHOUT A HOME AND WITHOUT A ROOF

NO BREAD, NO WATER DID WE GET
WE WERE HELD THERE A DAY AND A NIGHT
THE CHILDREN WERE TORN FROM THEIR MOTHERS
AND SOMEWHERE DRAGGED AWAY.
REFRAIN; WITHOUT A HOME AND WITHOUT A ROOF

WE ARE CHASED, WE ARE PLAGUED
WE ARE EXHAUSTED
AND THAT'S HOW THEY DRAIN OUR BLOOD
OY, OY THE BLOOD, OY OY THE BLOOD.
REFRAIN: WITHOUT A HOME AND WITHOUT A ROOF.

TO THE GATHERING "PUNKT" WE WERE CHASED
AND LIKE SHEEP WE WERE PICKED
AND FROM OUR PARENTS WE WERE TORN
AND OUR YOUNG ONES TO THE CAMP WERE CHASED.

REFRAIN: WITHOUT A HOME, AND WITHOUT A ROOF,
WANDERING WERE WE, ALL THROUGH THE NIGHT
NOT KNOWING WHERE
NOR WHAT WILL BE OUR ZEEL.

Chapter Nineteen

"All through time the victor wrote history. During Hitler's reign the vanquished made and wrote history. If it was not for the Germans, that documented their heinous deeds, the world would have never known all the horrors the Third Reich inflicted on their innocent victims."

Arnold L. Shay

TREES

SO MANY TREES
I HAVE COUNTED THEM
SMALL ONES, TALL ONES
NARROW ONES, WIDE ONES,
YOUNG ONES, OLD ONES,
THEY ARE ALL THE SAME,
THEIR SHRIVELED LEAVES
ARE TURNED TO DUST
THEIR BRANCHES, BLANCHED AND TWISTED
IN THE COLD WINTER'S NIGHT HANG NAKED.
YET, THEY LIVE
I KNOW
FOR I AM ONE OF THEM.
THIS MORNING WHEN THE S.S. MAN SAID "ANTRETEN"
THEY STOOD AT ATTENTION
AND FORMED INTO LINES
BUT THEY COULD NOT STAND ERECT,
THEY DO NOT LOOK
LIKE THE TREES I USED TO KNOW
THEY ARE DIFFERENT NOW
WITH VACANT EYES RECESSED IN DEEP SOCKETS
THEY LOOK AWAY AND DO NOT SEE ME NOW.
ARE THEY AFRAID TO LOOK AT ME,
BECAUSE I LOOK LIKE THEM?
NO LEAVES, NO BARK, NO ROOTS,
YET, WE STILL REMEMBER HOW IT USED TO BE.
BUT THIS IS OUR HOME NOW —
HOME?
HA!
THESE BARRACKS IN AUSCHWITZ
WHERE HORSES ARE SUPPOSED TO BE —
IS THIS OUR HOME?
WE, WHO LIVE, BELONG IN THE FOREST
WHERE WE MAY GROW

AND KNOW FREEDOM
AND FORM NEW LEAVES
AND GROW NEW BARK.
SILENTLY WE TALK, WITH OUR EYES
WE SEE AND WE KNOW.
WE DO NOT OPEN OUR MOUTHS.
OUR BRAINS TALK
THEY SAY, THERE WILL BE SUN ONE DAY
NO MORE SMOKE TO OBSCURE THE RAYS
THERE WILL BE FRESH AIR
AND FREEDOM
AND WE WILL PLAY AGAIN IN THE WOODS.
BUT WHEN? WHEN?
WILL IT COME TOO LATE
WHEN THE SMOKE ABAITS?
AND WE SHALL ALL BE CONSUMED?
THERE ARE MANY TREES IN THE WORLD
THEY ARE FREE TO BEND WITH THE WIND AND REACH TO THE SKY —
FREE TO LIVE AND PRODUCE
TO HAVE PARTNERS AND CARE FOR EACH OTHER.
WE HAVE GUARDS TO WATCH US
TO WATCH WHAT WE EAT
WHEN WE EAT
GUARDS TO WATCH THAT WE DO NOT EAT
WE TALK
WE TALK IN WORDS OF OUR OWN
TALK OF THE WOODS IN NEIGHBORING PLACES
WHERE TREES ARE ALLOWED TO GROW FREE
WHERE TREES CAN GROW AS GOD HAS GIVEN THEM THE RIGHT TO GROW
OH GOD!
DO YOU NOT SEE US?
DO YOU NOT HEAR US — OUR PRAYERS?
WHERE IS YOUR MERCY?
YOUR COMPASSION?
ARE WE NOT YOUR CHILDREN?
DO YOU NOT LOVE ME GOD?
I WAS SO GOOD.

MY FATHER WAS SUCH A GOOD MAN
MY MOTHER WAS AN "AISHES HAYE" (A WOMAN OF VALOR)
WHY DID THE NAZIS KILL MY FATHER?
THEY KILLED HIM ON HIS OWN BED
MY MOTHER AND I HAD TO LOOK ON.
WHY GOD DID THEY TAKE MY MOTHER TO AUSCHWITZ?
SEE THOSE CHIMNEYS OVER THERE —
THE TALL ONES BELCHING BILLOWS
OF STINKING BLACK SMOKE DAY AND NIGHT?
THAT IS WHERE MY MOTHER WAS SHOVED IN.
THOSE BODIES BURNING IN THE HELL OF AUSCHWITZ
ARE OUR MOTHERS, FATHERS, SISTERS AND BROTHERS
I CAN SEE THEM
IN THE STENCH OF THAT TERRIBLE SMOKE
THEY ARE GOING TO HEAVEN
BUT WHY NOW GOD?
SHLOIMELE IS ONLY TWO YEARS OLD
SURELE IS ONLY FIVE
KIVELE IS EIGHT.
THEY HAVE NOT BEGUN TO LIVE.
WHY DEAR GOD? WHY?
HOW CAN I TRUST IN YOU?
WHEN YOU HAVE DISAPPOINTED ME?
WHEN MY HEART HURTS ME SO.
CAN YOU SEE THOSE HAZY BODIES?
OH! THOUSANDS OF THEM, MORE
I CAN SEE THEM
THE DOCTORS, THE LAWYERS, THE SCIENTISTS,
THE RABBIS, THE WRITERS, THE TAILORS,
THE PHILOSOPHERS, THE SHOEMAKERS
I SEE MEN AND WOMEN NOT BORN YET
A FOREST RAVAGED
THEY COULD HAVE MADE A BETTER WORLD.
A BETTER PLACE TO LIVE IN
BUT WHO DESTROYED IT?
NOT ONE MAN ALONE.
BUT MEN WITH PHd's
MEN OF SCIENCE
MEN WHO ARE SUPPOSED TO KNOW HOW PRECIOUS LIFE IS

MEN WHO WERE SUPPOSED TO TEACH THE WORLD HOW TO BEHAVE.
WE THE TREES IN THE FOREST AUSCHWITZ
WHO CANNOT GROW
WE ARE NOT ALLOWED TO THINK
WE ARE THE LIVING DEAD,
WHY DEAR GOD DO YOU LET IT HAPPEN TO YOUR CHOSEN TREES?
THE TREES YOU PROMISED TO MULTIPLY LIKE SAND ON EARTH.
WE ARE NOT EVEN GOOD TREES
THEY USE GASOLINE TO MAKE US BURN.
I REMEMBER WHEN WE USED TO LAUGH
TO CRY, TO THINK, TO DANCE
GOD, WHY DID YOU LET THEM DO THIS TO US?
WHY GOD, DID YOU LET THEM BURN ALL THOSE BEAUTIFUL TREES?
I WANT TO CRY…I HAVE NO TEARS
I WANT TO LAUGH…I FORGOT HOW
I WANT TO SING…I HAVE NO VOICE.
I WANT TO DANCE…I HAVE NO STRENGTH
WILL THEY LET ME LIVE, WILL THEY LET ME GROW?
WILL I EVER HAVE A CHANCE TO BE IN MY WOODS AGAIN?
AND WATCH OTHERS PLAY?
I DO NOT KNOW
WILL ANYONE TRY TO STOP THE SLAUGHTER?
THEY HAVE CUT DOWN THE MOST BEAUTIFUL TREES.
ALL THE TREES THAT MADE THE WORLD WHAT IT IS TODAY.
THE TREES THE GAVE THE WORLD THE POWER
THE WISDOM TO CONDUCT THEMSELVES HUMANE
NOW THEY SAY THAT WE ARE DIFFERENT
MY KIND OF TREE IS DIFFERENT
AND WE ARE HATED FOR IT
WE ARE HATED FOR DOING THINGS
WE ARE HATED FOR NOT DOING THINGS
WE ARE DESPISED IF WE JOIN WITH OTHERS
WE ARE DESPISED IF WE DO NOT JOIN OTHERS
SO WHY DEAR GOD HAVE YOU CHOSEN US?
FOR WHAT? TO SUFFER?

WILL THE WORLD EVER CHANGE?
WILL TREES EVER STOP CUTTING DOWN OTHER TREES?
WILL THE FOREST EVER KNOW WHAT WAS DONE TO IT
AND TO HER MOST PRECIOUS TREES?
NOW FORTY YEARS LATER I AM TELLING THEM...
THAT THIS DID HAPPEN
I WILL KEEP ON TELLING AS LONG AS I CAN THINK
AS LONG AS I HAVE STRENGTH.
I HAVE TO
ALL THOSE TREES THAT WERE CUT DOWN ARE NOT HERE
I HAVE TO REPRESENT THEM
PLEASE HELP ME NOT TO FORGET THEM
I WILL NEVER FORGET THEM
AND YOU MUST NOT FORGET THEM EITHER.
WE OWE THEM THAT MUCH...WE OWE THEM A DEBT.

ARNOLD L. SHAY
WORCESTER, MASS.
MAY 3, 1984

I REMEMBER AUSCHWITZ

I WALKED IN THE SHADOW OF THE SMOKE
THE SMOKE THICK AND BLACK.
HOW CAN ANYONE LIVE WITH THAT STENCH
OF CHIMNEY STACKS OVER YOUR HEAD?
IN THAT JUNGLE OF TORTURE
NO FOOD, NO WATER.
WORK ONLY AND THE THREAT OF DEATH.
IN THE MORNING BEFORE DAWN
YOU'RE AWAKENED TO DO YOUR CHORES.
TO WASH-UP AND DO YOUR "DUTIES"
JUST TEN MINUTES YOU ALLOWED.
THEN ROLL CALL TO THE WILL OF YOUR MASTERS THE S.S.
YOU WORK AND SLAVE FROM DAWN TO DUSK
JUST TO STAY ALIVE.
SOMETIMES YOU ASK…IS IT ALL WORTH IT?
NOT KNOWING WHAT TOMORROW MAY BRING?
ANOTHER WIRE…ANOTHER HANGING.
YOU'RE USED TO IT…YOU CARE NO MORE.
JUST WAIT ANOTHER DAY, THEN IT IS YOUR TURN
JUST LIKE THE ONE BEFORE YOU.
SO YOU WAIT, AND WAIT,
MAYBE, JUST MAYBE
THE SUN WILL COME OUT AND WILL SHINE
YOU HOPE…YOU PRAY
WITHOUT MIND…WITHOUT STRENGTH
THAT YOUR DAY…WILL BE HERE SOON.
AND DAYS GO BY…WEEKS…MONTH
AND YEARS THAT COUNT NOW SIX
THE END MAY BE NEAR BUT YOU…CARE NO MORE
BY NOW YOUR BODY IS NUMB
YOU ENVY THE DEAD.
THEY HAVE NOW PEACE.
NO MORE WORRIES…NO MORE PAIN.
YET!!!
LIFE STILL GOES ON…WITH JUST ONE THOUGHT IN MIND
TOMORROW MAY BE BETTER, TOMORROW MAY BE THE END.

YES!!!
YOU ENVY THE GUY THAT TOOK HIS OWN LIFE,
TOMORROW IS NOT HIS ANY MORE.
YET!!!
YOU CAN NOT DO THE SAME,
JUST QUIT?...GIVE UP?
LIKE THE GUY...JUST THE ONE BEFORE?
AND THEN, THEY ARE HERE...THE ANGELS IN GREEN,
THE ONES WHO LIBERATED THE CAMPS.
AND YOU LAUGH...AND YOU CRY...AND YOU THINK.
WHAT CAN LIFE BRING NOW?
HOW CAN YOU START A NEW LIFE?
JUST FORGET OF THE LIFE BEFORE??
AGAIN QUESTIONS AND FEAR,
BUT LIFE MUST AND WILL GO ON.
AND YOU'RE NOT THE ONE TO STOP IT RIGHT HERE!
AND WE LIVE AND WE LAUGH
OUR PAIN WE STILL HIDE
THERE IS NO ONE THAT WILL OR CAN UNDERSTAND US.
WE ARE SAYING "SHEMA" DOES GOD REALLY HEAR US???
DOES GOD HEAR WHAT WE CAN NOT SAY ANY MORE???
CAN ANYONE SEE THE TEARS IN OUR HEARTS??
THE SUN NOW SHINES FOR ALL THE SAME
IT IS JUST THAT WE THE SURVIVORS
CAN SEE IT MUCH CLEARER AND BRIGHTER.
LIFE IS FOR THE LIVING
WE ARE BACK AGAIN AND WE SHALL LIVE
YES!!!!
WE SHALL LIVE.

ARNOLD L SHAY
SURVIVOR
AUSCHWITZ 135584
JULY 23, 1984

Chapter Twenty

…"There is within us some hidden power,
Mysterious and secret, which keeps us alive
Despite the natural law.
If we cannot live on what is permitted,
We live on what is forbidden…"

Chaim Kaplan wrote this
in his diary on March 10, 1940

The following three poems are included in the Jewish High Holiday services.

I took the liberty of enclosing these writings to express the feelings of all the survivors.

WHEREVER I GO...

WHEREVER I GO I HEAR FOOTSTEPS.
MY BROTHERS ON THE ROAD, IN SWAMPS, IN FORESTS,
SWEPT ALONG IN DARKNESS, TREMBLING FROM COLD,
FUGITIVES FROM FLAMES, PLAGUES AND TERRORS.
WHEREVER I STAND, I HEAR RATTLING;
MY BROTHERS IN CHAINS, IN CHAMBERS OF THE STRICKEN.
THEY PIERCE THE WALLS AND BURST THE SILENCE.
THROUGH THE GENERATIONS THEIR ECHOES CRY OUT
IN TORTURE CAMPS, IN PITS OF THE DEAD.
WHEREVER I LIE, I HEAR VOICES;
MY BROTHERS HERDED TO SLAUGHTER
OUT OF BURNING EMBERS, OUT OF RUINS,
OUT OF CITIES AND VILLAGES, ALTAR FOR BURNED OFFERINGS.
THE GROANING IN THEIR DESTRUCTION HAUNTS MY NIGHTS.
MY EYES WILL NEVER STOP SEEING THEM
AND MY HEART WILL NEVER STOP CRYING "OUTRAGE";
EVERY ONE WILL BE CALLED TO ACCOUNT FOR THEIR DEATH.
THE HEAVENS WILL DESCEND TO MOURN FOR THEM,
THE WORLD AND ALL THAT IS THEREIN WILL BE A
MONUMENT ON THEIR GRAVE.

Shin Shalom, translated by David Polish.

WE REMEMBER THE HOLOCAUST...

WE RECALL WITH BITTER GRIEF THE CATASTROPHE WHICH OVERWHELMED OUR PEOPLE IN EUROPE, ADDING AN UNPRECEDENTED CHAPTER TO OUR HISTORY OF SUFFERING.

WE MOURN FOR SIX MILLION OF OUR PEOPLE, BRUTALLY DESTROYED BY "CIVILIZED MEN" BEHAVING LIKE SAVAGES. THE CRUELTIES OF PHARAOH, HAMAN, NEBUCHADNEZZAR AND TITUS CANNOT BE COMPARED WITH THE DIABOLICAL SCHEMES OF THE MODERN TYRANTS IN THEIR DESIGN TO EXTERMINATE AN ENTIRE PEOPLE.

THE BLOOD OF THE INNOCENT WHO PERISHED IN THE GAS CHAMBERS OF AUSCHWITZ, BERGEN-BELSEN, BUCHENWALD, DACHAU, TREBLINKA, AND THERESENSTADT, CRIES OUT TO GOD AND MAN.

WE WILL NEVER FORGET THE BURNING OF SYNAGOGUES AND HOUSES OF STUDY, THE DESTRUCTION OF HOLY BOOKS AND SCROLLS OF TORAH, THE SADISTIC TORMENT AND MURDER OF SCHOLARS, SAGES, AND TEACHERS.

THEY TORTURED THE FLESH OF OUR BROTHERS AND SISTERS; BUT THEY COULD NOT CRUSH THEIR SPIRIT, THEIR FAITH, THEIR LOVE.

WE RECALL OUR BROTHERS AND SISTERS IN WARSAW GHETTO, JEWS WHO VALIANTLY DEFIED THE MONSTROUS ADVERSARIES.

AND WE RECALL THE HEROISM OF THOSE WHO, IN THE FACE OF UNPRECEDENTED AND OVERWHELMING FORCE, MAINTAINED JEWISH CULTURE AND ASSERTED JEWISH VALUES IN THE VERY MIDST OF ENSLAVEMENT AND DESTRUCTION.

LET US PRAY; O LORD, REMEMBER YOUR MARTYRED CHILDREN. REMEMBER ALL WHO HAVE GIVEN THEIR LIVES FOR THE SANCTIFICATION OF YOUR NAME.

EVEN AS WE MOURN, WE RECALL THOSE COMPASSIONATE MEN AND WOMEN OF OTHER FAITHS AND NATIONALITIES WHO, AT THE PERIL OF THEIR LIVES, SAVED SOME OF OUR PEOPLE. TRULY, "THE RIGHTEOUS OF ALL NATIONS HAVE A SHARE IN THE WORLD TO COME."

LET US PRAY AND WORK FOR THE DAY WHEN THEY SHALL

NOT LIFT UP SWORDS AGAINST NATION, NOR SHALL THEY LEARN WAR ANY MORE."

THE LETTER OF THE NINETY-THREE MAIDENS

WHEN THE NAZIS CAPTURED WARSAW, POLAND, THEY ORDERED PUPILS AND TEACHERS OF A BETH JACOB GIRL'S SCHOOL TO PREPARE THEMSELVES TO SERVE THE PLEASURES OF THE SOLDIERS. TO AVOID THIS DEFILEMENT, THE GIRLS OFFERED THEIR LAST PRAYER, TOOK POISON, AND DIED, "IN ORDER TO SANCTIFY THE NAME OF GOD BY THEIR DEATH AS WELL AS BY THEIR LIVES."

WE WASHED OUR BODIES AND WE ARE CLEAN;
WE PURIFIED OUR SOULS AND WE ARE AT PEACE.
DEATH DOES NOT TERRIFY US; WE GO OUT TO MEET IT.

WE SERVED OUR GOD WHILE WE WERE ALIVE,
AND WE SHALL KNOW HOW TO SANCTIFY HIM BY OUR DEATH.
WE MADE A COVENANT IN OUR HEARTS;
TOGETHER WE LEARNED THE TORAH AND TOGETHER WE WILL DIE.

WE READ THE PSALMS TOGETHER AND WE WERE RELIVED;
WE CONFESSED OUR SINS TOGETHER AND OUR HEARTS GREW STRONG.
NOW WE FEEL PREPARED AND READY TO DIE.

LET THE UNCLEAN COME AND DEFILE US; WE ARE NOT AFRAID.
WE WILL DRINK THE CUP OF POISON
AND PERISH IN FRONT OF THEIR EYES,
PURE AND UNDEFILED, AS BEFITS THE DAUGHTERS OF JACOB.

WE WILL COME TO MOTHER SARAH AND SAY;
HERE WE ARE!
WE MET THE TEST, THE TEST OF THE BINDING OF ISAAC!
ARISE AND PRAY WITH US FOR OUR PEOPLE ISRAEL.

O MERCIFUL FATHER, BLESS YOUR PEOPLE WITH YOUR
MERCY,
FOR THERE IS NO HUMAN MERCY.
REVEAL YOUR HIDDEN LIVING KINDNESS AND SAVE YOUR
OPPRESSED PEOPLE;
SAVE AND KEEP YOUR WORLD!

THE HOUR OF NEILAH HAS COME, AND OUR SOULS GROW
QUIET.
ONE MORE PRAYER WE UTTER;
BRETHREN, WHEREVER YOU ARE, SAY KADDISH FOR US,
FOR THE NINETY-THREE JEWISH MAIDENS.

Translated from the Hebrew of Hillel Bavli,
based on a letter by Haya Feldman,
One of the ninety-three young girls,
dated Rosh Chodesh Elul, 5704 (1944).

Chapter Twenty-one

"Thou shall teach it to thy children"
Exodus 13:8

"The sun rising over Poland-Lithuania
Will no longer find a Jew sitting by a light in the window
Saying Psalms,
Or at dawn on his way to synagogue.
Peasants with their carts will come to the town
But there will be no Jews there
To deal with them on market day…"

Yitzchak Katnelson-In
"Songs of the Slaughtered Jewish People"

This chapter I dedicate to my parents
with all my love

TO MY PARENTS WITH ALL MY LOVE

TO THE 35th ANNIVERSARY OF THE DEATH OF MY PARENTS. FATHER KILLED BY THE NAZIS ON APRIL 28th, 1942. MOTHER KILLED AT AUSCHWITZ, AUGUST 16, 1942.

YOUR BODY LIKE COAL
FOR THE FURNACE WAS USED
TO HEAT UP THE SOULS OF PAGANS
THE GERMAN SADISM AND LUST
NOT EVEN ASHES OR BONES WERE LEFT
ONLY PIECES OF SOAP OTHER BODIES TO CLEANSE
HOW FRIGHTFUL TO THINK OF THOSE HORRIBLE YEARS
WHEN PAGANISM RETURNED, AND LAUGHTER BECAME TEARS.
THE ONES WHO FAMILIES LOST
PAID THE HIGHEST OF A PRICE
BUT EVEN "MEN" OF APATHY
HAVE GIVEN A SLICE.
BECAUSE NOW ALL THOSE "MEN"
WHO STILL ARE ALIVE
HAVE TO LIVE — IF THEY CAN
AND WITH GUILT TO SURVIVE.
WHY DID NO ONE SAY
"HOW LONG CAN IT LAST"?
OR DID THEY BELIEVE
THAT THERE IS NO PAST?
NOW AS WE ALL LOOK
AT THOSE YEARS GONE BY
WE SHUDDER AT THE THOUGHT
WE EVEN SOMETIMES DO CRY

WHY IS HUMANITY
SO SOUGHTLESS — WITHOUT COMPASSION?
IS IT REALLY ALWAYS THE OTHER GUY
WHEN DEATH TAKES POSSESSION?
DO YOU REALLY THINK
WITH GOD YOU HAVE A PACT?
THAT NEVER TO YOU
CAN HAPPEN SO TERRIBLE AN ACT.
HOW MANY PEOPLE WERE THERE BEFORE
THAT THOUGHT THE SAME WAY
THAT THINK OF THOSE ACTS
THAT YOU DO ABHOR
YET SO FEW PROTESTED
INHUMANE CONDITION
AND NO ONE ARRESTED
BUT ALL IN SUBMISSION
TO THE CRUELTY OF POWER
OF A STATE OF BARBARIANS
WHERE ALL MEANT SO LITTLE
LIFE OF THE JEWS AND EVEN THE ARYANS.
WAKE UP LITTLE PEOPLE
NONE OF YOU IS BIG
NOT EVEN ADOLF HITLER
WHEN HE DID THE "JIG"
THOUGHT THAT HIS POWER
WILL COME TO AN END
SO THINK OF HUMANITY
AND DO WHAT YOU CAN.
TIME DOESN'T RUN OUT
BUT LIFE SURELY WILL
WHEN I THINK OF PAST YEARS
THEY GIVE ME A CHILL

ARNOLD L. SHAY

IN MEMORY OF MY MOTHER

THE TRAIN WINDING THROUGH THE OPEN MEADOW WITH THE ROAR OF THE HEAVY IRON WHEELS AGAINST THE TRACKS WHERE SO MANY TRAINS HAVE PASSED BEFORE. THIS TRAIN HOWEVER IS SO DIFFERENT. THE TRAINS THAT USUALLY PASS THIS WAY, CARRY PASSENGERS WHO LAUGH, ENJOY THE RIDE AND THE MOST BEAUTIFUL VIEW OF THE SHEARED FIELDS THAT LOOK LIKE A PICTURE POST CARD. THE VIEW, THE MOST MAGNIFICENT ONE YOU COULD WANT TO SEE.

THOSE BEAUTIFUL LITTLE HOUSES BUILT SO MANY YEARS AGO, STAND ON THE ROAD AS IF TO GREET THE PASSENGERS WHO, AFTER THE SNACK THAT THEY BROUGHT WITH, LIKE TO ENJOY THE VIEW.

AND ENJOY THEY CAN, BECAUSE THE RIDE IS A LONG ONE, AND YOU AS A CITY DWELLER, NEVER HAVE A CHANCE TO SEE.

COWS GRAZING OR JUST LAYING CROSSED LAZILY AS IF THE WORLD AROUND THEM DID NOT EXIST. AND SO THE PASSENGERS OF THE TRAIN HAVE A TREAT.

NOT SO WITH THIS TRAIN. NOW, THIS IS A SPECIAL TRAIN. YES! ON THE SAME TRACKS, YOU HEAR THE SAME ROAR OF THE IRON WHEELS ON THE IRON TRACKS AS ANY OTHER TRAIN, THAT HAS PASSED HERE SO MANY TIMES BEFORE WITH LUXURY COMPARTMENTS, AND THE CONDUCTOR WITH A SMILE ON HIS FACE TRYING TO PLEASE THE PASSENGERS.

THIS TRAIN...WELL...CATTLE CARS...CARRY HUMAN CARGO. THESE PASSENGERS CAN NOT ENJOY THE VIEW, THERE IS ONLY ONE SMALL WINDOW WITH BARBED WIRE ACROSS IT.

THE "PASSENGERS" INSIDE HAD A LONG JOURNEY, NO FOOD, NO WATER, NO PLACE TO SIT DOWN, SOME DIED DURING THE TRIP AND ARE JUST LAYING AROUND. NOBODY CARES. THE STENCH IS UNBEARABLE AND OH THAT HEAT. BUT THEY CAN NOT COMPLAIN. THEY ARE JEWS.

THEY ARE LOCKED IN THOSE TRAINS FOR THE LAST 3, 4, 5,

DAYS. WHO COUNTS? WHO CAN COUNT? TOO TIRED. TOO WEAK AND THE CARS ARE ROLLING ALONG. WHERE?! WHERE ARE THOSE CARS TAKING THOSE UNFORTUNATE SOULS? DESTINATION UNKNOWN. SOME TRY TO THINK OF THEIR FAMILIES THAT WENT BEFORE THEM. PROBABLY THE SAME ROAD, BUT NEVER HEARD FROM AGAIN.

THEY HAD FAMILIES TOO — BELIEVE IT OR NOT. BEAUTIFUL FAMILIES. HAPPY FAMILIES. SOME CAN STILL REMEMBER AND EVEN HEAR THE LAUGHTER OF THEIR CHILDREN, THE JOY OF SHABAT EVE, THE CANDLE LIGHTS, THE FATHER WITH THE CHILDREN GOING TO THE "BETH HAMEDROSH". THEN AT THE TABLE THE FATHER MAKING "KIDDUSH" AND MOTHER BUSYING HERSELF WITH THE DINNER, IT IS A BIG FAMILY SIX OR MAYBE EIGHT CHILDREN, BUT WHO COUNTS?

THE JOY IS SO GREAT YOU ARE AFRAID OF AN "AYIN HARAH" (EVIL EYE)…AND NOW IS BEDTIME. MOTHER IS PREPARING THE LITTLE ONES FOR BED, WHILE THE OLDER ONES ARE STILL SITTING AROUND THE TABLE AND TALKING POLITICS/RELIGION, AND EVERYTHING ELSE. OH HOW WE USED TO ARGUE DIFFERENT POINTS AND EVERYONE WANTED TO PROVE HIS POINT, BUT IT WAS FUN BECAUSE AT THE END WE ALL HUGGED AND KISSED JUST BEING HAPPY THAT WE COULD THANK GOD TO BE TOGETHER.

AND SO ALL THOSE GOOD OLD TIMES COME TO MIND. WE SEE ALL THIS IN FRONT OF OUR EYES AS IF IT WAS HAPPENING NOW.

ALL OF A SUDDEN A STOP, A WHISTLE BLOW THAT PIERCED THE EARS AND AWAKENED EVERYONE FROM HIS DAYDREAMS. WE CAN HEAR NOISES OUTSIDE, THE DOORS OPEN UP, AND ALL HELL LETS LOOSE. THE DOGS BARK, THE MEN IN BLACK UNIFORMS…WHO BARK LOUDER THAN THE DOGS, AND THOSE GUYS IN THE STRIPED UNIFORMS WHO LOOK HALF DEAD AND THEY TOO TRY TO SCREAM, AND ALL YOU COULD HEAR IS ORDERS…TAKE YOUR SUITCASES. LINE THEM UP IN FRONT OF YOU, STAY IN LINE, GO TO THE LEFT…GO TO THE RIGHT…WHO COULD KNOW WHAT ALL OF THIS MEANS. NO ONE!

NO ONE COULD EVER KNOW WHAT ALL THIS MEANS IF YOU WERE NOT THERE. NO ONE COULD IMAGINE THAT A

POINTING OF A FINGER BY ONE OF THOSE IN THAT BLACK UNIFORM WOULD MEAN LIFE OR DEATH. YET, THESE MEN WERE YOUR JUDGES. GOD HAD NOTHING TO SAY ANYMORE. I THINK THAT GOD HAD HANDED OVER HIS JOB TO THOSE BLACK UNIFORMED MEN. MAYBE IT WAS TOO MUCH FOR HIM.

YES! I READ SOME TIME AGO SOMEWHERE IN THE BIBLE, THAT THE "MALACH HAMOVET" THE ANGEL OF DEATH COMES DRESSED IN BLACK. BUT SO MANY??

AND NOW WE ARE ALL IN TWO DIFFERENT LINES. ONE LINE...STRONG YOUNG MEN, THE OTHER LINE...OLD PEOPLE AND CHILDREN. SCARED BUT SO INNOCENTLY GOING WHEN THEY ARE TOLD TO MARCH TOWARDS THE TRUCKS. NOT KNOWING THAT THOSE TRUCKS ARE GOING TO TAKE THEM TO THE GAS CHAMBERS AND CREMATORIA WHERE THE ASHES WILL BE AFTERWARDS STREWN AROUND NOT EVEN KNOWING WHERE ONE IS GOING TO FIND THEIR REMAINS. THE OTHER LINE IS LUCKIER(?), THEY WERE ASSIGNED TO WORK FOR THE GERMAN MACHINERY.

THEY ARE GOING TO THE "SAUNA", BEFORE TAKING A SHOWER THEY ARE TOLD TO LEAVE THEIR CLOTHES NEATLY BUNDLED UP, TIED TOGETHER SO THAT NOTHING GETS LOST AND THAT WHEN THEY COME OUT THEY SHOULD NOT HAVE TO LOOK FOR THEIR CLOTHES. (THE OTHER LINE WAS TOLD THE SAME)

THEN THEY WAIT DRIPPING WET UNTIL THE "SCHREIBER" RECORDER COMES IN TO TAKE THEIR NAMES...FOR THE LAST TIME. THEN THEY ARE BEING TATTOOED WITH A NUMBER ON THEIR LEFT FOREARM AND THEY ARE TOLD THAT THIS NUMBER IS ALL THEY HAVE TO REMEMBER SINCE THEIR NAME, BIRTHDATE, BIRTHPLACE, AND EVERYTHING ELSE THAT GOES WITH A PERSON, "DOES NOT MEAN ANYTHING AROUND HERE."

YOU ARE IDENTIFIED AND CALLED BY YOUR NUMBER, AND IF A BLACK UNIFORMED MAN COMES OVER TO YOU ASKING WHO YOU ARE, JUST STAY AT ATTENTION AND SAY 135584. THAT IS ALL YOU ARE NOW. A NUMBER AND YOU ARE CONSIDERED LUCKY ON TOP OF THAT. THE OTHERS. WELL!! THEY DO NOT NEED A NUMBER ANYMORE.

AND SO YOU HAVE YOUR NUMBER NOW, AND YOU GET IN LINE TO RECEIVE "CLOTHES." BECAUSE YOU WILL NEVER AGAIN SEE YOUR OWN CLOTHES. SEE. THE CLOTHES YOU CAME IN WITH WERE REMOVED WHILE YOU WERE TAKING A SHOWER AND IT IS NOW ON IT'S WAY FOR THE GERMANS TO WEAR.

OH!! I CAN NOT FORGET THE OTHER LINE. THE OLD MEN. OR THE LINE WITH THE WOMEN AND THEIR BABIES ON THEIR ARMS. THE SICK...THE...WELL ALL THOSE OTHERS THAT THE GERMANS CONSIDERED UNFIT FOR WORK. ALL THOSE INNOCENT PEOPLE AWAITING THEIR TURN TO THE GAS CHAMBERS.

NOBODY BOTHERS WITH THEM NOW. THEY ARE GOING TO A PLACE OF NO RETURN. THE TRUCKS ARE MOVING UP, THE REAR LOADING PLATFORM OPENS UP, THE PEOPLE ARE LOADED AND AWAY THEY GO. THE TRUCKS ARE ROLLING AWAY...AWAY...AWAY... THE ROAD SEEMS SO LONG AND YET IT IS ONLY ONE KILOMETER TO THE GAS CHAMBERS AND THEY TOO ARE GOING THROUGH THE SAME ROUTINE.

UNDRESS, TIE YOUR CLOTHES IN A NEAT BUNDLE NOT TO MAKE IT HARD TO FIND WHEN YOU COME OUT FROM THE "SAUNA." BUT THIS "SAUNA" IS DIFFERENT. THIS "SAUNA" SPEWS GAS, "ZYKLON B" INSTEAD OF WATER. AND AFTER A FEW MOMENTS, AGONIZING MOMENTS, THE DOORS ARE OPENED AND THE BODIES ARE TAKEN OUT BY THE "SONDER-COMMANDO" SPECIAL ATTACHMENT...INMATES ASSIGNED TO THAT SPECIAL PRIVILEGED JOB.

OH... NOT OF THEIR OWN FREE WILL THEY KNOW PERFECTLY WELL THAT AFTER A FEW WEEKS OR MONTH, THEY WILL BE THE ONES TO BE TAKEN OUT OF THOSE SAME GAS CHAMBERS BY OTHER INMATES AND THAT IS WHY, WHILE THEY WERE WAITING FOR THEIR BRETHREN TO BE GASSED THEY LAUGHED AND TALKED ABOUT EVERYTHING ELSE EXCEPT ABOUT THOSE PEOPLE IN THERE.

THEY DID NOT EVEN LOOK TO SEE WHEN THE S.S. MAN LOCKED THE DOOR AFTER THEY "BURIED" THOSE POOR SOULS INTO THE CHAMBERS. THEY DID NOT LOOK WHEN THAT BLACK UNIFORMED MAN AND HIS GUEST LOOKED THROUGH THAT LITTLE WINDOW...HOW THOSE PEOPLE

SLOWLY SUFFOCATE WITH THAT GAS. OR HOW BEFORE THAT ANOTHER UNIFORMED MAN WENT UP ON THE ROOF OF THAT SINGLE BUILDING, OPENED UP A LITTLE DOOR ON TOP OF THE ROOF AND JUST OPENED UP A CAN OF GAS, WHILE HE WAS PROTECTED WITH A GAS MASK, AND JUST PLACED THE CAN UPSIDE DOWN SO THE FUMES WOULD GO INSIDE THE ROOM.

THEY, THE "SONDERCOMMANDO" DO NOT SEE IT ANYMORE. THOSE MEN HAD SEEN IT SO MANY TIMES BEFORE THAT IT DID NOT BOTHER THEM ANYMORE. THEY ARE BY NOW IMMUNE TO THAT WHOLE PROCESS. MAYBE BECAUSE THEY CAN NOT HELP THEM ANYWAY? ...AND THEN THE DOORS OPENED, ACTUALLY ONE VERY HEAVY DOOR, AND THE BODIES ARE TAKEN OUT WITH BIG PITCHFORKS TO SEPARATE THE BODIES.

THE HAIR THAT WAS CUT OFF THE PEOPLE BEFORE GOING IN TO THE GAS CHAMBERS (SOMETIMES EVEN AFTER THE PEOPLE WERE GASSED) IS ALREADY BEING PACKED AND SHIPPED AWAY TO GERMANY TO BE USED. THE GERMANS DO NOT WASTE ANYTHING. IT WILL NOT BOTHER THOSE JEWS IF THE GERMANS USED THEIR HAIR FOR MATTRESSES OR SOMETHING ELSE AS LONG AS IT IS NOT BEING WASTED. IT MAKES GOOD INNERLINING (HORSEHAIR) FOR SUITS. AFTER ALL...YOU CAN NOT KILL HORSES, THEY ARE NEEDED FOR WORK, FOR MEAT OR EVEN FOR PLEASURE. WELL YOU KNOW WHAT I MEAN?! AFTER ALL IT DID NOT COST THE GERMANS ANYTHING, SO IT IS ALL "CLEAR" PROFIT.

THE DEAD BODIES ARE BEING LAID OUT ON THE GROUNDS. BECAUSE THE SPECIAL "DENTISTS" ARE COMING TO REMOVE THE GOLD TEETH FROM THE DEAD. WHY NOT?? GERMANY NEEDS GOLD. THE DEAD WILL NOT COMPLAIN. DOES ANYONE KNOW OF A CHEAPER WAY TO GET GOLD? AFTER ALL THE CORPSES WILL BE SHOVED IN THE OVENS ANYWAY.

SO MANY GERMANS ARE GETTING RICH ON THOSE CORPSES. SEE THE GERMANS ARE FREE TO DO ANYTHING THEY PLEASE WITH THE JEWS AND THE WHOLE WORLD WILL JUST LOOK ON. NO ONE WILL COMPLAIN.

WILL THE WORLD EVER CARE? I DO NOT THINK SO. NOW

ALL THIS IS BEING DENIED. NOW PEOPLE SAY THAT IT NEVER HAPPENED. WAS ALL THIS ONLY A DREAM? THEN WHERE ARE MY PARENTS? WHERE HAVE SIX MILLION JEWS DISAPPEARED?

BUT THERE ARE THOSE LIKE ME. WHO CAN NOT NOR WILL THEY EVER FORGET. THEY WILL KEEP ON REMINDING THE WHOLE WORLD THAT IT DID HAPPEN.

AND THEY ARE THE ONES THAT WILL SAY “KADDISH” FOR THE REST OF THEIR LIVES.

“KADDISH” THAT IS ALL THAT IS LEFT.

BY: ARNOLD L SHAY
TO THE 40th ANNIVERSARY
OF LIBERATION FROM THE NAZI CAMPS
1945-1985

Descriptive Contents

Index

A SELECT BIBLIOGRAPHY

CREDITS AND A HEARTY THANK YOU TO ALL OF YOU WHO HELPED ME SO MUCH WITH YOUR WRITING. GOD BLESS YOU ALL. I CANNOT MENTION HERE EVERY BOOK OR MONOGRAPH OR ARTICLE I READ ON THE HOLOCAUST, BUT I DO WANT TO THANK ALL OF YOU, EVEN THE ONES THAT ARE NOT MENTIONED HERE.

ABRAMSKI, CH. JAVCHYMNY AND POLANSKI. *THE JEWS OF POLAND*

MARTIN GILBERT. *THE SECOND WORLD WAR,* A COMPLETE HISTORY.

JUDAH PILCH, EDITOR. *JEWISH CATASTROPHY IN EUROPE*

ISAIAH TRUNK. *JEWISH RESPONSE TO NAZI PERSECUTION*

ISAIAH TRUNK. *THE JUDENRAT*

FILIP MULLER. *EYEWITNESS TO AUSCHWITZ*

ZALMAN GRABOWSKI. *CHRONICLES OF THE SONDERKOMMANDO*

DAVID G. ROSKIES. *THE LITERATURE OF DESTRUCTION*

KAZIMIERZ SMOLEN. *AUSCHWITZ 1940-1945*

ARNOLD L. SHAY. *CLINICAL PEDIATRICS 1964*

DONALD GRAY BROWNLOW AND JOHN ELUTHERE du PONT. *HELL WAS MY HOME, THE TRUE STORY OF ARNOLD SHAY*

RAUL HILBERG. *PERPETRATORS, VICTIMS, BYSTANDRS*

RAUL HILBERG. *THE DESTRUCTION OF EUROPEAN JEWRY*

NORA LEVIN. *THE DESTRUCTION OF EUROPEAN JEWRY*

NACHMAN BLUMENTHAL. *THE LAST LETTER FROM BENDZIN KATZETNIK, THE CONGREGATION COUNCIL*

D. STEINBOCK. *THE LOST YEARS, BOOK OF ZAGLEMBIE, PINKUS BENDIN*

JOSEPH FRIEDMAN. *OUR HEROS*

LAJB SHPEIZMAN. *JEWS IN ZAGLEMBIE DURING THE SECOND WORLD WAR*

PRIMO LEVI. *IF THIS IS A MAN*

PRIMO LEVI. *SURVIVAL AT AUSCHWITZ*

BERNARD MARK. *ZYCIE I WALKA MLODZIERZY WGETTACH W OKRESIE OKUPACJI 1939-1945* (THE LIFE AND STRUGLE UNDER THE GERMAN OCCUPATION), (IN POLISH)

WLODZIMIERZ BLASZCZYK. *BENDZIN* (IN POLISH)

KANTOR MORSKI. *DOMBROWSKIE FROM THE PAST OF ZAGLEMBIE* (IN POLISH)

TARSKI, EVERT AND MICHALSKI. *THE ILLUSTRATED* (IN POLISH)

BALINSKI AND LIPINSKI STAROZYTNA. *POLSKA* (POLAND OF OLD), (IN POLISH)

JANKO Z CZERNOWA. 1828 *SAMORZAD MIEJSKI* (SELF-GOVERNING)

PAUL WIEDERMAN. *PLOWA BESTIA* (THE BLOND BEAST), (IN POLISH)

GUTENBERG. *UNIVERSAL* (IN GERMAN)

זכור-געדענקן
REMEMBER–
from Generation to Generation!

זכור

REMEMBER